The Pocket Guide to Saint Paul

Dr Peter E. Lewis, BD Hons (London); MB, BS (Qld); DTM&H (Sydney); FRCS (England); FRACS, is a medical practitioner who practises on the Gold Coast in Queensland. He trained as a surgeon in England where he gained the Fellowship of the Royal College of Surgeons of England. He subsequently worked as a surgeon in Bangladesh and the Solomon Islands. In the 1970s he studied the History of Religions at the University of Queensland, and in 1990 he obtained an honours degree in Divinity from the University of London. He is a numismatist specialising in coins relating to the early history of Christianity. He is a member of the Australian Numismatic Society. He has recently published articles on the Tribute Penny in the Journal of the Numismatic Association of Australia.

Ron Bolden is a retired senior chemical technician who lives at Blaxland in the Blue Mountains. He has TAFE qualifications in Chemistry and Chemical Instrumentation, Supervision and Small Business Practice. His career commenced at Unilever (Australia) Pty Ltd and he later spent over twenty years in the New South Wales Department of Technical and Further Education in technical and laboratory managerial positions. His main numismatic interests are collecting and studying Biblical coins and the restoration of ancient coins. His particular interest is collecting coins mentioned in the Bible and coins of Biblical characters as well as acquiring related texts. In the area of ancient coin restoration he has done work for major numismatic dealers throughout Australia and for Macquarie University. He is a member of the Australian and American Numismatic Societies.

The POCKET GUIDE *to* SAINT PAUL

Coins encountered by the Apostle on his travels

PETER LEWIS AND RON BOLDEN

Wakefield
Press

Wakefield Press
17 Rundle Street
Kent Town
South Australia 5067

First published 2002

Designed and typeset by Clinton Ellicott
Printed and bound by Hyde Park Press

National Library of Australia
Cataloguing-in-publication entry
Lewis, Peter E.
The pocket guide to Saint Paul.

Bibliography.
Includes index.
ISBN 1 86254 562 6.

1. Paul, the Apostle, Saint – Journeys. 2. Bible. N.T. – Geography.
3. Mediterranean Region – Description and travel. I. Bolden, Ron. II. Title.

225.92

Wakefield Press thanks Fox Creek Wines and Arts South Australia for their support.

Contents

Foreword

This is a book that is concerned with the life of Paul the Apostle. Its approach is to tie together two professional disciplines, theology and numismatics. These disciplines are coupled throughout the book in an interesting and informative way, creating a new perspective on the life of Paul the Apostle. Each of the authors has a strong interest in both areas of this study, however the major theological component is the work of Peter Lewis and the numismatic research essentially that of Ron Bolden.

The book traces Paul's travels and details his various missionary journeys through Asia Minor, the Middle East, Greece and his last, the voyage to Rome. The writings in the New Testament, the Acts of the Apostles and the letters to the various Christian communities, provide the framework for the careful calculation of the chronology of these journeys. However, in addition to the biographical account of Paul's trips, a primary concern throughout the book is the examination of the diversity of contemporary coinage that circulated in the areas visited by Paul. The book focuses on that coinage which Paul most likely would have handled or seen and which, in all probability, he or his friends would have used. His movement from city to city and region to region from the years spanning the mid 30s to the mid 50s, exposed him to an extraordinary maze of small change, which still exists today, in the form of bronze coins. These coins differed from place to place, and consequently created a remarkable challenge to travellers trying to establish the relative value of each coin. The authors vividly demonstrate the rich diversity of coinage that Paul would have encountered in his travels. This must constantly amaze us today, where we live in a continent with one simple coinage, tied to other countries by well-publicised exchange rates. But in the first century of the Christian era no simple exchange mechanism existed. The precious metal struck at only a few mints was universally accepted. The minor bronze coinages, however, must have posed many problems for the moneychangers. No wonder then that these minor coins stayed in the general area of issue and hence rarely travelled, and then only as 'leftovers' from tourists, soldiers or travelling merchants who at times must have carried these 'lesser' coins to the communities they visited. Consequently each place visited presented a new monetary problem. Fortunately Paul had little need for moneychangers or cash as he stayed and travelled with other Christians who looked after his needs. Nevertheless it is certain that he would have seen and possibly handled that diversity of coinage in most of the places that he stayed.

The book also incorporates some new numismatic ideas as elsewhere proposed by Peter Lewis, such as his controversial views that the Antioch tetradrachm is in fact the 'tribute penny'. Naturally this book draws heavily on the first volume of the new standard work, *Roman Provincial Coinage*, which provides a synthesis of the numismatic evidence for 'Greek Imperial' coins issued or circulated in the areas visited by Paul.

The authors of this book have in a very special and exceptional way brought together numismatic material relevant to Paul's travels. The authors go beyond successfully linking the two main themes. They also provide supplementary material such as commentaries, discussion of Biblical truths, myths related to the sites or those portrayed on the coinage, the present status of the archaeological remains, other religions practised there and the principal activities in each of these cities or regions that Paul visited. Peter Lewis's theological training is very apparent throughout the book. The authors of this book are to be commended for presenting a very readable and enjoyable account of the life of Paul the Apostle. It is a book written with skill and considerable knowledge and is a must for any Biblical scholar or numismatist interested in coinage related to the Bible. I commend this book to all such readers as well as the lay public. You will be entertained, enlightened and enthused.

Colin E. Pitchfork, 2001
Australian Numismatic Society delegate to the Numismatic Association of Australia, Consultant to Noble Numismatics Pty Ltd

Preface

The Numismatic Association of Australia is dedicated to the promotion of numismatics in Australia. It represents all the major numismatic organisations in every State and provides a unified voice for the advancement of numismatics in all its aspects. I am therefore very pleased to commend this book, our third special publication.

The authors are well known to me. They combine expertise in the fields of theology and numismatics in making a particular study of the coins that Saint Paul might have handled during his lifetime. The result is a fascinating account which gives new insights into the life and work of a person whose importance for Christianity is second only to Christ himself.

Although the book deals primarily with coins it is not a catalogue but a discursive account covering areas such as archaeology and theology. It contributes to our knowledge of the whole environment in which Saint Paul worked.

This book is unique. As far as I know, coins have not previously been used in this way to chart the career of a famous person of the past. Unfortunately in many historical studies the numismatic aspects are ignored or mentioned only as an afterthought. This book gives numismatics its rightful place as an important key to the past and should appeal to everyone interested in Saint Paul, his first-century world, and to the part numismatics can play as a documentation of history.

Peter Lane
President

The Numismatic Association of Australia Inc.

Postal Address:	PO Box 1920R
	GPO Melbourne, 3001
	Australia
Web:	http://naa-online.com

Office Bearers:

President	P. Lane
Immediate Past President	M.B. Keain
Vice President	J. Hope
Secretary/Treasurer	J. Lane
Journal Editor	P. Lane
Assistant Journal Editors	P. Fleig
	J. Hope

Sponsoring Societies	Delegates
Australian Numismatic Society PO Box R4 Royal Exchange, Sydney NSW 2000	E. Pitchfork
Numismatic Society of South Australia PO Box 2029, Kent Town SA 5071	M.B. Keain
Perth Numismatic Society PO Box 259, Fremantle WA 6160	Dr W.R. Bloom
Australian Numismatic Society, Queensland Branch PO Box 78, Fortitude Valley QLD 4006	G.D. Snellgrove
Numismatic Association of Victoria GPO Box 615D, Melbourne VIC 3001	P. Hamilton
Tasmanian Numismatic Society, Inc. GPO Box 884J, Hobart TAS 7001	R.V. McNeice OAM
Elected Members of Council	Dr J. Chapman A. Flint J. Hope

Acknowledgements

The authors wish to acknowledge and thank the following institutions and persons for kindly granting permission to reproduce images of their coins: The British Museum for figures 8, 9, 13, 19, 31, 32, 33, 36, 40, 48, 51, 52, 53, 54, 55, 56, 57, 59, 62, 63, 64, 65, 66, 67, 68, 69, 70, 73, 74, 76 (obv.), 77 (rev.), 79, 81, 84, 85, 86, 87, 88, 89, 90, 102 (© Copyright The British Museum); Bibliotheque Nationale de France for figures 18, 20, 21, 24, 25, 30, 34, 43, 72, 82, 83; Staatliche Museen zu Berlin for figures 26, 29, 35, 37, 41, 71, 76 (rev.), 91; Ashmolean Museum, Oxford, for figures 23, 49, 75, 101; The American Numismatic Society, New York, for figures 9, 45, 100; The Royal Collection of Coins and Medals, National Museum, Copenhagen, for figure 61; Staatliche Munzsammlung, Munich, for figure 42; Noble Numismatics Pty Ltd, Sydney and Melbourne, for figures 2, 10, 11, 12, 16, 103, 110, 113; Mr David Hendin of New York for figures 3, 4, 5, 6, 7, 44, 93, 94, 95, 96, 97, 98 (these coins are illustrated in Mr Hendin's book *Guide to Biblical Coins*, 3rd edition, Amphora, New York, 1996); Spink and Son Ltd, London, for figures 38, 47, 92 (these coins are illustrated in *Greek Imperial Coins and their values* by David Sear, Seaby, London, 1982), and for figure 46 (illustrated in *Greek Coins and their values*, Volume 2, by David Sear, Seaby, London, 1979); Munzen und Medaillen AG, Basel, for figure 1.

Introduction

The importance of Paul of Tarsus for Christianity cannot be overestimated. His writings comprise a large part of the New Testament, and it has been said many times that without him Christianity would simply have faded away or at best continued as a minor Jewish sect. Therefore any study which throws light on his life and times will be of value.

Paul would certainly have been interested in coins. He earned his living as a tent-maker[1] and a knowledge of the local coins would have been essential in that trade. Even after his conversion to Christianity he continued his trade and found work in the various cities in which he stayed on his missionary journeys.[2]

Jesus himself knew what was on coins,[3] and so did the average citizen of the Roman Empire. In fact, at a later date the Christian people of Antioch rioted when they saw that the pagan emperor, Julian II, had issued coins displaying a bull, presumably to promote some pagan cult.[4]

In the period in which Paul lived, coins were more significant than they are today, but it was a different significance. Not only were they essential for commerce, but they were a vehicle of propaganda for the imperial and provincial authorities. Also the ability to mint coins gained prestige for a city, especially for the smaller cities. The coins advertised their temples and festivals,[5] and so gained profit for the citizens. Trade increased around temples and at festivals, and the city authorities provided small change and moneychangers to facilitate it, a proportion of the transactions going to the city.[6] Coinage helped to disperse information in the ancient world which had no newspapers or any other means of communication which we take for granted today. This information was very diverse, from who was the current emperor, to which god or goddess was worshipped in a particular city. So in many ways the coins which Paul encountered on his missionary journeys would have had an influence on him, even if at times only subtle.

It might be objected, however, that there are already many large books which deal with the coinage of the Roman Empire during the lifetime of Paul. Some books, such as *Roman Imperial Coinage*[7], deal with the coins issued from Rome for the whole empire; while others, such as *Roman Provincial Coinage*[8], deal only with the coins issued in the provinces; but all are in catalogue form and consist of long lists of coins. The present work attempts to interpret this large amount of data for a particular purpose, namely to determine its significance for Paul and to present a readable account which can be read from beginning to end. Hopefully the end result will be of interest to numismatists, historians, students of St Paul, and the general public.

The plan of the book is to trace the journeys of Paul as recorded in the book of Acts.[9] A brief account of each city will be followed by a description of the coins he would most likely have encountered there, and an attempt will be made to determine the significance of these coins for Paul. As the chronology of Paul's life is so relevant to the study of the coins, chronology will be briefly discussed at the beginning of each section.[10]

Our major source has been *Roman Provincial Coinage (RPC)*. Without this comprehensive catalogue of the provincial coins, the present work would not have been possible. In fact, none of the information in our work is the result of original research; we have simply mined the large amount of material which is already available. We have tried to indicate the sources in the end notes; to these scholars and to the many more whom we have not mentioned, we express our gratitude.

1. Tarsus 5–10 A.D.

I am a Jew, born in Tarsus in Cilicia . . .
Acts 22:3a

Paul was born in Tarsus. Just when this was is unknown, but there are a few clues in the New Testament which enable us to make a rough estimate. For example in his letter to the Galatians[1] Paul writes, 'I was violently persecuting the church of God and was trying to destroy it. I advanced in Judaism beyond many among my people of the same age'. In the book of Acts (Acts 7:58), he is called a young man at the martyrdom of Stephen. This suggests that Paul was in his twenties at the time he was persecuting the early church; and this time would have been a few years following Jesus' crucifixion which is generally considered to have occurred in 30 A.D.[2] So, as Professor Bruce[3] states, Paul was probably born in the first decade of the Christian era. Jerome Murphy-O'Connor[4] dates the birth of Paul to about 6 B.C. but his argument for this is rather tenuous.

Although he was born in Tarsus, Paul says he was brought up in Jerusalem at the feet of Gamaliel, a famous Jewish teacher. The term 'brought up', suggests that Paul's childhood was spent in Jerusalem. So, for our purposes, it seems reasonable to assume that Paul was born in Tarsus about 5 A.D. and moved to Jerusalem about 10 A.D.

In 5 A.D. Tarsus was already a very old city. It is mentioned in Hittite texts and listed on the black obelisk of the Assyrian ruler Shalmaneser (850 B.C.). Originally it was probably a native

Cilician town which was penetrated by Greek colonists in the eighth century B.C. Another era of Greek influence began with Alexander's conquests in 333 B.C., and the city subsequently became part of the Seleucid Empire, during which period Paul's ancestors probably arrived in the city. In 64 B.C., the Roman general Pompey organised the cities of the Cilician plain into a network of city states with Tarsus as its centre. From the 30s B.C. the area was incorporated into the province of Syria, the capital of which was Antioch on the Orontes river.

When Paul was born, Tarsus was an important[5], sizeable city of many thousand inhabitants. The clear, cold stream of the river Cydnus flowed through the city down to a lagoon which was only a few miles from the sea and provided an ideal harbour for the city. Into this harbour, only 46 years before, the royal Egyptian barge had floated bearing Cleopatra to her first, fateful meeting with Mark Antony who had been waiting in the city. Cleopatra was arrayed as Aphrodite arising from the sea, and Antony quickly succumbed to her charms.

We know little of what Paul's Tarsus looked like, because its remains[6] lie buried under the present city which has a population of 150,000. The river Cydnus no longer flows through the city and its once great harbour is a swamp. Writing in 1936, H.V. Morton[7] described the Tarsus he saw as 'a shabby little town where rows of wooden shacks faced each other across roadways of hard mud. And this was Tarsus, this dusty malarial town crouched in a swamp. I looked for something that might have lingered from the time of its pride, but there was nothing'. In the 1993 edition of the Lonely Planet guidebook for Turkey, the author devotes only one small paragraph to Tarsus and it ends with a brief word of advice, 'Don't waste your time here'. Such is the fate of the city of which Paul was so proud. Gone are the marble temples, colonnades, baths and public squares which once adorned the site.

During this period of Paul's early childhood, the coins which circulated in Tarsus were mostly coins minted in Antioch for use in the whole province. With one notable exception, all the silver coins which Paul's father would have handled were not minted in Tarsus. From 5 B.C. to the end of Augustus' reign in 14 A.D.,

Antioch had issued a large number of silver tetradrachms with the head of Augustus on the obverse and the Tyche of Antioch on the reverse[8]. They differ only in the date on the reverse. There were no Roman denarii in Syria at this time[9], and the circulation of the silver tetradrachms of Tyre was mostly confined to Judaea and Southern Syria.

There were two other silver coins not minted in Tarsus which Paul's father might have handled. One had the portrait of the long-dead Seleucid king Philip Philadelphus (92–83 B.C.) on the obverse and a seated Zeus on the reverse[10]. This coin was similar to the tetradrachms which had been issued by the Seleucid rulers for over two hundred years. They were revived by the Roman authorities about 50 B.C. and issued from Antioch until 16 B.C. Also there was a tetradrachm[11] which is now rare with a head of Augustus on the obverse and the seated Zeus on the reverse (*RPC* 4108), the mint of which is uncertain (?Anazarbus), but it was issued early in the first decade A.D. and it circulated in northern Syria and Cilicia. On the reverse in Greek letters is the inscription ΚΑΙΣΑΡΟΣ ΘΕΟΥ ΥΙΟΥ, meaning (a coin) of Caesar, Son of God. Octavian, who adopted the surname Caesar, claimed the deified Julius Caesar as his adopted father (actually he was Octavian's grand-uncle). Paul's father, a strict Jew, must have found such a title objectionable; but the point to make here is the title, 'Son of God', was known to Paul from an early age, and it was a term especially associated with his preaching[12]. The first recorded words of Paul after his conversion are found in Acts 9:20, 'For several days he was with the disciples in Damascus, and immediately he began to proclaim Jesus in the synagogues, saying, "He is the Son of God"'. The concept of a god having a semi-human son was of course well known in the ancient world from Greek mythology.

Like the silver it seems that hardly any bronze coins were minted in Tarsus. The bronze coins from Antioch were used instead, and again a common type was the Tyche of Antioch. However it is likely that Tarsus might have been the mint for a bronze coin with the head of Augustus on the obverse and the name ΣΤΡΑΤΗΓΟΣ ΡΗΓΛΟΣ (Strategos Reglos = General Reglos) on the reverse, because one specimen was found during excavations there.[13] The identity of the general Reglos (Regulus) is unknown and there is no date on the coin, but from the type of portrait *RPC* considers it to be from the last decade or so of Augustus' reign. Regulus was probably a Roman official in the province of Syria. The coin is rare today.

A more common coin was the silver coin minted at Tarsus during the period 1–10 A.D. (*RPC* 4004). It was a tetradrachm like the tetradrachms of Antioch with the head of Augustus on the obverse and a Tyche on the reverse, but it bore the monogram of Tarsus and this must have been a source of considerable pride for the citizens of the city. Paul's father was probably one of the leading citizens and could well have shown the shiny coin to his bright child. The legend on the obverse was ΚΑΙΣΑΡΟΣ ΣΕΒΑΣΤΟΣ (of Caesar Augustus), and on the reverse ΜΗΤΡ ΟΠΟΛΕΩΣ (of the metropolis). Metropolis meant mother-city and Tarsus was the chief or mother city of Cilicia.

Figure 1 – A silver tetradrachm of Tarsus. (*RPC* 4004)

Tyche was an important Greek goddess in Hellenistic and Roman times. She was equated with the Roman goddess Fortuna, although Fortuna tended to be more particular in her activities, affecting individual people, while Tyche tended to be universal in scope but with particular manifestations. The importance of Tyche (Fortuna) is made clear by Pliny the Elder (23–79 A.D.) when he writes that all through the world Fortuna alone is invoked; she is the one defendant, the one culprit, the one thought in men's minds, the one object of praise, the one cause; she is worshipped with insults, courted as fickle and often as blind, wandering, inconsistent, elusive, changeful, and friend of the unworthy.[14]

During Hellenistic times, as cities became more established, along the lines of the ancient Greek polis, they began to develop personalities of their own, with their own histories and advantages, and their own individual destinies; so it was inevitable that Tyche should become a city goddess. The cult of Tyche was widespread during Paul's time and some cities had elaborate shrines with priests and priestesses. Early in the third century B.C. the Greek sculptor Eutychides, from Sicyon near Corinth, created a wonderful bronze statue of Tyche for the city of Antioch. Pausanias, the Roman travel writer of the second century A.D., mentioned it in one of his books. A copy of the famous statue stands today in the Vatican museum. No doubt Tarsus had a similar statue of its Tyche.[15]

Like the statue, the Tyche on the tetradrachm of Antioch has a turreted crown on her head representing the city wall and sits on a rock representing the nearby mount Silpion. At her feet the river-god Orontes is vigorously swimming in the river (he seems to be doing the backstroke). In her hand she holds a palm branch, perhaps from a date palm, to symbolise prosperity and peace. The Tyche of Tarsus imitates her more important sister, though sitting on a rock representing a mountain seems inappropriate as Tarsus was built on a plain. The Tarsians probably considered that their mountain was the snow-capped range of the Taurus Mountains which was about 30 kilometres to the north and clearly visible from the city. The road which led north from Tarsus passed through a narrow gorge in the mountains called the Cicilian Gates and was the only way that wagons could cross these mountains.

In Asia Minor a great Mother-goddess had been worshipped since prehistoric times and newcomers like Tyche and Artemis tended to be assimilated to her, becoming manifestations of her. The Mother-goddess was also a nature goddess inhabiting the earth and mountains, so Tyche sits on a mountain to symbolise this aspect of her character.

Tyche was essentially a manifestation of the power of the gods. Writing in the fourth century A.D., Sallustius, a friend of the pagan emperor Julian, explains, 'The power of the gods which orders for the good, things which are not uniform, and which happen contrary to expectation, is commonly called Fortune, and it is for this reason that the goddess is especially worshipped in public by cities; for every city consists of elements which are not uniform'.[16] These words are reminiscent of Paul's famous statement in his letter to the Romans, 'We know that in all things God works for good for those who love him'.[17] Actually Paul's own life illustrated the meaning of this statement; for he suffered many hardships and was eventually martyred in Rome; yet all the while, events were working towards the triumph of Christianity. Not only during Paul's childhood in Tarsus but for years afterwards he would have been faced by Tyche on many of the coins that he handled. Did she tease him with thoughts of the unfairness of life?

Let us give the last word on Tyche to the ordinary citizens of the Roman empire. On headstones to be seen everywhere along the highways and byways of the empire, a common epitaph read:

> *I've escaped, I've got clear. Good-bye, Hope and Fortune.*
> *You've nothing on me. Play your tricks on others.*[18]

2. Jerusalem 10–36 A.D.

I am a Jew, born in Tarsus in Cilicia, but brought up in this city {Jerusalem}.
Acts 22:3a

Paul was educated in Jerusalem at the school of the famous rabbi, Gamaliel. The city was the centre of the Jewish world and Paul would have taken notice of all its aspects, including its coins.

How long he stayed in Jerusalem depends on the date of his conversion, which occurred when he was on his way to Damascus. Three years later, Damascus was under the control of Aretas IV, king of the Nabataeans (2 Corinthians 11:32) and Aretas would not have gained control earlier than the accession of the Roman emperor, Caligula, in 37 A.D.[1] So, if the three years are reckoned inclusively[2], the earliest date for Paul's conversion would be 35 A.D., and the latest date 38 A.D. because Aretas died in 40 A.D. Some scholars have suggested that the stoning of Stephen, which occurred in Jerusalem and at which Paul was present, would not have been allowed under Pontius Pilate who was the Roman governor of Jerusalem, and they date Stephen's death and Paul's conversion to the time of Pilate's recall to Rome in 36 A.D. Everything considered, a date of about 36 A.D. for Paul's conversion seems reasonable.

The Jerusalem that Paul saw was very different from what we see today, which is essentially a medieval walled city. The walls of modern Jerusalem date from 1540 A.D., and its central feature, the Dome of the Rock, was built by Caliph Abd el-Malik in 691 A.D. Paul's Jerusalem was destroyed in 70 A.D. and even more

9

thoroughly in 135 A.D. when even its name was obliterated and it was called Aelia Capitolina. All that remains today of Paul's Jerusalem are parts of the wall that surrounded Herod's temple. Fortunately, however, there exist today many of the coins that Paul might have handled when he was growing up in Jerusalem.

The Hasmonean rulers of Jerusalem had been producing coins since the time of John Hyrcanus I (135–104 B.C.), whose father and uncles had led the Maccabean Revolt to wrest the Jewish nation from the Seleucid kings of Syria. His coins would have been unknown to Paul, but the coins of his successor, Alexander Jannaeus (103–76 B.C.), are among the most common of ancient coins and archaeological evidence has shown that they were in circulation in Paul's time.[3] Apparently they continued to be produced long after the death of Alexander Jannaeus. Why this occurred is not obvious. Alexander Jannaeus was a drunk and a fornicator, hated by large sections of his people, many thousands of whom he put to death; but he was also a war-monger whose successful campaigns extended the boundaries of Israel, not only to include the coastal cities whose inhabitants he compelled to follow the Jewish law, but to equal in size the kingdom of Solomon (965–927 B.C.). So the people of many neighbouring areas would have recognised these coins.

The coins of Alexander Jannaeus are all small bronze ones. They carry designs of anchors, stars, lily flowers, and crossed cornucopias (with a pomegranate arising between them). Typically, on one side the inscription shows Alexander's Hebrew name, 'Yehonatan', often spelt with errors as the ancient Hebrew script was giving way to the Aramaic script, which is used for modern Hebrew. Where there was an inscription on the other side it was the Greek inscription, 'of King Alexander'.

One of the commonest of Alexander Jannaeus' coins, and a likely candidate to be the widow's mite of Mark 12:42, had an anchor on one side and either a lily or a star with eight rays on the other. The anchor may refer to the Jewish control of the coastal cities, or as one writer[4] states it may signify the reliability of God's promises. The anchor was the symbol of the Seleucid kings of Syria[5] and it was used on a coin of Antiochus VII (138–129 B.C.) with his name on the same side and a lily on the other side.

As these coins are mostly found in Judaea and the lily presumably symbolises this area, it has been assumed that the Jews under John Hyrcanus I were allowed to mint these coins in Jerusalem. Alexander Jannaeus may simply have based his anchor/lily coins on these.

The star on the reverse of Alexander Jannaeus' coin was an innovation and has been considered by some scholars[6] to typify the radiant sun, referred to in Malachi 4:2 as the sun of right-eousness. Dr P. Romanoff[7] says that the star on the coins of Alexander Jannaeus may suggest the morning star, the sun or the heavens, and as the Menorah (the seven-branched candle-stick) could symbolise the solar system, it would not be foreign to have such symbols on Jewish coins. He points out that the star with eight rays was employed numismatically in many lands, its earliest form being the star found on the coins of Itanus in Crete dating from the fourth century B.C. However it seems more likely that Alexander Jannaeus used the star symbol for a specific purpose and that was to refer to the ancient prophecy in Numbers 24:17b:

> *A star shall come out of Jacob,*
> *and a sceptre shall rise out of Israel;*
> *it shall crush the borderlands of Moab,*
> *and the territory of all the Shethites.*

and to suggest that he was that Messiah. When Paul handled this coin, as he would have on many occasions, he might have been reminded of the many prophecies of a coming Messiah in the Hebrew scriptures, and he might have noted, perhaps with a chuckle, that they certainly did not mean Alexander Jannaeus. During the Second Jewish Revolt in 132–5 A.D., the Jewish leader, Simeon bar Kosiba, was hailed as Bar Kochba (Son of a Star), and the star above the temple on coins of the Second Jewish Revolt probably refers to Bar Kochba. Even in Paul's time there would have been a prevailing expectation of a coming Messiah, and the star on the widow's mite would have intensified those feelings. Although as far as we know, Jesus did not refer to himself as the Star, in the Revelation to John, probably written about 95 A.D., John quotes, 'It is I, Jesus, who sent my angel to you with this testimony for the churches. I am the root and descendant of David, the bright morning star' (Rev. 22:16).

Figure 2 – A prutah of Alexander Jannaeus. (Hendin 469)

It is interesting to note that when the modern state of Israel issued its first series of coins in 1949, the coins had designs taken from ancient Jewish coins issued two thousand years before, and the first coin of the series, the one prutah denomination, which was made of aluminium, has the anchor of Alexander Jannaeus on the obverse. Although the eight-pointed star does not feature in this initial series, it appears on a one lira coin issued in 1958, where the star is present on either side of a menorah above a Hebrew legend, 'The Law (Torah) is Light'. Here the stars apparently are simply symbols of light. The well-known six-pointed star of David, which became the emblem of Judaism and appears on the flag of Israel, was adopted by the Jews in the Middle Ages and has no Biblical or Talmudic authority.

The cornucopias on the coins of Alexander Jannaeus were common in ancient Greek art and symbolised prosperity and abundance. The pomegranate between the cornucopias was a common fruit in the region and lends the motif an original Hebrew flavour. Romanoff[8] suggests that a symbol like the cornucopia may have been adopted to aid Jewish trade as it would have been understood by the neighbouring nations. He says that the pomegranate was one of the seven celebrated products of Palestine (Deut. 8:8), that pomegranates formed a decorative motif on Solomon's temple, and that they were part of Aaron's high-priestly attire (Ex. 28:33,34). Also, because of its refreshing juice and great number of seeds, it assumed the meaning of blessing and fertility. It also connoted piety, good deeds, and knowledge. It was therefore natural that the pomegranate should become the symbol of Israel.

The lily probably referred to one of the many wildflowers that grew in Israel at that time, but which specific flower was meant is not known as the flora of the region would have changed greatly over the millennia. The lily had special significance for the Jews because according to the prophet Hosea, God said, 'I will be like the dew to Israel, he shall blossom like the lily', (Hosea 14:5a), and lilies were also used to decorate the temple (1 Kings 7:19). No doubt Paul would have found these allusions pleasing. He would have noticed the wildflowers of Palestine and, like Jesus, been led to consider the lilies of the field, how they grow (Mt. 6:28).

Although one of the ten commandments had forbidden the making of a graven image, or any likeness of anything that is in heaven above, or that is in the earth beneath, or that is in the water under the earth, it seems that this commandment was referring to idols and not to the making of images for other purposes. After all, had not God ordered his temple to be decorated with lilies and pomegranates? So the people did not object to these simple designs on the coins, and the successors of Alexander Jannaeus continued to use them, mostly the double cornucopias with pomegranate.

Paul would have seen some of the coins of Herod the Great (40 B.C–4 B.C.). Herod had married into the Hasmonean family, and was from an Idumaean, not a Jewish family, but he tried to please the Jews by building the temple in Jerusalem, and on the whole was careful not to offend their religious sensitivities. Towards the end of his reign, however, he erected a sculptural representation of an eagle over the main gate of the temple in Jerusalem, and issued coins with the bird on the reverse. Why he did this is unknown. The eagle was the bird of Jupiter, the head of the Roman pantheon, and it was used as a symbol of power or victory, decorating the top of legionary standards. In any case Josephus[9] relates that the Jews considered the sculpture a forbidden image and rioters tore it down. What they thought of the coins is not recorded.

Figure 3 – A lepton of Herod the Great. (Hendin 501)

Other designs on the coins issued by Herod the Great include a tripod with bowl, a military helmet, a crested helmet, a decorated shield, a winged caduceus, a palm branch, and a cross surrounded by a closed diadem, although his commonest coin had an anchor on the obverse and a double cornucopia with a caduceus between on the reverse. The presence of a caduceus deserves some comment, as the caduceus was the staff of Hermes (Mercury), the messenger of the gods. Here, for the first time in Jewish coinage, was a symbol of a foreign god. It is possible that the caduceus is in fact just a stylised pomegranate or a Phoenician symbol unrelated to Hermes. If it is a caduceus, it may represent an aspect of Herod's Hellenising policy to which the theatre and temple to Augustus at his seaport of Caesarea bear witness. Herod was the first Jewish ruler to use exclusively Greek inscriptions on his coins.

Herod was succeeded as ruler of Jerusalem by his son, Archelaus (4 B.C.–6 A.D.). Although he treated his subjects cruelly and was eventually banished by Augustus, he was careful not to issue coins which might offend their religious feelings, and largely reproduced the designs on his father's coins. One of his designs which was not found on his father's coins was a bunch of grapes. Wine in its various forms was the general drink in Judaea, and the grapes were grown locally. The vine symbolised national peace and prosperity (e.g. Micah 4:4). Israel itself was a vine (Isaiah 5:7), brought out of Egypt (Psalm 80:8). Unfortunately Archelaus' reign resulted in loss of independence for the Jewish nation as his territory was annexed to the province of Syria and placed under the direct rule of a Roman governor.

When Paul was living in Jerusalem it was ruled by a succession of Roman governors, most of whom minted coins. Apart from Pontius Pilate, very little is known about these men. The first governor, Coponius (6–9 A.D.), began his rule by calling for a census in order to impose heavy taxes on the people. His small copper coins exhibit only two symbols, an ear of barley and a date palm, which would not have offended the Jews; but there was one enormous difference between his coins and all the preceding Jewish ones: on the obverse in Greek letters was **KAICAPOC** (of Caesar). They were now under the thumb of the emperor in Rome. Apart from two brief revolutions they would remain under foreign domination for the next two thousand years. At the time, however, the people may have welcomed the change after the terrible reign of Archelaus.

Figure 4 – A prutah of Coponius. (Hendin 635)

The next governor, Marcus Ambibulus (9–12 A.D.), minted similar coins with the same symbols. When the emperor Augustus died in 14 A.D., Valerius Gratus (15–26 A.D.) put the new emperor's name, **TIBEPIOC**, usually abbreviated to **TIB**, on his coins. He used a variety of innocuous designs: double cornucopias, a palm branch, three lilies, a vine leaf, an amphora, a cup. Some of his coins bore the name 'Julia' in Greek letters, **IOYΛIA**, referring to Julia Livia, the mother of the emperor Tiberius. No doubt Valerius wanted to ingratiate himself with the imperial family by issuing such a coin.

Figure 5 – A prutah of Valerius Gratus. (Hendin 646)

The next governor, Pontius Pilate (26–36 A.D.), was not as careful as his predecessors to respect the religious sensitivities of the Jews. According to Philo, the Jewish philosopher who lived in Alexandria in the first century A.D., Pilate infuriated the Jewish leaders by setting shields dedicated to the emperor on the walls of his residence in Jerusalem. Why this should upset the Jews is not clear; perhaps the shields bore inscriptions referring to Tiberius as the son of the divine Augustus, as on the coins issued at Rome. In any case Tiberius ordered that the shields be removed to the temple of Augustus in Caesarea. Josephus, the first-century A.D. Jewish historian, records an incident in which the Roman army in Jerusalem used standards that displayed images of the emperor, contrary to previous Roman practice. These were eventually removed after the people demonstrated. Although there were no images of the emperor on Pilate's coins they carried pagan cult symbols which must have been abhorrent to the Jews. There is no record of how the Jews reacted to them.

Pilate minted his first coin in 29 A.D. just before the crucifixion of Jesus. On the obverse was the name of the emperor's mother, Livia Caesar, in Greek.[10] Livia died in 29 A.D. at the age of 86, but whether the coin was issued before or after her death is unknown, probably the latter. In any case Pilate intended to honour Livia, and so ingratiate himself with the emperor. Pilate's plan, however, may have backfired because the emperor's relations with his mother had gradually soured over the previous fifteen years. In fact, Suetonius[11] writes that he visited her exactly once in the last three years of her life, and for only an hour or two at that. He did not even attend her funeral.

The design on the obverse of the coin is three bound ears of corn, with the centre ear upright and the outer two drooping. The design may simply be a symbol of abundance, but more likely it indicates the process of growing and dying, which was the centre of attention of the cult of the corn goddess, Demeter, (Ceres).[12] Ferguson[13] states that in Ephesus during the reign of Tiberius there was a priestess of Livia as Augusta Demeter. Pilate may have minted his coin in anticipation of the deification of Livia, but in this too, his plan backfired because Tiberius refused to allow Livia to be deified. She had to wait till the reign of her grandson Claudius before she could become a goddess. Pilate was removed from his post by Tiberius in 36 A.D.

On the reverse of Pilate's coin is the Greek inscription **TIBEPIOY KAICAPOC** (of Tiberius Caesar) and the image of a simpulum, or libation ladle, used by the Roman priests in their ceremonies. Apparently sacrificial wine was poured from the ladle. The emperor would have used such an implement in his capacity as High Priest (Pontifex Maximus) in Rome. Again, Pilate may have been hinting at Livia's deification by showing a simpulum on his coin. Also on the reverse was the date LIS (year 16) i.e. 29 A.D.

Figure 6 – A prutah of Pontius Pilate. (Hendin 648)

Pilate minted his next coin in 30 A.D. On the obverse is the same inscription as before, and a lituus, which was a staff with a curled end, used by the augurs in Rome to divine the will of the gods. Apparently the lituus was held up to the sky to mark out areas for the observation of the flight of birds. It probably represented one of the religious offices held by the emperor, although it has been suggested that it was used because of the word-play, augur-Augustus, and its use by Augustus led to its being employed as a general imperial symbol by subsequent emperors. On the reverse of the coin was the date LIZ (year 17), surrounded by a wreath. Pilate minted a similar coin in 31 A.D., but with the date LIH (year 18).

Figure 7 – A prutah of Pontius Pilate. (Hendin 649)

Paul may have seen some of the coins minted by Herod Antipas (4 B.C.–40 A.D.). Although his coins circulated only in his territory of Galilee and Peraea, some of them would have found their way to Jerusalem where they would have been changed into the local currency by moneychangers who set up their tables in the court of the temple. Herod Antipas was careful not to upset his Jewish subjects with his coins which have the innocuous design of a plant or palm branch on the obverse with the inscription ΗΡΩΔΟΥ ΤΕΤΡΑΡΧΟΥ (of Herod Tetrarch); and on the reverse ΤΙΒΕΡΙΑC (Tiberias), the name of the capital which Herod built on the shore of the sea of Galilee and which he named after Tiberius. The city was built about 20 A.D. and the earliest coins are dated LKΔ (year 24, i.e. 20 A.D.) so they were probably issued to commemorate Herod's founding of the city and to win favour with the emperor.

Figure 8 – A full denomination bronze of Herod Antipas.
(*RPC* 4918)

Concerning Roman Imperial coinage[14], it appears there was very little of it in Jerusalem at this time. Very few Roman denarii have been found there. D.T.Ariel[15] in *A Survey of Coin Finds in Jerusalem* mentions only one Republican denarius, one of Mark Antony, one of Augustus and one of Tiberius. The writers of *RPC*[16] state that Roman denarii were not made in Syria nor did they circulate there, and that the principal silver currencies in Syria, of which Judaea was part, were tetradrachms of Antioch and shekels of Tyre. If this is the case it is hard to explain how easily Jesus obtained a Roman denarius from the people when he made his statement, 'Give to Caesar what is Caesar's, and to God what is God's' (Mark 12:17), in answer to the question whether it is right to pay tax to Caesar. The most likely explanation is that the coin which Jesus held up to the people was not a denarius at all but a tetradrachm of Antioch. Because the writer of Mark's Gospel was writing for a Roman audience who had never seen a tetradrachm of Antioch, he referred to the coin as a denarius.

Mark's Gospel was probably the first Gospel to be written. The Gospels of Matthew and Luke largely reproduce the information in Mark's Gospel and they too refer to a denarius in their versions of the story. John's Gospel uses other sources and does not include this story. The evidence that Mark's Gospel was intended for a Roman audience includes the verse (Mk 12:42 in the Greek N.T.) where it is explained that two lepta equal one quadrans, which was a Roman coin not found in the eastern part of the empire. In any case, the story of Jesus showing a coin to a group of people and expecting them to answer questions about what was on it, requires a large coin like a tetradrachm not a small coin like a denarius.

The tetradrachm of Antioch which is most likely to be the coin actually held by Jesus is *RPC* 4161, which has the laureate head of Tiberius with the Greek inscription ΤΙΒΕΡΙΟΣ ΣΕΒΑΣΤΟΣ ΚΑΙΣΑΡ (Tiberius Augustus Caesar) on the obverse and the radiate head of Augustus with ΘΕΟΣ ΣΕΒΑΣΤΟΣ ΚΑΙΣΑΡ (God Augustus Caesar) on the reverse.

Figure 9 – The actual Tribute Penny. (*RPC* 4161)

Briefly, the argument for *RPC* 4161 being the Tribute Penny[17] runs as follows: Mark used the word δεναριον because he was writing for an audience in Rome who was familiar with this coin; no denarii circulated in Judaea in Jesus' time; the coin which Jesus held had the emperor's head on it and was used for paying the Roman tax in the province of Syria of which Judaea was part; Jesus would have been referring to the reigning emperor, Tiberius; only one silver coin was issued by Tiberius from Antioch during the lifetime of Jesus (*RPC* 4161). The detailed argument and discussion can be found in the *Journal of the Numismatic Association of Australia*.[18]

The coin which has usually been considered to be the Tribute Penny is the denarius of Tiberius with the laureate head of

Tiberius on the obverse and the seated figure of a woman, probably Livia, on the reverse (*RIC*, I, 30). The inscription on the obverse is TI. CAESAR DIVI AVG. F. AVGVSTVS (Tiberius Caesar, son of the divine Augustus, Augustus), and on the reverse it is PONTIF. MAXIM. (Pontifex Maximus = High Priest).

Figure 10 – A silver denarius of Tiberius. (*RIC*, I, 30)

Tiberius issued only two denarii during his reign. The other denarius has Tiberius driving a quadriga on the reverse (Sear 568). It is much less common than the denarius with Livia, and for this reason is not considered to be a candidate for the title of Tribute Penny. Harvey Shore[19] argued that the Tribute Penny was the denarius of Augustus with his laureate head on the obverse and the figures of his two grandsons, Caius and Lucius, on the reverse (*RIC* I, 207). This was the commonest denarius of Augustus, and it constituted the bulk of the 164 denarii in a hoard of coins found on Mount Carmel in 1960. The hoard had been buried sometime after 54 A.D. It was, however, a most unusual hoard as it also contained 4500 silver shekels and half-shekels of Tyre.

Figure 11 – A silver denarius of Augustus. (*RIC* I, 207)

Paul too would have been required to pay the tax to the Roman authorities and if *RPC* 4161 was the Tribute Penny, the reference on it to Augustus as Theos would have been objectionable to him, and to every other Jew; but it is not known whether the Jews objected in any way. *RPC* 4161 is rare today with only three specimens found by *RPC* in the major museums it surveyed. A possible reason for its rarity is that when Caligula succeeded Tiberius in 37 A.D. he melted down the tetradrachms of Tiberius to produce tetradrachms of lower silver fineness; or perhaps the Jews objected to the blasphemous inscription on the coin and it was withdrawn, as the Roman shields had been withdrawn from Jerusalem.

Throughout the Roman Empire and its client kingdoms the right to mint silver and gold coins was reserved by the Roman authorities and only base metal (copper, bronze or leaded bronze) coins were minted by provincial authorities or client kings, except when the right to mint silver was granted to certain cities such as Tyre and Antioch. Tyre had been minting silver tetradrachms (shekels) since 126 B.C. They were so integral to the economies of the surrounding areas that the Romans allowed the city to continue issuing its coins. These tetradrachms of Tyre were used by the Jews to pay the temple tax[20], and of all the coins that Paul must have seen in Jerusalem at this time, the tetradrachm of Tyre would have been very prominent. Jesus himself needed it to pay his temple tax, as well as the tetradrachm of Antioch to pay his tax to the Roman authorities. The thirty pieces of silver paid to Judas were probably tetradrachms of Tyre because the priests would have had a plentiful supply of them; for according to Exodus 30:13 each adult male was required to pay half a shekel for the upkeep of the temple. Half a shekel would have been equivalent to a Tyrian didrachm, but didrachms were much less common than the tetradrachm, so the Jews usually paid their temple tax in pairs, as in the story of Peter finding the coin in the fish's mouth (Mt. 17:27).[21] Moneychangers in the temple court would have been kept busy exchanging coins for these Tyrian tetradrachms.

There is little doubt that Tyrian coins were required for the temple tax. Ariel (op. cit.) lists 37 Tyrian tetradrachms found in various parts of Jerusalem. The Mishna stipulated that the temple tax be paid in pure silver of Tyrian currency (Mishna, Bechorot, 8.7). The usual reasons given for this situation are that Tyrian coins were of very fine silver (95 per cent) and that they did not have the image of any living person.[22] Nevertheless it seems strange that these coins should have been acceptable to the Jewish priests because they had the head of the Greek god Heracles on the obverse and an eagle, the symbol of Zeus (Jupiter), the chief of the Greek gods, on the reverse.

Figure 12 – A silver tetradrachm of Tyre. (Sear 5918)

There is no doubt that the head is that of Heracles as the paws of his lion's skin coat are shown knotted in front of his muscular neck. This Tyrian Heracles is often called Melqarth or Melqarth-Heracles, but the term Melqarth simply means king or lord of the city, in Phoenician. These coins were produced by Tyre from 126/5 B.C. when the city regained its autonomy, but the Greek influence would have been strong in the city since it was besieged and conquered by Alexander the Great in 332 B.C. Tyre was the only city in the area to resist Alexander and it paid a fearful price with ten thousand of its inhabitants put to death and thirty thousand sold into slavery. Henceforth Greek religion would have prevailed. Tyre, of course, was the nearest major commercial centre to Judaea and its Hellenising influence would have been felt throughout the region.

But the most likely explanation for the Jewish priests accepting these Tyrian coins is that Tyre had supplied timber and skilled workmen for building the original temple of Solomon in the tenth century B.C., and it would have been natural for Tyrian silver to be used for the building and the upkeep of Herod's temple. Jerusalem produced no silver coinage and Tyre fulfilled this need, just as Tyre supplied the needs of Solomon before the beginning of coinage. Tyre is frequently mentioned in the Bible as having close ties with Israel, and even Jesus visited the region of Tyre (Mt. 15:21). So although the polytheistic religion of Tyre was quite different from the monotheistic religion of Israel, Tyre was allowed to be involved in the building and upkeep of the temple in Jerusalem. The Jews may even have felt a sense of pride in having these foreign gods working in the service of their temple.

Ya'akov Meshorer[23] has suggested that from 18/17 B.C. these Tyrian tetradrachms were actually minted in Jerusalem. He says that from that date the style and fabric of the coin changes and it bears the monogram KP (? for kratos = power). The Roman historian Dio (54.7.6.) recorded that in 20 B.C. civil disturbances in Tyre led to Augustus reducing the city's level of autonomy. Brooks Levy[24] disagrees with Meshorer and suggests that the Kappa Rho monogram stands for Kaisar and simply reflects some degree of imperial intervention in Tyre's affairs after the disturbances of 20 B.C.

Heracles, who was equivalent to the Roman Hercules, was one of the most popular gods in the ancient world. He was the great hero who, having a human mother and a divine father, struggled on behalf of mankind. Zeus wanted to have a son who would be a champion for both gods and men, so he visited Alcmene in the guise of her husband and she became pregnant. The child grew to become very strong and through his physical prowess and great courage he overcame the many obstacles set before him. One of his adventures involved killing a lion who was terrorising the countryside. He skinned the lion and thereafter wore the pelt with its head as a sort of helmet and its paws knotted in front of his neck. This is the way Heracles is portrayed on the obverse of the tetradrachms issued by Alexander the Great, who likened himself to Heracles. On the reverse of Alexander's coin, one of the commonest in antiquity, is Heracles' divine father, Zeus. In the second century A.D. the emperor Commodus actually identified himself with Heracles, being so portrayed on his coins. In the third century A.D. the emperor Diocletian made Hercules second only to Jupiter. 'Above all, to Diocletian it is Jupiter who restores the world, or who protects the emperors. In his reorganization of the Empire into a tetrarchy, the senior emperors were placed under the protection of Jupiter, the junior under the protection of Hercules. The panegyrists make clear the distinction. Jupiter governs the heavens; Hercules brings peace on earth. Jupiter initiates policy; Hercules executes it. Jupiter plans; Hercules acts. The new pattern is amply represented on the coins with types of the protecting deities'.[25] So the influence of Heracles in pre-Christian and early Christian times was very great.

The parallels between Heracles and Christ are striking. Both were born from human mothers and divine fathers, and were therefore equally human and divine. They both worked for the good of mankind and suffered greatly before ascending to the divine realm. Christ was nailed to a cross, while Heracles put on a coat which caused severe pain and death. Both descended into hell. In Heracles' case this was to capture the dog of hell, Cerebus. In Christ's case it was presumably to indicate his victory over the infernal powers.

The similarities between the suffering deaths of the two heroes are so obvious that educated Jews of the period must have been aware of them. Paul was an educated Jew and it is possible that the portrait of Heracles on the ubiquitous Tyrian shekel had a subtle influence on his thinking. We know that Paul's religious thinking was radically changed at his conversion in 36 A.D. when his reliance on salvation through strict observance of the Jewish Law was displaced by his confidence in salvation through faith in Jesus Christ whom he now proclaimed the Son of God. Paul's great contribution to Christian theology was the concept of salvation through faith, and this differs from the concept of salvation through the observance of the Law only in that the human factor is introduced into the former. What part did the numismatic Heracles play in the introduction of this human factor into Paul's thinking? Although Paul never met Jesus during his earthly ministry, he would have seen the face of Heracles almost daily on the coins.

3. Damascus 36–38 A.D.

So they led him by the hand and brought him into Damascus.
Acts 9:8b

The chronology of this period is important, not only to determine which coins Paul would have seen, but for his subsequent career. The three relevant texts are 2 Corinthians 11:32–33, Galatians 1:15–18 and Acts 9:8–25. There is an apparent discrepancy between these accounts in that Acts does not mention Paul's sojourn in Arabia. If we marry the three accounts the complete story is that after Paul's conversion he went to Damascus but after 'several days' he went into Arabia for an unknown length of time before returning to Damascus; then three years after his conversion he escaped from Damascus which was under the control of Aretas IV, the king of Nabataea, by being lowered from the wall in a basket. The key issue for the chronology is that in 2 Corinthians Paul says that Damascus was under the control of Aretas IV when he escaped. This means that Paul's flight from the city must have occurred during the period 37–40 A.D., i.e. from the accession of Caligula to the death of Aretas. There were no Roman coins minted in Damascus during the reigns of Caligula or Claudius, which confirms that the city was part of the kingdom of Nabataea during those reigns. So a date of about 38 A.D. for Paul's flight from Damascus is reasonable. In keeping with this chronology Damascus would still have been in Roman hands when Paul arrived in 36 A.D., and probably after Caligula's accession on 18 March 37 A.D. it would have come under the control of Aretas IV.

Damascus at this time was a busy trading centre on the crossroads of important caravan routes.[1] One route led north to Antioch, the capital of the Roman province of Syria. One route led east across the desert to Palmyra and then on to Mesopotamia and the Persian Gulf. One route led south, passing east of the Dead Sea to reach the Nabataean capital of Petra, which was the destination of caravans from South Arabia via Mecca and Medina. Another route led west through the mountains to the port of Tyre. So Damascus would have been a bustling town with a great variety of goods to be seen: frankincense from South Arabia, pepper from India, even silk from China. There would have been a great variety of coins: tetradrachms of Tyre and Antioch, Nabataean and Syrian bronze coins, and silver drachms and tetradrachms of Parthia, the great empire which lay to the east of Syria and included Mesopotamia and Persia. The moneychangers would have worked hard in Damascus.

Caravans coming from desert areas must have been delighted to reach Damascus because it would have seemed a paradise of fertility with lush greenery and water flowing everywhere. The reason for this fertile environment was the Barada River which began in the snow-capped mountains to the west and flowed into the desert in the east, but before disappearing in the hot sands it nourished the oasis on which the city developed. It is no wonder that the gods worshipped there were concerned with fertility. The people naturally wondered at the miraculous change in the earth after the rain which came with storms and was heralded by thunder. So in Old Testament times there was a sanctuary to the storm god, Hadad, in Damascus. With the coming of the Romans Hadad was assimilated to Jupiter whose symbol was also thunder and by the third century A.D. there was a temple of Jupiter on the site. It is interesting to note that in 379 A.D. Theodosius I built a church dedicated to St John the Baptist on the site of Jupiter's temple and in 705 A.D. the caliph al-Walid began to build the Great Mosque which is still an important feature of the city.

There is very little left of the city that Paul knew. The present walls of the old city are probably built on stones which formed part of the wall down which Paul was lowered in a basket. There still exists the main east–west thoroughfare which is referred to in Acts 9:10,11 as the street called Straight: 'Now there was a disciple in Damascus named Ananias. The Lord said to him in a vision, "Ananias." He answered, "Here I am, Lord." The Lord said to him, "Get up and go to the street called Straight, and at the house of Judas look for a man of Tarsus named Saul."'

But this street is now 15 feet under the present thoroughfare called Bab Sharqi Street. H.V. Morton[2] wrote that there is a small mosque in the street called Straight which both Christians and Muslims believed was built on the site of the house of Judas, but a stronger claim to authenticity can be made by the chapel which tradition associates with Ananias. This underground chapel is to be found in an old part of the city which Morton says was the Jewish quarter in Paul's time. The chapel itself is not ancient but there are remains of an ancient church at the back of it which provides some evidence for its claim to authenticity.[3] Just as well all the coins Paul might have seen in Damascus are available to evoke and enlighten that distant period.

When Paul first arrived in Damascus it was under Roman control and the official coinage was that issued from Antioch for circulation in the whole province of Syria. Also, from the reign of Augustus, Damascus had been allowed to mint bronze coins for local circulation. The last issue under Augustus was in 13/14 A.D.[4] when four bronze denominations were minted. On the obverse two of them have the head of Augustus, another has a youthful head (?Tiberius), and another, a radiate head presumably that of Helios, the sun god who was popular in Syria. The later emperor, Elagabalus (218–222 A.D.) was high priest of the sun god, El Gabal, at his great temple in Emesa (modern Homs) which was only 150 kilometres from Damascus. On the reverses there are a male head (?Tiberius), a female head (?Livia), the head of Tyche, and on the reverse of the Helios coin, there is the head of his consort, Selene, on a crescent moon. The coins are dated by the Seleucid era which began in 312 B.C. and all have ΔΑΜΑΣΚΗΝΩΝ (of the Damascenes) or its abbreviation, on the reverse.

There were three issues of bronze coins minted at Damascus under Tiberius.[5] The first was in 16/17 A.D. when a large coin (26 millimetres) was produced with the head of Tyche on the obverse, and on the reverse the winged goddess of victory, Nike, advancing with a wreath or palm, all within a wreath (*RPC* 4797). The legend ΔAMACKHNWN[6] and the date are on the reverse. The Tyche, of course, is the city goddess of Damascus, but the reason for the Nike is not apparent. The only Roman victories at this time were in Germany by Tiberius' nephew and heir, Germanicus, and it seems unlikely that the Nike would be referring to him. In 17 A.D., however, Germanicus was made consul and sent to the eastern empire with extraordinary powers to solve the problems there, so a reference to him remains a possibility. Germanicus fell ill and died in Antioch in 19 A.D. under suspicious circumstances.

Figure 13 – A bronze of Tiberius. (*RPC* 4797)

Little did Paul realise that the Nike which he saw on the coins of Damascus would gradually be transformed in later centuries into an angel, characteristic of the Christian religion.

The second issue by Tiberius was minted in 23/24 A.D. It consisted of two denominations, both with the head of Tiberius on the obverse. On the reverse one has Tyche seated on a rock, and the other has a caduceus, symbol of Hermes. Hermes was in fact a very ancient god who played a variety of roles in Hellenistic religion. A likely reason for his symbol to appear on this coin of Damascus is that he was especially interested in fertility, for example his union with Aphrodite produced Hermaphroditus who retained the characteristics of both sexes. Fertility was a central concern of Syrian religion. Another reason might be that he was the protector of merchants and thieves, as well as travellers and roads generally.[7] All of these would have been in Damascus when Paul was there.

The third issue by Tiberius was minted in 33/34 A.D. It consisted of three denominations. On the obverse of two was the head of Tiberius, on the other was a veiled head (?Livia). On the reverses were a standing animal (?horse), a seated Tyche, and Hermes' symbol the caduceus.

When Paul first arrived in Damascus he 'went away at once into Arabia'. Luke does not mention this Arabian sojourn in Acts but it is commonly assumed that Paul went into the desert to commune with God and to reflect on his situation. It is more likely, however, that his purpose was to preach to the Nabataeans that Jesus was the Son of God. Perhaps Paul expected that such a concept might be more acceptable to the pagan Nabataeans than to the strictly monotheistic Jews.

Arabia did not, as it does today, denote the whole of the great peninsula between the Red Sea and the Persian Gulf. In Paul's time the term referred to the territory occupied by the Nabataeans who in the fourth century B.C. had settled the area south of Damascus and east of the rift valley which contained the Dead Sea. Their king was Aretas IV (9 B.C.–40A.D.) and his capital was Petra, 'a rose-red city as old as time',[8] which so impresses modern tourists with its facades cut out of the surrounding cliffs. Paul probably visited Petra during his Arabian sojourn but it would not have impressed him much, as the great facades were mostly created in the second century A.D.

It seems that the Nabataeans were not much impressed by Paul either. In fact his preaching may have aroused their animosity, which would account for the Nabataean governor of Damascus wanting to seize him. It is interesting to speculate how this Nabataean experience influenced Paul's later outlook. Unfortunately we know little of what Nabataean culture was like in 35 A.D. except for its reflection in the coins of Aretas IV. Dr Ya'akov Meshorer has comprehensively studied the coins of the Nabataean Kingdom and his monograph[9] includes a detailed account of the coins of Aretas IV.

Aretas' first wife, Huldu, died about 17 A.D. and Paul would more likely have seen the coins issued when his second wife,

Shuqailat, was queen. In 18/19 A.D. there were two issues: Meshorer 96, a silver coin which has a laureate bust of Aretas with long curly hair on the obverse and a laureate bust of Shuqailat on the reverse; and Meshorer 97, a bronze coin which has Aretas standing as a soldier with his right hand raised on the obverse and Shuqailat standing with her right hand raised to show the palm of her hand on the reverse.

Figure 14 – A Nabataean bronze of Aretas IV. (Meshorer 97)

In 19/20 A.D. there was an issue, Meshorer 98, in silver, which had a bust of Aretas with the Aramaic inscription, 'Aretas, King of the Nabataeans, the lover of his people', on the obverse, and a bust of Shuqailat on the reverse. From 20/21 A.D. to 39/40 A.D. there were almost yearly silver issues which differed from each other only in the date on the reverse (Meshorer 99 to 111). These had the bust of Aretas on the obverse and jugate busts of Aretas and Shuqailat on the reverse.

Figure 15 – A silver Nabataean coin of Aretas IV. (Meshorer 103)

Paul would not have seen the most common Nabataean coins which are bronze and have the jugate busts of Aretas and Shuqailat on the obverse and crossed cornucopias on the reverse, because they were not issued till 39/40 A.D.

What would Paul have thought of the coins he encountered on his Arabian sojourn? We know from his letter to the Corinthians (1 Corinthians 11:14) that he considered long hair on a man degrading. So he would have disapproved of the appearance of Aretas with his shoulder-length hair. Perhaps his

Nabataean experience planted the seed of this dislike which was so clearly expressed at a later date. There was nothing in the Hebrew scriptures against men having long hair; in fact it was the normal Israelite custom to let hair grow to a considerable length. Absalom cut his hair only once a year when it had become too heavy and 'in all Israel there was no one to be praised so much for his beauty as Absalom' (2 Samuel 14:25a).

Another feature which Paul would have disliked was the prominence given to women. The queen appears on nearly all the coins. This may reflect the status of women in Nabataean society or it may simply have been a reflection of the importance of the female deity in the Nabataean pantheon. In either case Paul, who is often accused of misogyny[10], would have disapproved.

The two chief Nabataean deities were the god Dusares and the goddess Al Uzza.[11] Dusares was concerned with fertility and associated with bulls, while Al Uzza was the deity of springs and water as befits a fertility goddess. These deities do not appear on Nabataean coins and it could be that the royal couple were their representatives in some way. The queen was probably involved in religious ceremony as she is shown on Meshorer 97 with her open hand displayed and we know that the open hand was important to the Nabataeans because it occurs on the reverses of King Malichus I (60–30 B.C.). The significance of this open hand is unknown today, but could have been known to Paul. The idea of a female deity would have been anathema to him, as the early history of Israel had involved a long struggle against the fertility religion of the Canaanites who originally inhabited the Promised Land of the Israelites.

Actually Paul would have found that the Nabataeans had little in common with his own society apart from the Aramaic language, and with Professor Bruce[12], 'we may wonder where he found a point of contact in their outlook which could dispose them to listen with some interest to his message that the crucified Jesus had been vindicated and exalted by God as universal Lord'. One point of contact may have been the concept of the ruler as the lover of his people. This seems to have been a title specifically awarded to Aretas IV as it is not found on his earliest coins or on coins of other Nabataean rulers. The concept of God loving his people was of course central to Paul's theology, and perhaps some misunderstanding arose with regard to the status of King Aretas so that Paul was suspected of inciting rebellion. In any case it seems his mission to Arabia was a failure.

When Paul returned to Damascus it was probably still part of the Roman province of Syria, but soon after his return it would have come under Nabataean control. It must have been difficult for the moneychangers in Damascus as a great variety of coins would have turned up on their tables. Caravans and travellers would have arrived frequently from Parthia, the great empire to the east of Damascus, and Paul would almost certainly have seen some of these Parthian coins.

At this time Parthia was the economic centre of the world.[13] Trade from the Roman Empire, India, China, and other areas all passed through its commercial centres. About the time of Paul's conversion, however, the great Hellenistic city of Seleucia on the Tigris rebelled against the Parthian king, Artabanos II (10–40 A.D.) and there would have been considerable upheaval in the Parthian kingdom.

Parthian drachms from the reign of Artabanos II are common today as in Paul's time. He would have been interested to see what the Parthian king looked like, but the bust of the king on the obverse was in quite a different style to the portraits he had seen on the tetradrachms of Tyre and Antioch. Instead of the natural Greek style it was a line-drawing caricature of the king in Persian style with long hair and beard, and an earring!

The typical reverse on these Parthian drachms has a seated figure inside a square formed by a seven-line legend. The figure is usually considered to be Arsaces, the founder of the dynasty. He wears a Persian headdress or bashlik and a cape, and holds out a bow, the pride of the Parthian soldier. This design was probably based on a coin of Antiochus I (Sear 6869) which shows Apollo sitting on the omphalos, the stone at Delphi which marked the centre of the world. The Greek legend tended to become blundered as the Parthian kingdom grew away from its Hellenistic past and the native language predominated.

A typical legend reads: ΒΑCΙΛΕΩC ΒΑCΙΛΕΩΝ ΑΡCΑΚΟΥ, ΕΥΕΡΓΕΤΟΥ ΔΙΚΑΙΟΝ ΕΠΙΦΑΝΟΥC

ΦΙΛΕΛΛΗΝΟC ((a coin) of the King of Kings, Arsaces, benefactor, righteous, illustrious, Greek-loving).

Figure 16 – A Parthian silver drachm of Artabanos II. (GIC 5774)

In his letter to Timothy (1 Tim. 6:15) Paul refers to Jesus as
the King of kings and Lord of lords. Although most modern
scholars consider that Paul did not write this letter and that it was
probably written after his death by one of his followers, it is
interesting to note that the title 'King of kings' was originally
one that eastern rulers applied to themselves. In 'The Revelation
to John', which was probably written during the reign of
Domitian (81–96 A.D.) the title is again used for Jesus
(Rev. 17:14 and 19:16). Since the eighteenth century this title has
become familiar to people all over the world as it is sung in
Handel's famous Hallelujah Chorus.

Jesus could have been thinking of a Parthian drachm when he
told the parable of the lost coin (Luke 15:8–10). In this parable,
which is recorded only by Luke, a woman has ten drachms and
loses one. She then lights a lamp, sweeps the floor and searches
until she finds it. At this time there were no drachms in circulation in Judaea but there must have been many Parthian women
who for various reasons had settled there. These women probably
wore silver coins in their headdresses as women did in the Middle
East until recent times. If the coins were not on her headdress it
is hard to imagine how she could lose only one of them. Of
course Luke may have used the Greek term 'drachm' because he
was writing for a Greek audience, but in any case the lost coin
was probably a Parthian drachm.

4. Tarsus 38–45 A.D.

They brought him down to Caesarea and sent him off
to Tarsus.
Acts 9:30b

When Paul escaped from Damascus in 38 A.D. he visited
Jerusalem for fifteen days (Gal. 1:18) before travelling to Tarsus,
his home-town. The next mention of Paul in the book of Acts is
when Barnabas goes to Tarsus to bring him to Antioch (Acts
11:25,26). He stays a year in Antioch during which he travels to
Judaea to take famine relief to the Christians there. Josephus
dates the famine generally in the time of the procurators Fadus
(44–46 A.D.) and Alexander (46–48 A.D.), and a date of 46 A.D.
for Paul's famine relief visit is not unreasonable. So it seems Paul
lived in Tarsus for about eight years, from 38–45 A.D., after an
absence of twenty-eight years.

We do not know if the city had changed physically during
Paul's absence but its intellectual life would have been flourish-
ing. This was largely due to the Stoic philosopher Athenodorus
(74 B.C.–7 A.D.) who was authoritative both in the city and
the university. After returning to Tarsus about 15 B.C., he
re-modelled the city's constitution and influenced its academic
life. He had been the teacher of the young Octavian, later to
become the emperor Augustus, and he continued to be the
emperor's close friend. Unfortunately none of his writings are
extant and he is known only through references by other writers
such as the philosopher Seneca (4 B.C.–65 A.D.) who was Rome's
leading intellectual figure during Paul's lifetime. Athenodorus

stands out as a man of lofty character[1], and Ramsay[2] maintains that the remarkable resemblance, both verbal and in spirit, which has often been observed between the sentiments expressed by Seneca and the words of Paul is due at least in part to the influence exercised on both by Athenodorus. Athenodorus was succeeded in his commanding position in the Tarsian state by Nestor, another Tarsian philosopher who lived to the age of 92 and was still living in 19 A.D. The geographer Strabo (64 B.C.–24 A.D.) gives a favourable picture of the University of Tarsus, praising the zeal for philosophy and the whole range of education which characterised the people of Tarsus in his time.

Although Paul was a Jew and part of the Jewish community of Tarsus, he would have been aware of the intellectual life of the city, and may even have played an active role in it. In his address to the Athenians (Acts 17:28) he quotes the Greek poet Aratus (died c. 240 B.C.) who came from Soli (Pompeiopolis) which was only about 40 kilometres from Tarsus. Moreover, Paul was a Roman citizen, which meant he was a member of a family which had raised itself so conspicuously in the city by wealth or by high office, or both, as to be admitted into the governing class of the Roman Empire. In estimating Paul's role in the city, this privileged and aristocratic position which he inherited should be taken into account. Unfortunately there is no record of Paul's life in Tarsus but it was probably a difficult time for him as many of the painful experiences related in 2 Corinthians 11:23–27 are not mentioned in the book of Acts and could well have occurred in Tarsus.

At least we do know which coins Paul would have handled when he was living in Tarsus. Most of these coins were minted in Antioch for use in the whole province of Syria, and will be dealt with in the next chapter. Also *RPC* considers that some of the undated bronze coins of Tarsus might possibly have been produced during this period although there are some stylistic differences between them and the Tarsian tetradrachms of the period. Then there is the whole series of Zeus tetradrachms (*RPC* 4108–4121) which *RPC* assigns to an uncertain mint but is tempted to think come from Cilicia. There were two issues of these silver tetradrachms under Tiberius (14–37 A.D.), one under

Caligula (37–41 A.D.) and ten under Claudius (41–54 A.D.). They all have the bare head of the emperor on the obverse and the seated Zeus type on the reverse. Although the seated Zeus was similar to the seated Ba'al of Tarsus on the coins of Tarsus minted before its conquest by Alexander the Great, the type is Greek in style and reflects the partly Greek origins of the city. The legends for Tiberius are ΤΙΒΕΡΙΟΥ ΚΑΙΣΑΡΟΣ ΘΕΟΥ ΣΕΒΑΣΤΟΥ (of Tiberius Caesar God Augustus) on the obverse, and ΥΙΟΥ ΣΕΒΑΣΤΟΥ (of the Son of Augustus) on the reverse. Jews who saw these coins would have been offended by the title 'God'. For Caligula the legends are ΓΑΙΟΣ ΚΑΙΣΑΡ ΣΕΒΑΣΤΟΣ (Gaius Caesar Augustus) on the obverse, and ΓΕΡΜΑΝΙΚΟΣ (Germanicus) on the reverse. Caligula's full name on his accession was Gaius Caesar Augustus Germanicus. His father's name was Germanicus, and he inherited it from his father, Nero Claudius Drusus, who was awarded the title after successfully campaigning in Germany. For Claudius the legends are ΤΙΒΕΡΙΟΣ ΚΛΑΥΔΙΟΣ ΚΑΙΣΑΡ (Tiberius Claudius Caesar) on the obverse and ΣΕΒΑΣΤΟΣ ΓΕΡΜΑΝΙΚΟΣ (Augustus Germanicus) on the reverse. Claudius' full name on his accession was Tiberius Claudius Caesar Augustus Germanicus. Claudius inherited the title Germanicus from his father, Nero Claudius Drusus. The issues of Claudius differ only in the abbreviated names, presumably of the issuing magistrates, which appear on the reverses.

It is possible that Paul might have seen some of the silver drachms minted at Caesarea in Cappadocia after it became a Roman province. Cappadocia was the highland area north of the Taurus Mountains. It was easily accessible from Tarsus through the Cilician Gates. From about 25 A.D. Caesarea became an imperial mint issuing silver and bronze coins for the eastern regions of the Roman Empire. According to Sydenham[3] the coinage of Caesarea differs from that of Antioch in that the latter preserves its Syrian characteristics down to the time of Valerian (253–260 A.D.) whereas the former, despite its use of Greek legends, is thoroughly Roman in feeling. At Caesarea the portraiture closely follows the styles adopted by the Roman mint; and, with the exception of Mount Argaeus, which is the only purely local type, most of the reverse types are stock personifications adapted from those which appear on coins of the west. Mount Argaeus was a snow-capped peak 4000 metres high, which overlooked the city. There is no record of Paul having been there and it is unlikely that he would have visited the city.

The coin which Paul would have seen during his stay in Tarsus was a silver tetradrachm minted in Tarsus under Tiberius (*RPC* 4005). It is undated but *RPC* suggests a date of about 35 A.D. because the portrait is similar to that issued from Antioch in that year. The coin has the letters TAP (for Tarsus) in the field on the reverse, and MHTP (for 'of the metropolis') in the exergue on the reverse; and so must have been a source of pride for the citizens of Tarsus. It was 84.75 per cent silver and 25 millimetres in diameter. It is rare today with *RPC* finding only two specimens in the museums it surveyed. On the obverse was the laureate head of Tiberius and the legend ΤΙΒΕΡΙΟΥ ΚΑΙΣΑΡΟΣ ΣΕΒΑΣΤΟΥ. On the reverse was Livia as Hera, seated on a throne, holding ears of corn and poppies, and the legend ΣΕΒΑΣΤΗΣ ΙΟΥΛΙΑΣ ΗΡΑΣ (of Augusta, Julia, Hera).

Figure 17 – A silver tetradrachm of Tiberius. (*RPC* 4005)

Why does the goddess Hera appear on this special coin of Tarsus? The answer is that Greeks from Argos and Jews formed the main body of the new colonists settled at Tarsus by Antiochus IV Epiphanes when he refounded the city in 171 B.C.[4], and Argos was the chief centre in Greece of the cult of Hera.[5] In Argos Hera had several temples, the oldest of which was called the Heraeum and housed a marvellous statue of Hera in gold and ivory. The goddess was represented seated on a throne and wearing a crown adorned with figures of the Horae and the Graces (Pausanias, Book 2, 17:4). It was the most celebrated work of the famous Argive sculptor, Polycleitus (fl. 450–420 B.C.). The Hera on this coin was probably based on Polycleitus' statue.

Why does the name 'Augusta Julia' appear in the legend with Hera? Livia assumed the names Julia Augusta, the feminine forms of Julius and Augustus, after the death of her husband, Augustus. She was the wife of the deified Augustus and the mother of the emperor Tiberius, and it was easy to equate her with Hera, the wife of Zeus, the king of heaven, and the mother of various divine beings including Ares (Mars), the god of war. Although Tiberius refused to allow Livia to be deified after her death in 29 A.D. and did not encourage divine honours for himself, the equation of Livia with Hera suggests that they were already considered divine beings. In the Middle East there had always been a tendency to treat kings and other exalted human beings as divine, except in Israel where strict monotheism was observed.

In Tarsus Hera was probably perceived as another form of the great Earth Mother, whose various forms included Artemis in Ephesus, Demeter in Eleusis, Cybele in Galatia, Atargatis in Syria, and Aphrodite in Cyprus.[6] The goddess on the coin of Tarsus appears to be holding ears of corn (usually associated with Demeter) and poppies (usually associated with Aphrodite), which suggests she may have been worshipped in a syncretistic form, as at Hierapolis where sacrifices were offered to Hera-Atargatis.[7] Syncretism was widely practised in the religious life of the Roman Empire at this time. In Tarsus there was probably a temple to Hera, if only as an adjunct to the temple of Baal/Zeus.[8]

Paul would have had mixed feelings when he saw the coin that Tarsus issued. Firstly, Hera was alien to his religious outlook but he may have approved of the veil which trailed from the back of her head, because he writes to the Corinthians that 'if a woman will not veil herself, then she should cut off her hair; but if it is disgraceful for a woman to have her hair cut off or to be shaved, she should wear a veil' (1 Cor. 11:6). Paul's attitude to women could well have been moulded by his life in Tarsus because the complete veiling of women in the oriental style was practised in that city. Dio Chrysostom (40–112 A.D.) a famous orator who visited Tarsus, could find little that was good in Tarsian manners, but he did praise the extremely modest dress of Tarsian women.

Secondly, Paul, a Roman citizen, may have respected Livia as a member of the governing Roman hierarchy, but he would not have approved of her identification with the goddess Hera. The polytheistic religions and their syncretistic tendencies would have been offensive to him.

Thirdly and most importantly, the coin was essentially Hellenistic in style and content, and would have been just one more Hellenistic element in Paul's environment in Tarsus. Although the tendency of modern Biblical scholars is to emphasize the Hebrew background of Paul, the influence of Hellenistic culture on his life was considerable, as it was on the development of early Christianity. Some liberal scholars have gone so far as to say that a non-Hellenised Christianity would not have insisted that Jesus Christ was God incarnate.[9] As far as Paul is concerned Tarsus would have been a rich source of Hellenism, although he probably did not have to move far outside the Jewish community, for the Jews of the Diaspora were already much influenced by Hellenistic thought. As Professor Peters says, 'Paul is far less Hellene than he at first appears; it was Judaism itself that was Hellenised'.[10]

Tarsus was a city in which the ancient culture of the Middle East met the culture of the Hellenistic West. It was therefore peculiarly suitable to produce Paul, the Apostle to the Gentiles. Ramsay[11] says that Tarsus was not an important university city like Athens but its crowning glory, the reason for its undying interest to the world is that it produced the apostle Paul, and that it was the one city which was suited by its equipoise between the Asiatic and the Western spirit to mould the character of the great Hellenistic Jew.

5. Antioch 46 A.D.

Then Barnabus went to Tarsus to look for Saul, and when he had found him, he brought him to Antioch.
Acts 11:25,26a

Paul stayed a whole year in Antioch meeting other Christians. According to Acts 11:19–21, persecution in Jerusalem had caused Christians to flee as far as Phoenicia, Cyprus and Antioch, but it was only at Antioch that some of them began preaching to Gentiles, a great number of whom were converted. It was in Antioch that they were first called Christians. So Antioch was of vital importance for the spread of Christianity to the non-Jewish world, and Paul was brought from Tarsus to be part of this exciting development.

Professor Downey[1] summarises the special contribution of Antioch to the spread of Christianity. Firstly, the success of preaching to the Gentiles and the acceptance of them without insistence on their observance of the Jewish Law, determined the ecumenical character of Christianity. Secondly, the Christians of Antioch were wealthy enough to support early missionary journeys such as those of Paul and Barnabus, and to send famine relief to the Christians in Judaea. Thirdly, because of Antioch's position at the centre of a network of well-established communications radiating in all directions, it served effectively as a focal point for expansion and as a headquarters to which the missionaries could return for spiritual and physical rest and replenishment.

During his year at Antioch Paul together with Barnabus took

the famine relief to the Christians in Judaea. Exactly what form this relief took, whether a sum of money or actual supplies of food, is unknown. According to Josephus (Ant., Book XX, Chapter 5:2) the famine occurred during the procuratorships of Fadus (44–46 A.D.) and Alexander (46–48 A.D.), so a date of about 46 A.D. for Paul's stay in Antioch is reasonable. Claudius (41–54 A.D.) was the emperor in Rome, and Antioch had been the capital of the Roman Province of Syria since 64 B.C. The city was founded by Seleucus I, one of Alexander the Great's generals, in 300 B.C., and named after his father Antiochus, who had been a general of Philip II of Macedonia. Antioch soon became the western capital of the Seleucid Empire, while Seleucia on the Tigris was the eastern capital. Seleucia Pieria was the seaport for Antioch.

While the population was always mixed, Josephus (Ant., Book XII, Chapter 3:1) records that the Seleucids encouraged Jews to migrate to Antioch in large numbers and gave them citizenship rights. The Jewish quarter was in the southern part of the city.

Antioch enjoyed a beautiful site and abundant water supplies from springs in the suburb of Daphne, eight kilometres south of the city. It lay between Mount Silpius in the east and the Orontes river which at this point flows from north-east to south-west. The city was 22 kilometres from the sea. In Paul's day the river divided to form an island on which part of the city was built, but the eastern arm of the river has long silted up. The modern Turkish city of Antakya now occupies the site but from 1932 to 1939 excavations were carried out by a team of archaeologists, and foundations from Roman times were unearthed including a number of fine mosaic floors which indicated how wealthy the city had been.

Situated at the base of a mountain and on a river bank the remains of the city that Paul knew have become covered by metres of silt washed down from the mountain and deposited by the river in flood. However, the main street which runs parallel to the river in the eastern part of the modern city follows roughly the line of the principal thoroughfare of the ancient city, and traces of this thoroughfare were found in the excavations. It was a monumental, colonnaded street, the pride of the city, with marble paving supplied by Herod the Great of Judaea and roofed colonnades built by Tiberius who also ornamented the whole street with statues. The street was angled slightly near the centre of the city where a bronze statue of Tiberius stood on a stone column, so that the vista of the street was not indefinitely straight but concentrated on the statue of Tiberius. Tiberius extended the walls of the city and at the north-eastern end of the main thoroughfare he built a large gate surmounted by the she-wolf nursing Romulus and Remus, the legendary founders of Rome. The statue was erected to provide the city with a symbol of Roman sovereignty, and for travellers arriving from the hinterland of Syria this gate would be the first monument of the city that they would see.

Before Paul the city had been visited by many famous people including Hannibal, Julius Caesar, Pompey, Mark Antony and Cleopatra (who held their wedding there), and Augustus. Since its founding the city had been embellished with many public buildings and monuments, including a great temple of Jupiter built by Antiochus IV Epiphanes (175–163 B.C.). The temple had a ceiling panelled with gold and walls covered with gilded plates. Tiberius restored or completed this temple and it has been suggested that the cult statue was a representation of himself.

Augustus issued Tyche tetradrachms from Antioch regularly to the end of his reign in 14 A.D., but Tiberius authorised only two issues of tetradrachms and the surviving number of these coins is very small. *RPC* could find only three specimens for each issue. The first undated issue (*RPC* 4161) has the radiate head of Augustus on the reverse with the inscription ΘΕΟΣ ΣΕΒΑΣΤΟΣ ΚΑΙΣΑΡ (God Augustus Caesar) but for the second issue (*RPC* 4162) in 35/6 A.D. Tiberius reverts to the innocuous Tyche of Antioch type.

During Caligula's brief reign (37–41 A.D.) there were six issues of tetradrachms of Antioch (*RPC* 4163–4168) and Paul probably saw them all during his stay. The first (*RPC* 4163) is undated. It has the laureate head of Caligula (Gaius) with the inscription ΓΑΙΟΣ ΚΑΙΣΑΡ ΓΕΡΜΑΝΙΚΟΣ (Gaius Caesar

Germanicus) on the obverse and the laureate head of Caligula's father Germanicus with the inscription ΓΕΡΜΑΝΙΚΟΣ ΚΑΙΣΑΡ on the reverse.

Figure 18 – A silver tetradrachm of Caligula. (*RPC* 4163)

Caligula inherited the title Germanicus from his father who was Tiberius' nephew. In 17 A.D. Tiberius sent Germanicus to the East with extraordinary powers to solve the political problems there. Germanicus was young, handsome, friendly and popular with the people. Unfortunately differences of opinion between himself and the imperial legate in Antioch, Piso, came to a head and Germanicus dismissed the legate. Soon after Piso's departure from Antioch Germanicus became ill and died. Although the preserved description of his symptoms indicated a fever, Germanicus was convinced that he had been poisoned. The incident caused a sensation throughout the Empire and many people blamed Tiberius for the death of his nephew. Germanicus was only 33 when he died in 19 A.D., and his unclothed body was displayed in a public place at Antioch before being cremated. Among the children of Germanicus who witnessed his death at Antioch was the future emperor Caligula. According to Downey[2] Caligula's pious respect for the scene of his father's death led him, after he became emperor, to issue a coin at Antioch commemorating Germanicus. Caligula also showed great generosity to Antioch when it was damaged by an earthquake early in his reign.

The subsequent issues of Caligula (*RPC* 4164–4168) have a draped bust of Caligula's mother, Agrippina I, on the reverse with the date according to the year of the reign (A, B or Γ). The last two issues are further differentiated by the presence of a dot in the reverse left field (*RPC* 4166 and 4168 have the dot).

Figure 19 – A silver tetradrachm of Caligula. (*RPC* 4164)

Agrippina, who was the grand-daughter of Augustus, returned with her children and the ashes of her dead husband to Rome where she subsequently fell out of favour with Tiberius and was banished to an island where it is said she starved herself to death. She died in 33 A.D. One of her daughters was Agrippina II, the mother of Nero.

Claudius (41–54 A.D.) issued silver tetradrachms from Antioch but not until about 50 A.D. when the bust of the young Nero makes its appearance on the coins. So Paul would not have seen them.

As far as the bronze coins minted at Antioch are concerned, Augustus issued four types: civic, archieratic, legate and SC bronzes. As well, *RPC*[3] claims there is evidence from style that Antioch participated in the production of the CA coins which were more common in the province of Asia. The letters CA within a wreath occurred on the reverse, with a bust of Augustus on the obverse. What CA stood for is still disputed but suggestions have included Commune Asiae (by the Commonwealth of Asia), Caesaris Auctoritate (by the authority of Caesar) and Caesar Augustus. *RPC*[4] considers that the CA coinage of Augustus which was of brass and bronze and produced in the 20s B.C., probably represented an attempt to impose a unified currency on the communities of the eastern Empire, but it was abandoned.

The civic bronzes, of course, did not bear portraits of Augustus, but featured the laureate head of Zeus, a ram running, a tripod, three ears of corn or Tyche; and the name of the city was prominent on the coins. The types no doubt referred to cults practised in Antioch at the time. The archieratic bronzes probably referred to Augustus's acceptance of the title of Archiereus (High-Priest) at Antioch. They have Augustus's laureate head on the obverse and the inscription, ΑΡΧΙΕΡΑΤΙΚΟΝ ΑΝΤΙΟΧΕΙΣ (belonging to the high priest, people of Antioch) in a wreath on the reverse. The legate bronzes bore the name of the current legate of Syria on the reverse with the Tyche of Antioch (or later a running ram), while the laureate head of Zeus was on the obverse. Zeus was an important deity in Antioch and his cult was probably encouraged by the Romans in order to promote respect for sovereign power which at the time resided with them. The SC bronzes had the laureate head of Augustus on the obverse and a large SC within a wreath on the reverse. The SC probably stood for Senatus Consulto (by decree of the Senate), which suggests that this coinage was connected with imperial expenditure, e.g. army pay. These SC coins had no mark of origin as they were not financed by the city of Antioch but by the Roman authorities. Under the Roman system bronze coinage was issued by the authority of the Senate, whereas precious metal (silver and gold) was under the direct authority of the emperor. Butcher[5] states that the Roman legions countermarked these SC coins more than any other, which confirms that the troops certainly used them.

For his bronze coinage Tiberius continued only the legate and SC coins. In 14/15 A.D. he issued legate bronzes in two sizes (RPC 4270, 4271) with his bare head instead of the laureate head of Zeus on the obverse and the name of the legate, Silanus, in an inscription on the reverse within a laurel wreath of six leaves. The inscription read ΕΠΙ ΣΙΛΑΝΟΥ ΑΝΤΙΟΧΕΩΝ (of the Antiochenes in the time of Silanus). A. Caecilius Metellus Creticus Silanus was the imperial legate in Antioch from 11 to 16/7 A.D. He was also a prospective relative by marriage of the imperial family and Tiberius allowed the mint of Antioch to honour him by putting his name on its coins. Tiberius also allowed a later legate, L. Pomponius Flaccus, to be similarly honoured and in the issue of 33/34 A.D., again in two sizes (RPC 4274, 4275), the name Flaccus appears in the inscription. Flaccus was legate probably from 32 to 35 A.D. This practice was occasionally adopted in other parts of the Empire.

Figure 20 – A bronze of Tiberius. (*RPC* 4274)

In 31/32 A.D. Tiberius issued SC bronzes in two sizes (4272, 4273) with his laureate head and TI CAEΣAR AVG TR POT XXXIII on the obverse, and SC within a laurel wreath of six leaves on the reverse.

Figure 21 – A bronze of Tiberius. (*RPC* 4272)

Despite his six issues of silver tetradrachms, Caligula (Gaius) issued no bronze coinage, although many of the bronze SC coins of Tiberius and Augustus bear his countermarks e.g. ΓΑ–Β, ΓΑ–Γ. Claudius issued a lot of bronze SC coinage, although Paul in 46 A.D. would have seen only the SC and legate issues of 41/2 A.D. when the legate was Petronius.

Apart from the tetradrachm bearing the Tyche of Antioch which was issued by Tiberius in 35/6 A.D. all the silver and bronze issued after 14 A.D. which Paul would have seen in Antioch bore types which were Roman in character. They spoke of Rome as the sovereign power of the world. Paul would have been impressed by the beautiful city of Antioch with its great colonnaded street and its wonderful monuments, and by the imprint of Roman power upon it and its coins. Perhaps even at this stage in his career he realised he would have to go to Rome; for he firmly believed that the ultimate sovereign power resided not in Rome but in the God his fellow Christians worshipped at Antioch.

6. Seleucia 47 A.D.

*So, being sent out by the Holy Spirit, they went down
to Seleucia.*

Acts 13:4a

Seleucia (Greek Seleukeia) was the port for Antioch. It was 25
kilometres from Antioch and eight kilometres north of the mouth
of the Orontes River. It was situated at the foot of Mount Pierius,
a spur of the Amanus Mountains. Mount Pierius is known today
as Musa Dagi (or Jebel Musa). The district was called Pieria,
after the mountain, and Seleucia was called Seleucia Pieria to distinguish it from about ten other cities called Seleucia.

Seleucia was on the northern side of a wide bay. On the
southern side was Mount Casium, whose peak towers 1729
metres into the sky. The god who was worshipped on Mount
Casium was a Semitic deity who was identified with Zeus and
honoured with annual festivals on the mountain.[1] This god was
known as Zeus Casius (Greek Kasios).

Seleucia was founded by Seleucus I about 300 B.C. Ptolemy
III of Egypt captured it in the middle of the third century B.C.
but it was regained by Antiochus III in 219 B.C. In 146 B.C. the
Egyptians under Ptolemy VI again controlled the city for a short
time. In 108 B.C. it became independent and remained so even
when Pompey conquered Syria in 64 B.C.

Seleucia was built on a mountain that sloped steeply to some
level ground beside the sea. The port occupied this level ground
and the adjacent steep slopes were honeycombed with caves and
warehouses where goods were stored. Also in this lower city were

the suburbs and business district of the city. A winding stairway
cut in the rock led to the upper city where there was a paved
agora, an amphitheatre, and a large Doric temple.[2] Even higher
was the acropolis, or fortress, of the city. Actually the city was
very well fortified with strong walls and was considered impreg-
nable. H.V. Morton[3] called it a Syrian Gibraltar, implying that it
had all the inadequacies of that rocky port-fortress.

One of the major problems with the city in Paul's time was a
stream which flowed down from the mountain, through the
lower city and into the harbour. When it was in flood this stream
became a raging torrent which disrupted the life and work of the
city. One of the most remarkable feats of Roman engineering was
the building of a tunnel to divert this stream. The tunnel was 1.5
kilometres long, six metres wide, and over six metres high. Two
sections of it are cut through the mountain. At its entrance is an
inscription in the stone, DIVVS VESPASIANVS ET DIVVS
TITVS, which suggests that the work was begun under
Vespasian (69–79 A.D.).

Nowadays the ruins of Seleucia extend widely over the mountain slopes about six kilometres north of the modern town of
Samandag, a seaside suburb of Antakya (ancient Antioch) about
28 kilometres away. According to Tom Brosnahan[4] the ruins are
not much to look at. One of the reasons for this is that the
ancient stone buildings have been broken up in the course of the
centuries so that the ground is strewn for kilometres with sharp
splinters of marble and limestone. The harbour has silted up and
the sea has retreated, enabling the local people to plant trees on
the flat, rich land. H.V Morton[5] describes what he saw when he
visited this area: 'Sections of the harbour walls, and what appear
to be the foundations of a lighthouse, still stand in these mulberry
groves. Beneath a covering of brambles, I saw a flight of harbour
steps which led down through the branches of fig trees; it was on
such steps – possibly these steps – that Paul, Barnabas, and Mark
stepped aboard at the outset of their immortal voyage to Cyprus
and Asia Minor'.

Seleucia issued bronze coins from the second century B.C. and
silver coins after its independence in 108 B.C. During the reign
of Augustus (27 B.C.–14 A.D.) the city issued two silver

tetradrachms, *RPC* 4328 and 4329. The former is 26 millimetres in diameter and 74.75 per cent silver.[6] On the obverse there is the laureate head of Augustus and the inscription ΚΑΙΣΑΡΟΣ ΣΕΒΑΣΤΟΥ (of Caesar Augustus). On the reverse there is the symbol of a thunderbolt on a cushion placed on a throne, and the inscription ΣΕΛΕΥΚΕΩΝ ΤΗΣ ΙΕΡΑΣ ΚΑΙ ΑΥΤΟΝΟΜΟΥ (of the people of Seleukeia, the sacred and independent). Under the throne are the letters ΙΔΡ, indicating 114 years since independence in 108 B.C., i.e. 6 A.D. On either side are the letters A and H, of unknown significance, and the whole is surrounded by a laurel wreath.

Figure 22 – A silver tetradrachm of Augustus. (*RPC* 4328)

RPC[7] mentions that there are many examples of *RPC* 4328 which are silver-plated. *RPC* 4329 is similar except that the date is 8 A.D. The thunderbolt (Greek keraunos, Latin fulmen) is the symbol of Zeus, and when holding this symbol he is called Zeus Keraunios. Across the bay Paul would have seen the peak of Mount Casium where Zeus was worshipped, but it seems that the thunderbolt (probably in the form of lightning) was involved in selecting the site of the city of Seleucia, because Appian, a Greek historian of the second century A.D., wrote, 'They say that when he settled the people of Seleukeia, the city by the sea, Zeus sent lightning as a sign to guide them, and through this, lightning became divine to them and even now they worship and sing praises to lightning'.[8]

Paul was a Jew, and for him thunder and lightning were simply part of God's wonderful creation and of no religious significance in themselves, although they usually accompanied any manifestation of God, such as his presence on Mount Sinai (Exodus 19:16,17; 20:18,19). Paul's own conversion experience was accompanied by 'a great light from heaven' (Acts 22:6). In Psalm 18, however, Paul's God is portrayed in much the same way as Zeus or Hadad might have been:

> The LORD also thundered in the heavens,
> and the Most High uttered his voice.
> And he sent out his arrows, and scattered them;
> he flashed forth lightnings, and routed them.
> Psalm 18:13,14

The words of Psalm 18 are also found in the book of Samuel (2 Samuel 22:14,15), which suggests it was an ancient song of the Jews.

In 16 A.D. during the reign of Tiberius (14–37 A.D.) Seleucia issued three bronze coins: *RPC* 4330, 4331, and 4332. *RPC* 4330 is 27 millimetres in diameter and has the bare head Tiberius on the obverse with the inscription ΚΑΙΣΑΡ ΣΕΒΑΣΤΟΣ ΣΕΒΑΣΤΟΥ (Caesar Augustus, of Augustus). On the reverse is the inscription ΕΠΙ ΣΙΛΑΝΟΥ ΣΕΛΕΥΚΕΩΝ (in the time of Silanus, of the people of Seleukeia) enclosed in a laurel wreath. Above the inscription is Γ (year 3 of Tiberius, i.e. 16 A.D.), and below it is ΖΜ (year 47 of the Actian era). Q. Caecilius Metellus Creticus Silanus was Legate of Syria from 11 to 17 A.D. His name on these coins indicates that although Seleucia may have been nominally independent, it was very much under the thumb of the Romans. His name also appears on coins of Antioch.

RPC 4331 is 18 millimetres in diameter and has the laureate head of Zeus on the obverse, and his symbol of a thunderbolt on the reverse with the inscription ΣΕΛΕΥΚΕΩΝ ΕΠΙ ΣΙΛΑΝΟΥ (of the people of Seleukeia, in the time of Silanus). *RPC* 4332 is 13 millimetres in diameter and has the laureate head of Apollo on the obverse, and his symbol of a tripod on the reverse with the same inscription. It is appropriate that this last coin should honour Apollo because he was an important god at Antioch and it was the Christians of Antioch who sent Paul out on his first missionary journey. Apollo was worshipped particularly at Daphne[9], a beautiful place nine kilometres south of Antioch. At Daphne there were forests and waterfalls, and the people of Antioch enjoyed visiting the area, as they still do today. In Paul's

time there was a temple of Apollo there. One of the many functions of Apollo was that he sent people out to colonise distant
lands[10], and in so doing they spread Greek culture. Apollo was
the god of culture. He was also the god of light; and for the
Greeks, the spread of their culture meant enlightenment for the
recipients. In Paul's case it was 'the light of the gospel of the glory
of Christ' (2 Corinthians 4:4) which he was bringing to the
western world. But as he and his friends walked down the stone
harbour steps to embark on the waiting vessel, he could not
know what the future held for him, or could he? Apollo was
also the god who predicted the future, and the tripod was his
symbol as god of prophecy.[11] We can be sure that someone connected with Paul's expedition would have consulted Apollo about
the future, and that the reply was favourable.

7. Cyprus 47 A.D.

So, being sent out by the Holy Spirit, they went down to
Seleucia; and from there they sailed to Cyprus. When they
arrived at Salamis, they proclaimed the word of God ...
When they had gone through the whole island as far as
Paphos ...
Acts 13:4–6a

Paul's first missionary journey must have lasted about two years
because we know that he was in Antioch about 46 A.D. and
that he was in Jerusalem for the Apostolic Council which probably occurred in 49 A.D. The evidence for the latter date comes
from Paul's letter to the Galatians (Gal. 2:1) where he states that
after fourteen years he went up again to Jerusalem. Apparently[1],
he meant fourteen years after his conversion which, as has already
been discussed, probably occurred about 36 A.D. So it seems Paul
was in Cyprus in about 47 A.D.

According to the account in Acts Paul arrived at Salamis in
the east of Cyprus and after some time preaching to the Jews of
the city he travelled to Paphos in the west of the island. Although
Salamis was the major city, Paphos was the political capital
during the Roman period and the seat of the Roman governor.
Acts relates how Paul met the governor, Sergius Paulus, in Paphos
and how he was converted. If the period of his governorship was
known it would provide an anchor for the chronology of Paul's
career, but unfortunately no evidence has been found. There is a
Latin inscription (Corpus Inscriptionum Latinarum, IV, 31545)
which mentions a Lucius Sergius Paullus as one of the curators of
the banks of the Tiber river during the reign of Claudius, but
there is no evidence that this person was ever a governor in

Cyprus. A few other inscriptions[2] have been found but no definite conclusions can be made from them.

Cyprus was confirmed as a possession of Cleopatra by Mark Antony, but after the battle of Actium in 31 B.C. Octavian claimed the island and put it under the administration of the Roman Senate in 22 B.C. When Paul arrived in Salamis it was the most important city in Cyprus, having been founded in the second millennium B.C. It seems to have been the first city on Cyprus to strike coins, and from their inscriptions a list of kings from about 500 B.C. can be made. The city was totally destroyed by the Arabs in 647 A.D. and the site has been abandoned ever since. The harbour in which Paul arrived and which made it a great commercial centre has now completely silted up, but the ruins[3] of the city can still be seen about five kilometres north of the modern city of Famagusta.

Excavations carried out by the Cyprus Department of Antiquities from 1952 to 1974 have revealed that Salamis was an impressive Hellenistic city in Paul's time. A long, wide agora (market place) was situated in the central part of the city and at one end of the agora stood the temple of Zeus Salaminios who featured on the coins of Cyprus. Paul could not have avoided seeing this temple where human sacrifice was practised up to the first century A.D. Although the remains of the temple indicate that it was not large, it added considerable prestige to the city as Zeus was the chief of the gods. A gymnasium and a theatre with a capacity of 15,000 were built during the reign of Augustus in the northern part of the city which formed a kind of cultural centre. A stadium was also situated there.

Paphos was famous in the ancient world as the legendary birthplace of Aphrodite, the goddess of beauty and sexual love, and her temple there dated back to the second millennium B.C., being originally a shrine of the Phoenician goddess Astarte whose cult was adapted by the Greeks to the worship of Aphrodite. According to the legend first recorded by Hesiod (fl. c. 700 B.C.), when Cronus overthrew the sky god Uranus he castrated him and threw the genitals into the sea. Where they fell, white foam (aphros) formed and from this the goddess arose. She stepped ashore at Paphos and where she stood flowers and grasses grew.

Although she subsequently married the deformed blacksmith god Hephaestus, she had a passionate, adulterous affair with Ares (Mars), the vigorous and handsome god of war.

In Paul's time there was old Paphos where the shrine of the goddess stood, and new Paphos, about 16 kilometres to the north-west, which was the Roman capital of the island. Considerable Roman remains have been found at new Paphos, including city walls, a theatre, mosaic floors, and harbour moles. At old Paphos the site[4] of Aphrodite's temple can still be seen. It was a very unusual temple by Greek standards. It consisted of a central tower open to reveal a baetyl, a sacred stone which represented the divinity. On each side of the tower were side porticos in which stood incense burners. The whole complex was built on a platform, and in front of it was a semicircular courtyard of large stone slabs enclosed by a lattice fence with gates at the front. No doubt the worship of Paphian Aphrodite required a special ritual which dictated this architectural form. There were probably cult prostitutes associated with this temple which must have brought considerable wealth to the city. Such financial considerations would have influenced the Romans in their choice of Paphos as the administrative centre of Cyprus.

The temple of Aphrodite featured on the coins of Cyprus. Although *RPC* states that the question of mints is open, it would be reasonable to attribute these coins to the mint of Paphos, and those coins which feature Zeus to the mint of Salamis.

It is unlikely that Paul would have seen the coins issued by Augustus, but he probably saw the coins of Tiberius and Claudius. Caligula issued no coins at all in Cyprus, nor were there any silver coins minted there.

The first coins of Tiberius (*RPC* 3917–3919) were issued after 15/16 A.D. because the radiate head of Augustus on the reverse was copied from asses struck in Rome in 15/16 A.D. On the obverse was the bare head of Tiberius and the Latin inscription TI CAESAR AVGVSTVS. On the reverse of the largest coin was the radiate head of Augustus with a thunderbolt in front and a star above, with the inscription DIVOS AVGVSTVS PATER PATR (Divine Augustus, Father of the Nation). On the reverse of the smallest coin was the seated Livia, with the inscription **IVLIA AVGVSTA**. These coins were issued to celebrate the deification of Augustus and to honour his wife. The thunderbolt, of course, was a symbol of Zeus and apparently Augustus was being equated with the chief of the gods. The title 'Pater Patriae' had been awarded to Augustus by the Senate in 2 B.C. and it may have prompted Paul to think of the God whom Jesus referred to as 'Abba', Daddy. Paul too thought of God as father, and of his thirteen letters, eleven have the following phrase in the opening passage, 'Grace to you and peace from God our Father and the Lord Jesus Christ'.

The second issues of Tiberius (*RPC* 3920–3926) occurred in 22/23 A.D., and all have the head of Drusus, the son of Tiberius, with the inscription **DRVSVS CAESAR** on the obverse, and either Zeus Salaminios, the temple of Paphian Aphrodite, or both, on the reverse. After the death of Germanicus at Antioch in 19 A.D. Drusus, who was the son of Tiberius and his first wife Vipsania, became the heir, and in 22 A.D. he was granted the Tribunician Power, an indication that he was considered the eventual successor of Tiberius. *RPC* suggests that these coins may have been struck in 22 A.D. when Paphos and Salamis were confirmed in the right of asylum long enjoyed by their temples.

Figure 23 – A bronze of Tiberius. (*RPC* 3921)

The first issues of Claudius (*RPC* 3927–3931) are undated. They have the laureate head of Claudius with the Latin inscription **TI CLAVDIVS CAESAR AVG PM TR P IMP** on the obverse and the Greek inscription **ΚΟΙΝΟΝ ΚΥΠΡΙΩΝ** in a laurel wreath on the reverse. The reverse inscription means 'Confederation of the Cypriots', and the function of this body, which was established when Cyprus was under Egyptian rule, had been centred around the cult of the Ptolemaic rulers. When Cyprus came under Roman rule, the Koinon became responsible for religious activities throughout the island including the cult of the emperors as well as the control of bronze coinage. The most important annual festival that the Koinon organised was that of Aphrodite at Paphos.

Figure 24 – A bronze of Claudius. (*RPC* 3927)

In 43/44 A.D. Claudius issued coins (*RPC* 3932–3933) with his head on the obverse and the name of the governor, Cominius Proculus, on the reverse. It is unknown why Claudius should have honoured him in this way but he would have been a predecessor of Sergius Paulus who summoned Paul in order to hear his preaching. The complete inscription on the reverse was ΚΥΠΡΙWΝ (of the Cypriots) in large letters in the centre, surrounded by ΕΠΙ ΚΟΜΙΝΙΟΥ ΠΡΟΚΛΟΥ ΑΝΘΥΠΑΤΟΥ (in the time of Cominius Proculus, Proconsul). The official title of the governor of Cyprus was Proconsul, which meant that he had consular, i.e. virtually absolute, power over the province. When Paul saw these coins with the governor's name on them he would have been reminded that Cyprus was a province of the Roman Empire.

Figure 25 – A bronze of Claudius. (*RPC* 3932)

When Paul saw the coins with Drusus' head on them a much more complex impression would have been made; for behind the portrait of Drusus lay a drama of Shakespearian proportions which virtually every citizen of the Roman Empire must have known by 47 A.D. The key players in this tragic drama were firstly Drusus himself, the son and heir of the emperor. Drusus was described by Tacitus[5] as violent tempered, and by Suetonius[6] as having vicious and dissolute habits. His coin portraits reveal an ugly man with a cruel expression. His wife was Livilla, grand-niece of Augustus. Although unattractive in her earlier years, she grew into a woman of great beauty. Then appeared Sejanus, the vigorous commander of the Praetorian Guard. He was an ambitious man who wanted the empire for himself. He wooed Livilla, professing undying devotion, and seduced her. Tacitus[7] relates, 'Then, this first guilty move achieved (since a woman who has parted with her virtue will refuse nothing) he incited her to hope for marriage, partnership in the empire, and the death of her husband. So the grand-niece of Augustus, daughter-in-law of Tiberius, mother of Drusus' children, degraded herself and her ancestors and descendants with a small-town adulterer; she sacrificed her honourable, assured position for infamy and hazard'. Sejanus and Livilla contrived to poison Drusus, and in 23 A.D. they were successful; but their plans to gain the empire were thwarted by Tiberius who refused to allow them to marry and subsequently had Sejanus executed.

When Paul saw these coins with Drusus on the obverse he would have been reminded of this tale of lust, greed, and murder. Perhaps on this island of Aphrodite he was moved to consider the all-pervasiveness of sin in the human condition. 'All have sinned and fall short of the glory of God', he later wrote to the Romans (Romans 3:23). According to Paul the Jewish Law made the human condition worse, giving no hope: 'All who rely on observing the law are under a curse, for it is written "Cursed is everyone who does not continue to do everything written in the Book of the Law". Clearly no one is justified before God by the law' (Galatians 3:10–11a, NIV).

No wonder the proconsul Sergius Paulus was convinced by Paul's preaching! The proconsul was an intelligent man, and although Paul performed a miracle in his presence by blinding his Jewish magician, it was because of Paul's reasoned arguments that he believed; 'for he was astonished at the teaching about the Lord' (Acts 13:12). Sergius Paulus probably suggested that Paul continue his journey on to Pisidian Antioch where he had relatives and estates. Inscriptions relating to the family of Sergius Paulus have been found at Pisidian Antioch. 'The journey from Paphos to Pisidian Antioch was determined in large measure by the fact that Antioch was Sergius Paulus' home city'.[8]

8. Perga 48 A.D.

Then Paul and his companions set sail from Paphos and came to Perga in Pamphylia.
Acts 13:13

Paul spent about two years on his first missionary journey, returning about 49 A.D. for the Apostolic Council in Jerusalem. So he would have been in Pamphylia and Galatia about 48 A.D. He sailed directly to Perga in Pamphylia indicating that Perga was reachable by ship. The vessel carrying Paul was not large because it had to navigate the Kestros river for about 15 kilometres to reach the environs of the city.

Perga was one of the Greek cities which flourished on the plain of Pamphylia situated on the south coast of Asia Minor. It was the starting point for a mountainous road which wound into the hinterland of Anatolia. Paul took this route on the next leg of his journey to South Galatia. What the political situation[1] was in Pamphylia in 48 A.D. is not clear, but it was probably part of the Roman Province of Lycia-and-Pamphylia.

According to tradition Perga was founded by the Greeks from the Peloponnese after the Trojan War, but its origins probably go back to the Hittites in the second millennium B.C. So it was already an ancient city when Paul visited it, but in his time it had all the features of a typical Greek city, including an acropolis on a rocky outcrop and a theatre built in the Hellenistic period with an eventual seating capacity of 14,000. The city was divided into quarters by two broad streets which intersected each other. These colonnaded streets were paved with mosaics and lined with statues, and its sidewalks opened onto arcaded shops.

The mathematician Apollonius was born in Perga about 260 B.C. and although he worked mostly in Alexandria and Pergamum the city would have taken great pride in its illustrious son. Anybody who has ever struggled over geometrical problems can appreciate just what a genius Apollonius of Perga was, for not only did he develop the mathematics of conic sections, he was the first to devise a system of eccentric orbits which enabled Ptolemy (fl. 127–145 A.D.) to formulate his explanation of the universe. With Apollonius we are dealing with one of the greatest minds of ancient times, or any time for that matter.

Perga was famous for its temple of Artemis Pergaea, which the orator Polemo, speaking during the reign of Hadrian (117–138 A.D.), described as a marvel of size, beauty and workmanship. Surprisingly no trace of this great temple has ever been found by modern archaeologists. The site of Perga has been uninhabited since the Byzantine period and modern tourists are impressed by its extensive ruins[2]. In the stage building of the theatre they can see reliefs from the life of Dionysius, the god of the theatre as well as wine. His festivities were wild ecstatic celebrations, and one of the reliefs depicts a religious procession where he is carried in a chariot drawn by two panthers and crowned with vine leaves and ivy. Another relief shows Dionysius with Artemis who initiated him into the rites of her cult and taught him the cultivation of the vine. Artemis was the daughter of Zeus and the twin sister of Apollo. In Greece she was worshipped particularly in the Peloponnese where she was believed to roam the rugged woodlands of Arcadia as a chaste huntress armed with a bow and arrows. Sometimes she holds a torch symbolising her light-bringing powers[3]. In Perga, as in Ephesus, she probably became assimilated to the fertility goddess who was worshipped in the region before the coming of the Greeks.

Artemis Pergaea features on all the reverses of the bronze coins issued before Paul's visit. Tiberius produced three denominations (*RPC* 3369–3371), and an uninscribed issue (*RPC* 3372) may have been produced by Claudius. Except for *RPC* 3371 which has Nike advancing with a wreath, they all have the emperor's head on the obverse. The reverse has either the running figure of Artemis holding a torch in her right hand and a bow in her left or a temple with two columns enclosing a cult statue of the goddess. The largest denomination (*RPC* 3369) is 24 millimetres in diameter and has TIBЄPIOC CЄBACTOC on the obverse and APTЄMIΔOC ΠЄPГAIAC (of Artemis Pergaea) on the reverse. *RPC* 3370 (17 millimetres) is similar except for the addition of KAIΣAP in the inscription on the obverse.

Figure 26 – A bronze of Tiberius. (*RPC* 3370)

The smallest denomination (*RPC* 3371) is 16 millimetres and has NЄIKH TIBЄPIOY (Victory of Tiberius) on the obverse and APTЄMIΔOΣ ΠЄPГAIAΣ on the reverse. The shape of the letter Σ (S) suggests that the coin was minted early in his reign, in which case the figure of Nike might refer to his victories in the Danube region during the final years of Augustus' reign. A denarius (Sear 568) issued at Rome about 14/15 A.D. shows Tiberius in a quadriga celebrating these triumphs.

Figure 27 – A bronze of Tiberius. (*RPC* 3371)

In going from Paphos to Perga Paul was going from one extreme to another as far as the female divinities were concerned, for Artemis was the god of chastity while Aphrodite was the goddess of sexual love. According to Matsson[4], 'Artemis was often conceived of as the goddess of chastity, the protectress of young men and maidens, who defies, and is also disgusted by, the power of Aphrodite'. This probably made little difference to the ordinary citizens as life in an ancient Greek city allowed a considerable degree of freedom in sexual matters. The guilt-ridden attitude to sex of modern western civilization probably developed in the Christian Middle Ages. In a typical Hellenistic city of Paul's time there was freedom in all aspects of life. There was freedom in philosophical and scientific thought, as demonstrated by Apollonius. There was freedom in political life, for example there was no despotic ruler, only a city council. There was freedom in art, nakedness was often depicted. Also the coins of Perga show Artemis running freely with flowing robes, looking like an activated form of the American Statue of Liberty.

Paul would have sensed this freedom when he arrived in the city, and the coins would have confirmed that he was in a Greek environment. From Perga Paul journeyed north to preach to the Galatians, to whom he subsequently wrote his letter to the Galatians. In this letter he re-emphasised the special message he preached to them: freedom in Christ. Apparently at this moment in the history of Christianity the key issue was whether Gentile Christians should be bound by the Jewish law and in particular by circumcision. Paul's great contribution was his insistence that they were not bound: 'In Christ Jesus neither circumcision or uncircumcision counts for anything; the only thing that counts is faith working through love' (Galatians 5:6). Paul welcomed Gentiles; for 'we know that a person is justified not by works of the law but through faith in Jesus Christ' (Galatians 2:15). Paul's doctrine of Justification by Faith enabled Christianity to expand throughout the Roman Empire and beyond, and when taken up by Martin Luther in the sixteenth century it led to the Reformation and modern Christianity. Paul was careful to point out that the freedom brought by faith in Christ did not mean sexual licentiousness: 'Do not use your freedom as an opportunity for self-indulgence, but through love become slaves to one another' (Galatians 5:13b). Freedom meant living by the Holy Spirit, and 'the fruit of the Spirit is love, joy, peace, patience, kindness, generosity, faithfulness, gentleness, and self-control.

There is no law against such things' (Galatians 5:22). From Paul's letter to the Galatians we know that as he set out on the north road from Perga he was already convinced of 'the freedom we have in Christ Jesus' (Galatians 2:4).

After Perga, Saul is called by his Greek name, Paul, in Luke's account of these missionary journeys; and it is by this name that Paul is remembered today. Perga was a very appropriate point in Acts for Luke to make this change because Perga was essentially a Greek city and even its coins may have influenced the attitude of this 'Apostle of the Free Spirit'.

9. Pisidian Antioch 48 A.D.

They went on from Perga and came to Antioch in Pisidia.
Acts 13:14a

As previously discussed Paul probably reached Pisidian Antioch in about 48 A.D. This Antioch was one of many Antiochs founded by Seleucus I (312–280 B.C.) or his son Antiochus I (280–261 B.C.). It was not actually in Pisidia, which was the mountainous area separating Pamphylia from Phrygia to the north. Strictly speaking it was in the eastern part of Phrygia which at this time was incorporated into the Roman province of Galatia. The geographer Strabo, writing in the early part of Tiberius' reign, named the city Antioch towards Pisidia, to distinguish it from another Antioch on the Meander River in Caria.

The city was located on a plateau on the right bank of the Anthius River which flowed south into a large fresh-water lake. The site is about one kilometre from the modern village of Yalvaç. According to Ramsay[1] the situation of Antioch was very fine, but the locality is now deserted, forlorn and devoid of any ruins that possess any interest or beauty. There are still standing some arches of an aqueduct that brought water from the snow-capped Sultan Dag mountains to the east. Apart from the city walls there are ruins of a theatre, a temple to the Anatolian god, Mên[2], and a temple to Augustus. The Seleucids probably founded the city at the site of the temple of Mên, the god of the indigenous Phrygian people. Mên was portrayed as a standing, draped male figure with a crescent moon behind his shoulders. Ramsay[3] points out that he was not really the principal deity of Anatolia; he was always subordinate to the Great Mother who was to the Phrygian peoples the true and supreme embodiment of the divine nature. The temple to Augustus should not be a surprise as his cult was widely promoted throughout the Roman empire, especially in the east, following his deification in 14 A.D.

The Seleucids brought Greek colonists from Magnesia in Ionia for their Hellenistic city, and according to Josephus (Ant. XII,3:4) two thousand Jewish families were brought to Phrygia from Babylonia. Some of them would have settled in Pisidian Antioch. The native Phrygians, of course, would have occupied the lowest social classes.

In 39 B.C. Mark Antony gave the city and its surrounding territory, as well as the whole of Pisidia, to Amyntas, the king of Galatia. When Amyntas was killed in 25 B.C. fighting the unruly Pisidian mountaineers, his whole kingdom passed to the Romans and became the province of Galatia. As Antioch was situated on the east-west highway from Ephesus to Syria, and was both militarily and economically important, Augustus in about 20 B.C. decided to found a Roman colony there. It was called Colonia Caesareia Antiocheia. The original core of the colony was formed by veterans of the Skylark (Alauda) legion, formed in Gaul by Julius Caesar and named for its helmet decoration of a skylark. For the next two hundred years the city had a distinctly Roman character, and it was in this Roman colony that Paul arrived in 48 A.D. Morton[4] describes what Paul would have felt:

When he came to Antioch along the mountain road from Perga, Paul must have looked at the Latin inscriptions on the public buildings and on the statues with the feeling that he was nearer Rome than he had ever been before. He had preached the gospel in Syria, in Cilicia and in Cyprus. But he had not yet preached in a Roman colony. When he went to bed in Pisidian Antioch he would hear the night-watch give their commands in Latin; and he would think that on this hillside in Asia Minor had been flung a reflection of the capital of the world.

To celebrate the foundation of the colony the city issued bronze coins in three sizes (*RPC* 3529, *RPC* 3530, *RPC* 3531). *RPC*[5] guesses, on the basis of the portraits, that they were struck in about the tens B.C. The types are the standard colonial types: two legionary eagles between two standards, and a togate figure performing the religious ceremony for the formation of a Roman colony. In this ceremony the founder of the colony traces a furrow around the area to be occupied by the new city using a plough drawn by a bull and a cow yoked together. He wears a toga usually girded up to allow free movement and part of the toga is pulled up to cover his head like a Roman priest conducting a religious ceremony. Presumably a local Roman priest or official performed the actual ceremony for the founding of Pisidian Antioch in place of Augustus himself. It is very unlikely that Paul would have seen these coins which were minted more than fifty years before his visit.

No more coins were issued by Pisidian Antioch until about 65 A.D. when Nero was emperor. The coins which circulated in the city in Paul's time were almost certainly minted at Caesarea in Cappadocia. In fact *RPC*[6] considers that for the whole of Galatia one might expect the use of silver coinage from Caesarea in Cappadocia, given its proximity. According to Sydenham[7], from the time of Tiberius, the mint of Caesarea became the great imperial mint for the Roman dominions on the eastern frontier and issued silver as well as bronze coins. He maintains[8] that during the period from Tiberius to Gordian III (238–244 A.D.) the bulk of the imperial coinage of Asia Minor was supplied by the mint of Caesarea.

Cappadocia was the large area to the east of Galatia. Tiberius made it a Roman province in 17 A.D. on the death of King Archelaus. It was a rough, mountainous country with few towns except for Tyana and the ancient capital of Mazaca, which Tiberius made the capital of the province. It had been renamed Caesarea by Archelaus. The modern city of Kayseri occupies the site which lies at the foot of the impressive, snow-capped Mount Argaeus. The mountain rises to 13,000 feet and features on the coins of the ancient city.

According to Sydenham[9] the issues of bronze coins from Caesarea in the first century A.D. were intermittent and extremely scanty. None were issued by Tiberius and Caligula, and the bronze coins minted by Claudius have Greek inscriptions, which suggests they were city issues intended for local circulation only. So Paul probably did not see these bronze coins.

Except for the first issue under Tiberius the silver coins minted at Caesarea have Latin inscriptions and are often catalogued under Roman Imperial Coinage: Eastern Mints, because they have the same character as coins minted at Rome. They were intended for wide circulation in the Eastern provinces and Paul probably would have seen them. They tend to have a characteristic oval flan and were issued in two denominations, drachms and didrachms. The drachm had the same weight as the Roman denarius, but it is not clear how it was valued against the denarius or the Syrian and Asian tetradrachm, whether three or four to the tetradrachm.

The first issue of silver was in about 25 A.D. and there were subsequent issues in 32/33 and 33/34 A.D., once under Caligula, and in about 46 A.D. under Claudius. The first issue (*RPC* 3620) is undated but *RPC* suggests a date between 17 and 32 A.D. It has the laureate head of Tiberius with the Greek inscription ΤΙΒΕΡΙΟΣ ΚΑΙΣΑΡ ΣΕΒΑΣΤΟΣ (Tiberius Caesar Augustus) on the obverse, and a nude male figure standing on the summit of Mount Argaeus on the reverse with the inscription ΘΕΟΥ ΣΕΒΑΣΤΟΥ ΥΙΟΣ (Son of God Augustus). Sydenham[10] considers that attempts to identify the nude figure who is radiate and holds a sceptre and globe, with the Greek god Helios, or to connect the mountain with Serapis are unsatisfactory and it seems more in keeping with eastern notions to regard the radiate figure primarily as the Genius (or Spirit) of Argaeus. However he goes on to say that some sort of religious compromise was arrived at by which the Genius Argaei was identified for state reasons with the Genius Augusti, while to satisfy local custom the mountain itself might still be regarded as an object of veneration.

The subsequent issues of Tiberius in 32/33 and 33/34 A.D. (*RPC* 3621, *RPC* 3622) show Tiberius on the obverse with the bare head of his son, Drusus, on the reverse. These coins were issued on the tenth anniversary of the death of Drusus, which occurred in 23 A.D. According to *CNR*[11] Tiberius wished to commemorate Drusus, having discovered only ten years later that his assassination had been brought about by Sejanus.

Tacitus[12] relates how Apicata, the discarded wife of Sejanus, revealed the whole story of Drusus' murder to Tiberius. In 31 A.D. Tiberius had ordered the execution of Sejanus.

RPC considers that the drachms struck for Germanicus and the divine Augustus (*RPC* 3623) should probably be associated with the issues of Tiberius in 32/33 and 33/34 A.D. These drachms have the radiate head of Augustus on the obverse and the bearded head of Germanicus on the reverse. The obverse inscription is DIVVS AVGVSTVS (Divine Augustus). Augustus had been deified by Tiberius in 14 A.D.

The only issue of silver from Caesarea in Cappadocia during the reign of Caligula (37–41 A.D.) was a drachm with his bare head and a Latin inscription on the obverse, and a simpulum and lituus on the reverse (*RPC* 3624). The Latin inscription on the reverse reads IMPERATOR PONT MAX TR POT (Commander, High Priest, with the Tribunician Power). The simpulum symbolised Caligula's office of High Priest, while the lituus symbolised his office of Augur. On seeing this coin Paul would have realised that Caligula, like all the Roman emperors, claimed to be the head of both the civil and religious realms. In Jewish terms he was in the order of Melchizedek, i.e. both king and high-priest. No doubt, as a learned Jew, Paul would have known the implications of this claim and that the followers of Jesus understood his office in these terms. 'You are a priest forever, according to the order of Melchizedek', writes the author of the letter to the Hebrews (Heb. 7:17), quoting Psalm 110:4, but referring to Jesus.

Paul probably observed priestly implements like the simpulum and the lituus being used in the temple to Augustus in Pisidian Antioch. When this temple was built is unknown but it would have been standing when Paul visited the city. In Rome Caligula completed the building of the great temple to Augustus which Tiberius had begun.

Between 43 and 48 A.D. Claudius issued a large series of silver coins from Caesarea in Cappadocia. They were drachms and didrachms with a variety of types. As Paul's visit occurred in 48 A.D. these coins would have looked bright and new in his hand.

The types on these coins can be divided into two groups:

those referring to the family of Claudius and those celebrating his personal achievements. The former was no doubt issued to affirm the solidarity of the Julio-Claudian family, although the family life of Claudius was actually rather complex as he had already been married three times by 48 A.D. His wife at the time was Messalina and one of the didrachms (*RPC* 3627) has a beautiful bust of her on the obverse with her hair in a long plait. The obverse inscription reads MESSALINA AUGUSTI. On the reverse are the three children of Claudius: Octavia, Britannicus, and Antonia. The reverse inscription reads OCTAVIA, BRITANNICVS, ANTONIA.

Figure 28 – A didrachm of Claudius. (*RPC* 3627)

Although Messalina appears regal and dignified, the reality behind the portrait was a monster of depravity and cruelty. Having complete influence over her husband she caused the death of many distinguished Romans and led a life of lustful licentiousness. Her lifestyle was notorious in Rome and rumours would have spread even to the eastern end of the empire. Like modern movie stars the rich and famous of Paul's time would have enjoyed little privacy.

In 48 A.D. when Paul visited Pisidian Antioch Claudius was convinced by his secretary, Narcissus, that his wife was plotting against him and had in fact secretly married her lover, Gaius Silius. Claudius therefore ordered her execution. In 49 A.D. he married his niece, Agrippina II who was the daughter of Claudius' famous brother, Germanicus, and Agrippina I, and the mother of the future emperor Nero. According to *RPC* Claudius issued two coins in honour of Germanicus who had died in Syrian Antioch in 19 A.D. The first (*RPC* 3629) was a didrachm with the head of Germanicus on the obverse, and on the reverse the

figure of Germanicus crowning Artaxias whom he had proclaimed king of Armenia in 18 A.D. The second was similar
but a drachm (*RPC* 3630).

Figure 29 – A didrachm of Claudius honouring Germanicus.
(*RPC* 3629)

To complete the family series Claudius issued a didrachm
(*RPC* 3628) in honour of his father, Nero Claudius Drusus, who
was awarded the title Germanicus for his campaign against the
Germans. He was born in 38 B.C., the brother of Tiberius. He
married Antonia the daughter of Mark Antony; so, although
Octavian was the victor of the decisive naval battle of Actium, it
was Mark Antony's genes which were passed to Gaius, Claudius,
and Nero. No Roman emperor possessed the 'divine' genes of
Octavian except Gaius (Caligula).[13]

Nero Claudius Drusus was the father of Claudius and
Germanicus. After his successful campaign in Germany he was
killed by a fall from a horse at the summer camp of 9 B.C. The
coin has his laureate head with the inscription **NERO CLAVD
DRVSVS GERMANICVS IMP** on the obverse, and on the
reverse a triumphal arch surmounted by an equestrian statue
between two trophies. On the architrave is the inscription **DE
GERMANIS** (concerning the Germans).

Figure 30 – A didrachm of Claudius. (*RPC* 3628)

The coins celebrating Claudius' achievements both have his laureate head on the obverse. Suetonius[14] says that he was tall, well-built, with a handsome face, a fine head of white hair and a firm neck, but he stumbled as he walked owing to weakness of his knees. Suetonius mentions several disagreeable traits: slobbering at the mouth and running at the nose when under the stress of anger, a stammer, and a persistent nervous tic of the head, which was apparent at all times but especially when he exerted himself. There can be little doubt that Claudius suffered from what is known today as cerebral palsy. Although his family considered him to be a fool he was in fact very intelligent, and as emperor proved to be an able administrator.

Claudius' successful invasion of Britain in 43 A.D. was celebrated on the reverse of a didrachm (*RPC* 3625) which shows him in a triumphal quadriga holding an eagle-tipped sceptre. The inscription on the reverse is DE BRITANNIS (concerning the British).[15]

Figure 31 – A didrachm of Claudius. (*RPC* 3625)

Finally, Claudius' achievement is summed up by the reverse of a didrachm (*RPC* 3626) which has the Corona Civica, a wreath of oak leaves, surrounding the inscription PP OB CIVES SERVATOS (Father of the Nation, for saving the citizens). The Corona Civica was awarded to a person for saving the lives of Roman citizens. It was awarded to Pompey in 63 B.C. and to Augustus in 27 B.C. for saving lives by bringing peace. It was subsequently awarded to the Roman emperors almost as a routine.

Figure 32 – A didrachm of Claudius. (*RPC* 3626)

Paul had previously seen coins on which the emperor is called Father, but not one where he is considered to be a saviour. Before Paul's time kings had used the title Saviour (Soter) on coins in the Middle East e.g. Antiochus Soter of Syria, Ptolemy Soter of Egypt; but the Roman approach was much more subtle, using the Corona Civica rather than the blatant title. It is an interesting coincidence that when Paul addressed the Jews of Pisidian Antioch he referred to Jesus for the first time as the Saviour: 'God has brought to Israel a Saviour, Jesus, as he promised' (Acts 13:23).

Sir William Ramsay[16] considered the imperial system to be a parody of the Christian Gospel. The whole Roman cult of the emperor was a ridiculous imitation of the Christian Faith. Terms such as Father and Son of God, and concepts such as Saviour and Priest-King, were used in the imperial system to refer to a person who in reality was a travesty of his titles. Caligula, for example, far from being a divinely ordained priest-king in the order of Melchizedek, was a cruel and insane megalomaniac. Claudius was perhaps a little better, as we know that he was a capable administrator and scholar, but the reality behind the facade is glimpsed in the account by Suetonius[17], a writer fairly tolerant of the abuses of the age, 'His cruelty and bloodthirstiness appeared equally in great and small matters ... At gladiatorial shows, whether or not they were staged by himself, he ruled that all combatants who fell accidentally should have their throats cut – above all net-fighters, so that he could gaze on their death agony'.

Nevertheless Paul respected the Roman government.[18] He knew that it was only because of the peace and stability brought by the Romans that he was able to travel in Galatia at all. So when Paul made his way to the next city, he would have been mindful of the Pax Romana and the god who governed all.

Pisidian Antioch was the place where Paul first preached to the Gentiles (Acts 13: 46–48). It is, therefore, a place of tremendous importance to the history of Christianity. Today, at the lonely windswept site, there are the ruins of a church which dates from the beginning of the third century. It was built on the foundations of a synagogue and was dedicated to Saint Paul. Engraved on the stone font are a large cross and the words, Hagios Paulos (Saint Paul).

10. Iconium 48 A.D.

So they shook the dust off their feet in protest against them, and went to Iconium.
Acts 13:51

As the crow flies Iconium was 125 kilometres south-east of Pisidian Antioch. Paul would have travelled on the Roman road enjoying the magnificent scenery and eventually descending from the mountains on to the great plain on which the city stood. He would have been struck by the similarity between the situations of Iconium and Damascus: both have lofty mountain ranges to the west and vast plains to the east. Both have large streams descending from the mountains and watering the fertile ground before disappearing in the earth. Like Damascus, Iconium was an important crossroads of the Roman empire, with five roads radiating from it, and it was a centre of commerce and agriculture.

The city was in the Roman province of Galatia, but close to the border between the ancient districts of Phrygia to the west and Lycaonia to the east. In ancient times it was regarded as Phrygian. Its inhabitants were of Phrygian descent and spoke the Phrygian language. Their religion was the worship of the Phrygian Mother Goddess, Cybele. From the time of Alexander the Great, however, Greeks began to settle in the town, and by the first century A.D. the more educated citizens took pride above all in their Hellenism. So it would have been to an essentially Hellenistic city that Paul came in about 48 A.D. Unlike Pisidian Antioch, Iconium was not a Roman colony and the Roman presence would have been minimal.

In Paul's time Iconium was already a very ancient city. Like Damascus it was one of the oldest continually inhabited cities in the world. The site is now occupied by the modern Turkish city of Konya which has a population of 600,000, but in the centre of the city there still exists a great mound of earth and ruins, called Allaeddin Hill, which contains all the previous layers of habitation. Limited archaeological excavations indicate settlement dating from at least the third millennium B.C. According to a Phrygian legend of the great flood, Konya was the first city to rise after the deluge that destroyed humanity. The Iconians prided themselves on their ancient origins and believed that Phrygian was the primitive language of mankind. According to Ramsay[1] this had been proven to be true by a scientific experiment conducted by the Egyptian pharaoh Psammetichus (c. 600 B.C.), who found that infants brought up out of hearing of human speech naturally spoke the Phrygian language!

On the coins of Iconium one would expect to see Cybele, but in fact no traces of the Phyrigian religion appear on the coinage. Ramsay[2] considers that the seated figure of Fortuna (Tyche) which appears on later coins of Iconium is partly influenced by representations of the seated figure of Cybele as the ordinary Roman type shows Fortuna standing, but this is doubtful. The absence of Cybele from the Iconium coinage may be because the Phrygians were considered to be the lower classes of the city, or perhaps because the Roman authorities did not want to detract from their own Cybele who resided in a great temple on the Palatine Hill in Rome. During Hannibal's invasion of Italy in 204 B.C. the Romans followed a Sibylline prophecy that the enemy could be expelled if the Great Mother were brought to Rome. So the Roman Senate sent an embassy of five officials to Pessinus, a centre of her cult in Asia Minor, to bring back the sacred black stone which was identified with the goddess. She was duly installed in Rome but what the Senate had not realised was that the priests of Cybele were eunuchs whose initiation into her service included self-castration while in an ecstatic trance. The Romans were naturally reluctant to enter her priesthood and eunuch priests were brought from Phrygia for her orgiastic cult.

The first coins minted at Iconium were apparently issued in the second half of the first century B.C. They were bronze coins, 21 and 15 millimetres in diameter. The larger (Sear 5504) has a bust of Perseus on the obverse and Zeus enthroned on the reverse with the inscription ЄΙΚΟΝЄΩΝ (of the Iconians) and the names of two magistrates. The smaller (Sear 5505) has the head of Zeus on the obverse and a naked Perseus holding the harpa (a sickle-shaped blade) and the severed head of Medusa on the reverse with the inscription ЄΙΚΟΝЄΩΝ. It is unlikely that Paul would have seen these coins unless they were restruck at a later period, which seems unlikely.

Perseus was important for Iconium. The Greek legend relates how Perseus, the son of Zeus and a mortal woman, was given the task of obtaining the head of Medusa, one of the three terrifying Gorgons. Medusa was a winged monster, with huge ugly teeth, glaring eyes, a protruding tongue, claws of brass, and locks composed of numerous snakes instead of hair. She had the power, by simply gazing at men, to turn them into stone. Athena assisted Perseus in his task by warning him not to look directly at the Gorgon but to watch her reflection in the polished shield that she gave him. Hermes also assisted Perseus by giving him the harpa with which to decapitate Medusa. Having completed his task, Perseus came to Lycaonia and vanquished his enemies through the power of Medusa's severed head, the Gorgoneion, which turned them into stone. Ramsay[3] thought that the victory of Perseus represented the triumph of the Hellenistic constitution over the native Phrygian system in Iconium.

Having conquered his enemies Perseus converted a local village into a Greek city, and called it Eikonion from the εικων or image of the Gorgon. He erected in front of the new city a statue of himself holding up the Gorgon's head, and there was probably such a statue standing in the city when Paul visited it. Ramsay[4] states that there can be little doubt that it was a Hellenistic work modelled after the famous statue of Perseus by Myron, the great Attic sculptor of the fifth century B.C. The figure of Perseus which appears on the coins of Iconium is very likely copied from the statue which stood in the city. Unfortunately no copy of Myron's famous work exists today, but is was probably similar to the magnificent bronze statue of Perseus by Benvenuto Cellini (1500–1571 A.D.) which can be seen in the Loggia dei Lanzi in Florence.

In about 41 A.D. Claudius honoured the city by changing its name to Claudiconium. Claudius allowed the city to strike a bronze coinage in three denominations (*RPC* 3541, 3542, 3543). As Agrippina II, the fourth and last wife of Claudius, appears on the reverse of one of these coins, they can be dated from about 49 A.D. when Claudius married her, to about 54 A.D. when he died. All the coins bear the name of the governor, Annius Afrinus, and so his period of office can be similarly dated. As Paul visited Iconium in about 48 A.D. he could not have seen these coins, but as he probably saw them on subsequent visits to the city, they will be dealt with here.

RPC 3543 is the smallest denomination with a diameter of 17 millimetres. On the obverse it has the bare head of Annius Afrinus with the Greek inscription **ΑΝΝΙΟC ΑΦΡϵΙΝΟC**. He obviously must have been in favour at Rome as this was an unusual honour for a governor. On the reverse we again find the standing figure of Perseus. He holds the harpa in his right hand and Medusa's severed head in his left. The portrait of Perseus is interesting in that, like Cellini's statue, he averts his gaze from the dreaded Gorgoneion. The inscription reads **ΚΛΑΥΔϵΙΚΟΝΙϵWΝ** (of the Claudiconians).

Figure 33 – A bronze of Claudius. (*RPC* 3543)

What would Paul have thought of Perseus? First of all Perseus was in many ways similar to Heracles, who would have been familiar to Paul from the Tyrian tetradrachms needed to pay the temple tax in Jerusalem. Perseus and Heracles were both sons of the chief Greek god, Zeus, and mortal mothers, and they were both heroic figures who strove against evil. Of greater significance, however, would have been Perseus' achievement of overcoming and using for his own purposes that which turns men into stone. Paul would have remembered God's words as quoted by the prophet Ezekiel, 'I will remove from your body the heart of stone and give you a heart of flesh. I will put my spirit within you, and make you follow my statutes and be careful to observe my ordinances' (Ezekiel 36:26a–27). On his way to Iconium Paul was 'filled with joy and the Holy Spirit' (Acts 13:52), and in the city he spoke 'boldly for the Lord, who testified to the word of his grace by granting signs and wonders to be done through them' (Acts 14:3b). So, that which removes hearts of stone was certainly active in Iconium when Paul was there.

RPC 3542 is 20 millimetres in diameter. It has the laureate head of Claudius on the obverse with the inscription ΚΛΑΥΔΙΟC ΚΑΙCΑΡ CΕΒΑ (Claudius Caesar Augustus). On the reverse it has the draped bust of Agrippina II and the inscription CΕΒΑCΤΗ ΕΠΙ ΑΦΡΕΙΝΟΥ ΚΛΑΥΔΕΙΚΟΝΙΕWN (Augusta, in the time of Afrinus, of the Claudiconians). She has her hair set in an intricate short style with two plaits on either side of her neck and a looped plait at the back. The portrait is very much like the marble bust which can be seen in the National Archaeological Museum in Naples.

Agrippina was the eldest daughter of Germanicus and Agrippina Senior, and was born in 15 A.D. in an encampment on the Rhine which was later given the name of Colonia Agrippina in her honour, and where the present city of Cologne now stands. At the age of 14 she married the senator Cn Domitius Ahenobarbus and gave birth to a son, the future emperor Nero. When her brother Caligula was emperor he banished her to an island, but her uncle Claudius recalled her from exile in the first year of his reign. Now a widow she married a rich patrician whose murder she arranged in order to gain his inheritance. After Messalina's death Claudius wanted to marry her, but as Tacitus[5] relates, marriage with a niece was unprecedented – indeed it was incestuous, and disregard of this might, it was feared, cause national disaster. However, after an impassioned speech by one of his supporters in the Senate, Claudius requested a decree legalising future marriages with a brother's daughter. After arranging for Claudius to adopt her son and for him to marry Claudius' daughter Octavia, she had Claudius murdered by eating poisoned mushrooms. So, on Claudius' death in 54 A.D. she was de facto ruler of the empire, as Nero was only seventeen. According to Scullard[6] Agrippina was an ambitious and unscrupulous woman who 'struck down a series of victims: no man or woman was safe if she suspected rivalry or desired their wealth. Her weapons were poison or a trumped-up charge, often of magic'. But gradually Nero gained power and eventually in 59 A.D. he arranged his mother's murder. On seeing Agrippina's beautiful portrait on these coins of Iconium Paul could not imagine the evil web of intrigue that she was weaving in Rome, nor that her son would be the ruler who would finally be responsible for his own death.

Figure 34 – A bronze of Claudius. (*RPC* 3542)

RPC 3541 is the largest denomination at 24 millimetres diameter. It has the laureate head of Claudius on the obverse with the inscription ΚΛΑΥΔΙΟC ΚΑΙCΑΡ CΕΒΑCΤΟC (Claudius Caesar Augustus). On the reverse it has a type rare for ancient coinage: Hades, the ruler of the Underworld. The seated figure of Hades holds a long sceptre, and Cerebus, the dog who guards the entrance to the Underworld, lurks under his throne. The reverse inscription reads ΚΛΑΥΔΕΙΚΟΝΙΕWΝ ΕΠΙ ΑΦΡΕΙΝΟΥ (of the Claudiconians, in the time of Afrinus).

Figure 35 – A bronze of Claudius. (*RPC* 3541)

Hades was little venerated in the ancient world. He was stern and without pity, and hated not only by men but by the gods as well. It was useless to address prayers to him since he took no notice of them nor of sacrifices. However, shrines to him might naturally develop at points which seemed to be entrances to or exits from the Underworld. Thus deep caverns or places where rivers flowed underground or where subterranean streams came to the surface were likely sites. Lord Kinross[7] mentioned that 80 kilometres west of Konya was a spring where legend maintained that Plato had blocked, with cotton, pitch and large stones, the outlet of a subterranean river which threatened to flood Konya. Although Ramsay does not even mention Hades, he says that copper mines in the mountains have been worked from a remote period as is proved by extensive old shafts. Ramsay[8] considered that this underground wealth revealed to the Phrygians the presence of the Mother-Goddess Cybele. But to the Greek mind all this would have pointed to the ruler of the Underworld, Hades. So, though there is now no trace of it, a sanctuary dedicated to Hades must have existed in the region of Iconium.

Cerberus was the monstrous three-headed dog who guarded the entrance to the Underworld. A dead person, after being properly buried, would arrive at the river Styx where for a fee of one obol he would be rowed across the black water by the ferryman Charon. It was customary for the relatives of the deceased to place the coin in the corpse's mouth before burial. Most numismatists may not realise that many of the obols in their collections have been in the mouths of decomposing corpses, although John Melville Jones[9] states that finds in graves do not suggest that this denomination was particularly favoured. Presumably the relatives wanted their departed loved ones to have a little extra, just in case. The destination of most of the dead was the Plain of Asphodel where they continued a shadowy existence in continuation of their former lives. A fortunate few who earned the gods' favour went to the blessed realm called Elysium, but a few went to Tartarus for punishment. Michael Stapleton[10] points out that Hades should never be thought of as the Devil, a concept alien to Greek thought which believed that man committed evil or good deeds himself, without any prompting from a good or evil force.

Nor was Hades a punisher: he was never feared in that way because the Greeks never thought in that way. Any man who was arrogant or stupid or foolhardy enough to offend the gods was punished by the gods, the lord of the Underworld having no more or less to do with it than the other Olympians. Hades was accorded universal respect and revered by those who cared for the condition of the departed. He was rarely depicted in art but when he was he looked rather like his brother Zeus. This is how he is shown on *RPC* 3541.

The figure of Hades would have made Paul think of death. The Jews, like the Greeks, thought that the dead went to a shadowy realm called Sheol, but for Paul the whole concept of death was given a new twist by the death and resurrection of Jesus Christ. Paul believed that Christ had robbed death of its power: 'Our Saviour Christ Jesus ... abolished death and brought life and immortality to light through the gospel' (2 Timothy 1:10).

For Paul biological death was like sleep: 'Christ has been raised from the dead, the first fruits of those who have fallen asleep' (1 Corinthians 15:20). Far more important was spiritual death, and everyone ruled by sin is 'dead' in Paul's theology: 'God, who is rich in mercy, out of the great love with which he loved us even when we were dead through our trespasses, made us alive together with Christ' (Ephesians 2:4,5a). Christ destroyed death making it irrelevant: 'If we live, we live to the Lord, and if we die, we die to the Lord; so then, whether we live or whether we die, we are the Lord's' (Romans 14:8).

On his journeys in Asia Minor Paul would have passed wayside tombs where the epitaphs spoke of the sad state of the occupants who were asleep forever without hope. Ferguson[11] quotes a typical example: 'Here in my tomb I drain my cup more greedily because here I must sleep and here must stay forever'. Paul was full of joy because the good news he preached spoke of Jesus' victory over death, negating the message of *RPC* 3541.

11. Lystra 48 A.D.

When an attempt was made by both Gentiles and Jews, with
their rulers, to mistreat them and to stone them, the apostles
learned of it and fled to Lystra.
Acts 14:6

Lystra was a small, out-of-the-way town in a beautiful valley
30 kilometres south-south-west of Iconium. Paul and Barnabus
would have crossed a mountain range to reach it. Ramsay[1] thinks
it was not originally on Paul's itinerary as it was an unimportant
agricultural town, but it was a place of refuge from the turmoil
which resulted from his preaching. Paul probably chose Lystra
because it was a Roman colony and he was a Roman citizen.

As mentioned in the book of Acts Lystra was a city of
Lycaonia, which was the plateau district north of the Taurus
Mountains, west of Cappadocia, and east of Pisidia and Phrygia.
It was the south-east part of the Roman province of Galatia,
although the old tribal area of Galatia lay further to the north.
The origins of the people of Lycaonia are not clear but LaSor[2] suggests that the 'lu-' element indicates that Lycaonia and Lystra
were connected to the Luwian people, an Indo-European people,
who migrated to Asia Minor before the group which later became
known as the Hittites. They had their own language and culture,
and it seems Lystra was not much affected by Hellenistic influ-
ences. Presumably the town was not one which attracted Greek
settlers.

When Paul healed a crippled man the people shouted in the
Lycaonian language, 'The gods have come down to us in human
form'. Acts 14:12 relates how the people called Paul 'Hermes',

because he was the chief speaker. They called Barnabus 'Zeus', presumably because he was a quiet person in the background seeming to overseer the activity. The priest of the temple of Zeus, which stood just outside the town, came with garlanded oxen to be sacrificed to the two gods in human form, but Paul and Barnabus tried to restrain the crowd, shouting out that they were only mortals.

The attitude of the Lycaonians on this occasion has usually been attributed to their knowing the Greek legend of Zeus and Hermes coming down to earth disguised as poor mortals. The Latin poet Ovid tells the story in the 'Metamorphoses' (Changes):

> *Here once in mortal shape*
> *Came Jupiter and his son Mercury,*
> *Lord of the wand, but of his wings bereft.*
> *House after house they tried, in search of rest;*
> *House after house was barred; save one alone,*
> *A tiny cottage thatched with reeds and straw.*[3]

However, it seems unlikely that the Lycaonian citizens of Lystra would have been familiar with this story, and having witnessed the miraculous healing of the crippled man they simply identified Paul and Barnabas with the two main male gods in their pantheon.

Ramsay[4] explains that the distinction between the supreme deity and the working god was one which lay deep in the Anatolian religion and was expressed by the simple peasants of Lystra when they saluted Paul and Barnabas as gods. Paul was the working god, called Hermes in Luke's text, but the crowd would have used a Lycaonian name. Ramsay[5] refers to the god, sculptured of colossal size on the rocks at Ibriz on the north side of the Taurus Mountains, who is represented as the Peasant-God, dressed simply in a short tunic and bearing in his hands corn-ears and grapes, the gifts he has bestowed on mankind by his toil. He was sculptured long before the Hellenic period of Central Anatolian history, but he was not the supreme male deity who gives rains and fruitful seasons without exertion by the simple power of his word.

Lystra today is a forlorn site over a kilometre north of the

Turkish village of Hatun Sarai. Morton[6] describes his impression, 'We saw a long, low hill covered with stones and minute fragments of ancient pottery. I scraped with my stick and unearthed the rim and the base of a red bowl. There was not one ancient building left, yet the earth had that uneasy look which suggests that something is concealed beneath it'. No systematic archaeological excavation has been undertaken but it was probably inhabited from pre-historic times.

A coin led to the discovery of Lystra in 1885 by Professor J.R.S. Sterrett. Ramsay[7] relates that although the coins of Lystra are very rare one was bought on the spot by Professor Sterrett, and his discovery of an inscription in addition to the coin revealed the hitherto unknown fact that Lystra was a Roman colony. The Latin inscription discovered by Professor Sterrett was on a massive carved stone[8] about one metre high and 30 centimetres thick. It read: DIVVM AVG COL IVL FELIX GEMINA LVSTRA CONSEGRAVIT D D, in seven lines. It probably means 'The Colonia Julia Felix Gemina Lystra consecrates the divine Augustus by order of the decurions'. A literal translation of the name is 'Lystra, fortunate, double, Julian Colony'. 'Double' (Gemina) refers to Augustus simultaneously designating Lystra and Pisidian Antioch Roman colonies, to be linked by a Roman road, so that they were in a sense twin cities.[9] 'D D' stood for Decreto Decurionum, meaning by decree of the members of the Colony Council. The inscription presumably refers to a temple, statue or altar of Augustus. The stone would have been standing when Paul visited the town.

Augustus decided to make Lystra a Roman colony in about 6 B.C., probably to provide a defensive outpost against the mountain tribes to the south and west. There would have been Roman soldiers garrisoned there as well as a number of Roman officials. The first coins of Lystra celebrate the founding of the colony with the typical Roman type of a man ploughing with two oxen. He has a fold of his toga pulled up over his head and traces the limits of the new city with the plough. Because of the mature portrait of Augustus, *RPC* dates these coins to the last two decades of his reign. Although they were minted over 35 years before Paul's visit their circulation would have been very limited in such a small community and it is possible that Paul might have seen them in 48 A.D.

The largest coin (*RPC* 3538) is 26 millimetres in diameter and has the laureate head of Augustus on the obverse with the inscription IMPE AVGVSTI ((a coin) of the emperor Augustus). The S is retrograde. Behind the head of Augustus is a cornucopia, the symbol of fertility and prosperity. It is often associated with Ceres, the Roman corn-goddess. On the reverse is a figure ploughing with two hump-backed oxen and the inscription COL IVL FEI GEM LVSTRA. *RPC* 3539 is slightly smaller at 25 millimetres diameter. It has no cornucopia and FEL instead of FEI.

Figure 36 – A bronze of Augustus. (*RPC* 3538)

RPC 3540 is a unique and important coin in the possession of the Staatliche Museum in Berlin. It is 19 millimetres in diameter. It has been attributed to Lystra by Michael Grant because the same reverse occurs on Lystran coins of Antoninus Pius. Also the style of the obverse is like the Lystran coins of Augustus. The obverse has a laureate head with the inscription IMP AVG[. The reverse has the seated figure of Ceres holding ears of corn and poppies over an altar. She is also holding a torch or cornucopia. The inscription on the reverse is CERERIS (of Ceres). The English word 'cereal' is derived from Ceres, but how often do we think of this Roman goddess of corn and agriculture when we eat our breakfast?

Figure 37 – A bronze of Augustus. (*RPC* 3540)

On this coin we should see Ceres as only a Roman veneer; for according to Ferguson[10] she was just one of the manifestations of the Great Mother. The concept of the Great Mother or Earth Mother was, as we have seen, vital to the native religion of Anatolia. In the case of Paul and Barnabas, however, they were mistaken for the two male gods concerned with the fertility of the earth. So Ceres can also be seen as a Roman veneer for these male agricultural deities. Just as the Greek Hades was a 'stand in' for the Phrygian Cybele on the coin of Iconium, the Roman Ceres was a 'stand in' for the Lycaonian agricultural gods on the coin of Lystra. Paul and Barnabas were hailed as these fertility gods by the people of Lystra, and it is significant that the only recorded words of Paul to these people should refer to the fruitfulness of the earth, 'We bring you good news, that you should turn from these worthless things to the living God, who made the heaven and the earth and the sea and all that is in them. In past generations he allowed all the nations to follow their own ways; yet he has not left himself without a witness in doing good – giving you rains from heaven and fruitful seasons, and filling you with food and your hearts with joy' (Acts 14:15b, 16 17). Paul, of course, was more concerned with the fruitfulness of the spirit, as he later wrote to these very same people when the turmoil of his first visit had settled, 'The fruit of the Spirit is love, joy, peace, patience, kindness generosity, faithfulness, gentleness, and self control' (Galatians 5:22a). How appropriate that Ceres should be on this coin of Lystra!

12. Derbe 48 A.D.

Then they stoned Paul and dragged him out of the city,
supposing that he was dead. But when the disciples surrounded
him, he got up and went into the city. The next day he went on
with Barnabas to Derbe.
Acts 14:19b,20

The location of Derbe had been unknown until recently. Ramsay
was way off the mark when he suggested a site about 80
kilometres south-east of Konya. Unfortunately some modern
historical maps[1] still place Derbe in this area. In 1956 Michael
Ballance[2] found a stone block with an inscription which was a
dedication by the council and people of Derbe. The stone was
found at Kerti Hüyük, which is a sizeable, though not prominent, mound located 25 kilometres north-north-east of the town
of Karaman (ancient Laranda). It is about 40 kilometres north-
east of the area suggested by Ramsay.

The stone can be dated to 157 A.D. It is 105 centimetres
high, 69 centimetres wide and 68 centimetres thick. Ballance
considered that it may have formed the shaft of a large statue
base. It weighed half a ton and could not have been moved prior
to its discovery on the gently sloping skirt of the mound. The
stone has been transported to the Museum for Classical
Antiquities in Konya.

Another discovery supports Kerti Hüyük or its vicinity as the
site of Derbe. In 1962 Bastiaan Van Elderen[3] saw an inscription
on a stone in the village of Sudaraya near Kerti Hüyük. The
inscription mentions 'the most God-fearing Michael, Bishop of
Derbe'. It can be dated to the last quarter of the fourth century.
The natives of Sudaraya told Van Elderen that the stone had

been found on Kerti Hüyük, but Ballance[4] reported that it had been found at Devri Sehri about two-and-a-half miles south-south-east of Kerti Hüyük. In any case Derbe must be located in the area and most probably at the mound of Kerti Hüyük.

The new location places Derbe more towards the centre of Lycaonia, but the chief city of Lycaonia since the fourth century B.C. was Laranda. In 36 B.C. Mark Antony gave Lycaonia to Amyntas whom he made king of Galatia in that year. In 30 B.C. Augustus confirmed Amyntas in his kingdom and added Cilicia Tracheia. Tracheia means rough or rugged, and referred to the mountainous western part of Cilicia, as distinct from Cilicia Pedias, i.e. Cilicia of the plain, which was the flat eastern part. On the death of Amyntas in 25 B.C. the central part of Cilicia Tracheia was granted to Archelaus, king of Cappadocia.[5] When this king died in 17 A.D. his territory was added to the province of Galatia. Also in 17 A.D. Antiochus III, king of Commagene, died, and his territory became a Roman province.

Commagene was the most northerly district in Syria and lay east of Cilicia. It was founded as an independent kingdom in 163 B.C. when Samos, the governor, revolted against the Seleucid king of Syria. Samosata, the capital of the kings of Commagene, was on the Euphrates River. The son of Antiochus III was a friend of Caligula and in 38 A.D. Caligula restored the kingdom to his friend, who became Antiochus IV. Cilicia Tracheia was added to the kingdom of Commagene. Before his assassination in 41 A.D. Caligula deposed Antiochus IV, but on his accession Claudius again restored him to his kingdom. According to Jones[6], either Caligula or Claudius detached southern Lycaonia from Galatia and granted it to Antiochus IV, king of Commagene and Cilicia Tracheia. It is very likely that Derbe was in the territory granted to Antiochus IV.[7] Laranda certainly was as it issued coins inscribed with his name. In fact the whole point of Paul's flight to Derbe was to remove himself from the Roman province of Galatia and to seek refuge in the kingdom of Antiochus IV. It was probably Antiochus who renamed the city Claudioderbe in honour of Claudius.

No coins were issued by Derbe or Claudioderbe until the second century A.D. So the coins of Laranda probably circulated in that area when Paul was there. Exactly when they were issued is unknown, but Paul could well have seen them on one of his three visits. Actually there is no indication where they were minted but Laranda is the likely source as it was the chief city.

The coin usually attributed to Laranda is a large bronze one, 27 millimetres in diameter (*RPC* 3533). It has the diademed bust of Antiochus IV on the obverse with the Greek inscription ΒΑΣΙΛΕΥΣ ΑΝΤΙΟΧΟΣ. On the reverse is a large scorpion with the inscription ΛΥΚΑΟΝΩΝ (of the Lycaonians), all within a laurel wreath. According to Head[8] the scorpion was the zodiacal sign under which Commagene stood.

Figure 38 – A bronze of Antiochus IV. (*RPC* 3533)

There is also a coin of Antiochus IV which has a beautiful bust of his queen, Iotape, on the reverse (*RPC* 3534). The specimen shown in the Lindgren Collection[9] has the inscription ΒΑΣΙΛΙΣΣ[Α ΙΩΤΑ]ΠΗ ΦΙΛΑΔΕΛΦΟΣ (Queen Iotape, fond of her brother) on the obverse. On the reverse it again has a large scorpion with the inscription ΛΥΚΑΟ[ΝΩΝ]. Antiochus honoured his wife by naming the port-city of Iotape in Cilicia Tracheia after her. The ruins of Iotape can be seen today 12 kilometres north-west of the village of Gazipasa on the coast road.

Figure 39 – A bronze of Antiochus IV. (*RPC* 3534)

Three other coins are listed by *RPC* as having been minted in Lycaonia under Antiochus IV. It is unknown when they were minted. The first (*RPC* 3535) is 19 millimetres in diameter and has the two sons of Antiochus, Epiphanes and Callinicus, riding horses on the obverse with the inscription ΒΑΣΙΛΕΩΣ ΥΙΟΙ (sons of the king). On the reverse is a capricorn and a star, with an anchor above, all in a wreath. The inscription is ΛΥΚΑΟΝΩ. The anchor probably refers to the access to the sea that the kingdom now enjoyed as a result of the acquisition of Cilicia Tracheia. The capricorn[10] was well known as the zodiacal sign of Augustus[11] and on this coin it was probably intended as deference to Claudius who was the grandson of Livia, Augustus' wife. In 72 A.D., when Antiochus IV was deposed on a charge of conspiracy with the Parthians against Rome, his two sons held on to power for a while but could not prevent the incorporation of the kingdom into the Roman province of Syria.

The second coin (*RPC* 3536) is also 19 millimetres in diameter and on the obverse it has an anchor between crossed cornucopias, each surmounted by a youthful male head, with a star above. Although there is no inscription the heads must be those of the young sons of Antiochus. On the reverse is an Armenian-type tiara[12] with the inscription ΛΥΚΑΟΝΩΝ. On similar coins minted elsewhere in the kingdom it can be seen that the tiara is ornamented with a scorpion. The coin type of heads on cornucopias seems bizarre to us today but it apparently impressed the ancient mind[13] as Antiochus copied it from a sestertius of Drusus (Sear 587) which was minted in Rome between 19 and 23 A.D. and showed his twin sons. This suggests that the sons of Antiochus IV were also twins.

The third coin (*RPC* 3537) is only 14 millimetres in diameter and on the obverse it has clasped hands and a caduceus with the inscription ΠΙΣΤΙΣ (faith). On the reverse is an anchor with ΛΥΚΑΟΝΩΝ. The clasped hands no doubt referred to the relationship between Antiochus IV and Claudius which depended on mutual trust. For Paul this symbol would have pointed to his relationship with God which depended on his faith. Having been stoned nearly to death in Lystra one would have expected that Paul's faith would have been very weak indeed when he reached Derbe, but this was not the case, for we read in the book of Acts that at Derbe, 'they proclaimed the good news to that city and had made many disciples' (Acts 14:21a). In the letter which he wrote a year later to the Christians of South Galatia (and Derbe) he said 'I have been crucified with Christ; and it is no longer I who live, but it is Christ who lives in me. And the life I now live in the flesh I live by faith in the Son of God, who loved me and gave himself for me' (Galatians 2:20).

In Derbe Paul would have seen Antiochus' emblem of a scorpion either on official buildings and notices or on the coins he handled. Perhaps these scorpions prompted him at a later date to make his famous statement, 'Where, O death, is your victory? Where O death is your sting? The sting of death is sin, and the power of sin is the law. But thanks be to God, who gives us the victory through our Lord Jesus Christ' (1 Corinthians 15:55–57).[14] These verses are well known to lovers of Handel's 'Messiah'.

Scorpions, of course, were found throughout the Middle East and the poison in their tails was very painful and sometimes fatal. In the Old Testament (e.g. 1 Kings 12:11) and the New Testament (e.g. Revelation 9:5) scorpions are seen as instruments of punishment. For Paul, because Christ had overcome sin, the fear of death had gone. Death, the Great Scorpion, had no sting in its tail.

13. Attalia 48 A.D.

When they had spoken the word in Perga, they went down to Attalia.
Acts 14:25

From Attalia in Pamphylia Paul sailed back to Antioch in Syria. Attalia (Greek Attaleia) was a busy seaport serving the rich district of southern Phrygia and it was on the preferred route to Syria and Egypt. It stood on a flat limestone terrace about 35 metres above the Catarrhactes River (modern Düden-su) which flowed directly into the sea. The river has now completely disappeared, its waters having been diverted for irrigation purposes.

Attalus II Philadelphus, king of Pergamum, built the city either during his co-regency with his brother (165–159 B.C.) or during his own reign (159–138 B.C.). He needed a port in Pamphylia for the Attalid kingdom which had become an extensive domain covering most of western Asia Minor. According to Jones[1] it is not known whether the city was an entirely new foundation or had existed previously under another name. Attalus intended the city to be the principal Pergamene port on the Mediterranean coast and enclosed it with a line of powerful defence walls and towers which were rebuilt in Roman times. The entrance to the outer harbour was closed by means of a chain, while the inner harbour was merely a recess in the cliffs. The city itself was surrounded by two walls with a moat protecting the outer wall. Attalus III (138–133 B.C.), the last king of Pergamum, bequeathed his kingdom to the Romans. In 48 A.D. it would have been a cosmopolitan, though basically Hellenistic, harbour-city at which Paul arrived.

The modern city of Antalya is the chief tourist resort on the Turkish Riviera. It has grown explosively since the 1960s because of the tourist boom, and now has a population of about 400,000. Parts of the old wall which Paul would have seen are still standing and the little harbour from which Paul departed is now a marina for charter yachts.

According to Jones[2] the Attalians claimed kinship with the Athenians. He suggests this indicates that Attalus, who was always on cordial terms with Athens, persuaded the Athenians to send colonists to his new foundation, or it may, on the other hand, merely mean that the Pamphylian population had some legendary connexion with Athens. In any case the goddess Athena was important at Attalia because she featured on all the coins minted at the city from the reign of Augustus to the arrival of Paul. Although there is now no trace of it there must have been a temple of Athena there.

RPC lists four bronze coins *RPC* (3363–3366) minted in Attalia from the time of Augustus to Paul's arrival, but points out that the early imperial coinage is difficult to classify because the portraits are not labelled before Trajan. Coins with Ω are considered earlier than those with W. *RPC* 3363 is 19 millimetres in diameter and the portrait on the obverse seems most like Augustus. On the reverse is a bust of Athena wearing a Corinthian helmet pulled back on her head. The inscription on the reverse is ΑΤΤΑΛΕΩΝ (of the Attalians). *RPC* 3364 is 18 millimetres and the portrait is very reminiscent of that on Tiberian denarii. *RPC* 3365 is also 18 millimetres in diameter and its attribution to Caligula is suggested by the shape of the head and the lips. The reverses are similar to *RPC* 3363. *RPC* 3366 is 20 millimetres in diameter and has been confidently attributed to Claudius because the portrait is distinctively Claudian with a long muscular neck. The reverse is similar to *RPC* 3363 except for W.

Figure 40 – A bronze of Claudius. (*RPC* 3366)

There is no doubt that Paul would have seen these coins as he would have needed small change to buy provisions and other items for his intended sea journey. As far as numismatics is concerned this is the first time Paul would have come face-to-face with the great goddess Athena, known to the Romans as Minerva. Athena was one of the most important goddesses to the Greeks. She was a member of the triad which, with Zeus and Apollo, represented the embodiment of divine power.[3] Apollo was the god of light, but like Athena, he had many aspects.

Ferguson[4] considers Athena to be the Great Mother in another guise. The Great Mother is powerful indeed, controlling the powers of the earth and of nature. This female power is 'awful and unpredictable. It may heal or it may destroy. It may work for life or it may work for death. The Great Mother thus has many manifestations, many faces as it were'.[5] So Athena is different from Artemis who is wild and free, the goddess of the outdoors, while Athena is concerned with cities and civilization, using her power to guard cities and protect heroes like Perseus and Heracles who fight the chaotic forces in the world.

Athena was probably a pre-Hellenic mother goddess who became involved in the war-like culture of the Mycenaeans, as her most famous cult centre, on the Acropolis of Athens, was originally a Mycenaean palace. She is usually portrayed in war-like pose with a helmet, shield and spear.

The mythological origin of Athena would have been known to Paul. She was the daughter of Zeus by his first wife, Metis, who personified wisdom. Zeus was warned by the gods that his children by Metis would surpass him in wisdom and could usurp his place as king of the gods. So when Metis became pregnant he swallowed her whole, but soon afterwards he began to suffer from agonising headaches. Hermes found him sitting on the bank of a river howling with pain and rage and, knowing what the trouble was, he summoned Hephaestus, the smith god, who, with a mighty blow from his hammer, cracked open Zeus' head and Athena, fully armed, sprang forth with a shout that shook the heavens. Sir William Smith, the English classicist, stated, 'As her father was the most powerful and her mother the wisest among the gods, so Athena was a combination of the two, a goddess in whom power and wisdom were harmoniously blended'.[6]

These coins of Attalia would have reminded Paul of those passages in the Hebrew scriptures which personify wisdom:

> *I, Wisdom, live with prudence,*
> *and I attain knowledge and discretion . . .*
> *I have good advice and sound wisdom;*
> *I have insight, I have strength.*
> Proverbs 8:12,14

But for Paul the combination of divine power and wisdom meant Jesus Christ. Paul preached about the crucifixion of Christ, knowing that what seemed foolish to those without faith, was wiser than human understanding and stronger than any human power. 'For Jews demand signs and Greeks desire wisdom, but we proclaim Christ crucified, a stumbling block to Jews and foolishness to Gentiles, but to those who are called, both Jews and Greeks, Christ the power of God and the wisdom of God' (1 Corinthians 1:22–24).

14. Antioch and Jerusalem 49 A.D.

From there they sailed back to Antioch ... and they stayed
there with the disciples for some time ... Paul and Barnabas
and some others were appointed to go up to Jerusalem ...
When they came to Jerusalem they were welcomed ...
They went down to Antioch.
Acts 14:26a, 28; 15:2b,4a,30a

As previously explained[1] the visit to Jerusalem in Galatians
2:1–10 is the same as that described in Acts 15 when Paul went
to Jerusalem to discuss with the apostles whether Gentiles should
be circumcised, and therefore this Apostolic Council occurred in
49 A.D. and Paul's stay in Antioch this time would also have
occurred in that year. Paul had last been at Antioch in 46 A.D.
and at Jerusalem in 36 A.D., not counting the famine-relief visit
or the fifteen-day visit after his escape from Damascus.

Neither city would have changed much in these few years
although in Jerusalem building work continued on the temple
which was not finished until 64 A.D. In fact this magnificent
structure of cream stone and gold was scarcely completed before
it was destroyed by Roman soldiers at the end of the First Jewish
Revolt (66–70 A.D.)

In Antioch no silver coinage was minted by Claudius until
about 50 A.D., so Paul would not have seen it on this visit.
However, although it is usually stated that very little silver was
minted at Antioch by Tiberius and Claudius (in contrast to
Augustus, Caligula, and Nero), Claudius issued a considerable
number of the so-called Zeus tetradrachms from an unknown
mint, which *RPC* suggests was somewhere in northern Syria or

Cilicia. It seems that Claudius issued these Zeus tetradrachms, which were only 54 per cent silver, in place of the usual Tyche tetradrachms of Antioch, which were 76 per cent silver when minting restarted about 50 A.D. The Zeus tetradrachms (*RPC* 4112–4121) all have the bare head of Claudius with the Greek inscription ΤΙΒΕΡΙΟΣ ΚΛΑΥΔΙΟΣ ΚΑΙΣΑΡ (Tiberius Claudius Caesar) on the obverse, and on the reverse a seated Zeus holding a long sceptre in his left hand and in his right a Nike (Victory) who leans towards him with a wreath. The Greek inscription on the reverse is ΣΕΒΑΣΤΟΣ ΓΕΡΜΑΝΙΚΟΣ with the magistrate's initials to the left. The ten issues (28 coins and 8 dies in *RPC*) differ only in the magistrates' initials.

Figure 41 – A silver tetradrachm of Claudius. (*RPC* 4114)

A quantity of bronze coinage was minted at Antioch while Paul was away. It is dated to year 96 of the Caesarian era, i.e. in 47/48 A.D. The Caesarian era is calculated from June 48 B.C. when a great battle occurred at Pharsalus in Thessaly between Julius Caesar with only 22,000 soldiers and Pompey with 52,000 soldiers for control of the Roman world. Caesar's eight reserve cohorts moved up against Pompey's cavalry, using their spears as stabbing weapons, and caused a rout. Six thousand men were killed and 29,000 taken prisoner.[2]

This bronze coinage was issued under the authority of a Roman official called Cassius, who was most likely the legate of Syria at the time. *RPC* 4278 is part of this so-called Legate Series because it mentions Cassius on the reverse. On the obverse is the laureate head of Claudius with the Latin inscription IM. T[ ]VG. GER (Imperator Tiberius [ ] Augustus Germanicus). It is 23 millimetres in diameter. The full Greek inscription on the reverse is ΕΠΙ ΚΑΣΣΙΟΥ ΑΝΤΙΟΧΕΩΝ ΕΤ Ϟϛ within a laurel wreath of eight leaves. The translation is: 'In the time of Cassius, of the Antiochians, in the year 96'. The letters ET are an abbreviation of ETOS (year) or the genitive ETOUS (of year). Ϙ (koppa) was an obsolete Greek letter used in Hellenistic Greek to stand for the number 90. The lower case sigma (ϛ) stood for number 6.

Figure 42 – A bronze of Claudius. (*RPC* 4278)

Two other bronzes (*RPC* 4279 and 4280) were issued under Cassius, but they were part of the SC Series because they have a large SC (for SENATUS CONSULTO, by decree of the Senate) within a laurel wreath of eight leaves on the reverse. *RPC* 4279 is 23–26 millimetres in diameter, while *RPC* 4280 is only 18–20 millimetres. The laureate head of Claudius appears on the obverse with the Latin inscription IM. TI. CLA. CAE. AV. GER (Imperator Tiberius Claudius Caesar Augustus Germanicus).

Figure 43 – A bronze of Claudius. (*RPC* 4279)

When Paul visited Jerusalem in 49 A.D. the Roman governor of Judaea was Ventidius Cumanus (48–54 A.D). He was the fifth Roman governor after Pontius Pilate (26–36 A.D.). The others were Marcellus (36–37 A.D.), Marullus (37–41 A.D.), Cuspius Fadus (44–46 A.D.), and Tiberius Alexander (46–48 A.D.).[3] None of these governors issued any coins.

In the period between 41 A.D. and 44 A.D. Judaea was part of the kingdom of Agrippa I, the grandson of Herod the Great.

During this period Agrippa struck five bronze coins[4], four of which are rare and one is common. The rare coins are: Hendin 554 which has the bust of Claudius on the obverse and on the reverse a distyle temple containing four unknown figures; Hendin 557 which has Agrippa and King Herod of Chalcis crowning Claudius on the obverse and on the reverse a wreath enclosing two clasped hands celebrating the alliance between Agrippa and Claudius; Hendin 556 which has a bust of Agrippa on the obverse and on the reverse an anchor; and Hendin 555 which has a bust of Agrippa on the obverse and on the reverse a standing Tyche who holds a palm branch in her left hand and has her right hand on a rudder, and a surrounding inscription which reads 'Caesarea, beside Sebastos Harbour'. According to *RPC* these four coins were minted at Caesarea Maritima. These coins would not have been intended for circulation in Jerusalem but in other parts of Agrippa's kingdom because the portraits on them would have upset the Jews.

The common coin of Agrippa was struck in 41/42 A.D. It is 17 millimetres in diameter. On the obverse is an umbrella with a fringe and the Greek inscription ΒΑΧΙΛΕWC ΑΓΡΙΠΑ (of King Agrippa). On the reverse are three ears of barley growing between two stylised leaves and on either side of which are the letters L and S. The S was the letter for the number 6, while the L was a date symbol thought to have developed from a word in the Egyptian demotic script meaning 'year'. The years are dated from Agrippa's accession in 37 A.D. as king of the territory which formerly belonged to his uncle, Philip the Tetrarch. He also acquired another tetrarchy to the north of his uncle's territory at that time.

Figure 44 – An bronze prutah of Agrippa I. (Hendin 553)

The exact significance of the ears of barley is unknown today. Paul, of course, understood it. Ears of grain usually symbolise

abundance and prosperity, and barley was one of the products of
the land to which God led his people (Deuteronomy 8:7,8). The
umbrella was a unique symbol and Paul would have noticed it on
this coin of Agrippa. Umbrellas were used in ancient Egypt and
Mesopotamia to protect important people from the sun. They
were often large and needed strong bearers to hold them. They
served as signs of honour and authority and could be seen from a
distance. Agrippa could not put his portrait on this coin but he
certainly wanted people to know that he was a very important
royal person.

The story of Agrippa's life is quite amazing and Paul would
have been familiar with it. It is recorded by Josephus in books
XVIII and XIX of his 'Antiquities of the Jews'. Agrippa was born
in 10 B.C. When his father was executed by Herod the Great,
Agrippa's grandfather, he was sent to Rome for security and education. He grew up with Tiberius' son, Drusus, and became well
known in Roman aristocratic circles. After his mother's death he
squandered his inheritance and acquired large debts in a careless
and extravagant lifestyle. When Drusus died in 23 A.D. he
retired to the fortress of Malatha in the Idumean desert, leaving
many angry creditors in Rome. Agrippa contemplated suicide but
his wife pleaded with Herodias, his sister, to seek help from her
husband, Herod Antipas. About 28 A.D. Antipas, who was his
uncle and brother-in-law, gave him a minor position in his civil
service as an inspector of markets in his new capital of Tiberias.
They fell out, however, when they had too much wine during a
banquet and Antipas humiliated Agrippa by pointing out to
the guests that even the food he ate was owed to Antipas.
Agrippa returned to Rome where Josephus says he repaid his
debts by incurring new ones.

When he returned to Rome Agrippa befriended Caligula,
but a flattering remark by Agrippa to the effect that Caligula
should be emperor rather than Tiberius was overheard by a
servant and reported to Tiberius who immediately put Agrippa
in prison. When Tiberius died and his friend Caligula became
emperor Agrippa's fortunes were reversed. Caligula made him
ruler of the former territory of his uncle Philip and an adjoining
territory with the coveted title of king. Herodias and Antipas

became jealous and in 39 A.D. Antipas departed for Rome to seek the title, but Agrippa sent one of his freedmen to accuse Antipas of conspiracy against Rome. Caligula banished Antipas to Gaul and added his tetrarchy to the kingdom of Agrippa. Caligula was becoming megalomaniac with delusions of divinity and in about 41 A.D. he ordered that his statue be set up as an object of worship in the temple at Jerusalem. On the advice of the legate of Syria and realising the upheaval such an action would cause, Agrippa persuaded Caligula to desist from his plan. When Caligula was assassinated Agrippa supported Claudius in his accession and Claudius added Judaea and Samaria to Agrippa's territory so that his kingdom was as large as his grandfather's had been.

Agrippa was popular with the Jews but he persecuted the Christians, killing the apostle James, the son of Zebedee, and imprisoning Peter. In 44 A.D. Agrippa became angry with the people of Tyre and Sidon who depended on him for food. In Acts 12 Luke relates how ambassadors from these cities came to Agrippa who 'put on his royal robes, took his seat on the platform, and delivered a public address to them. The people kept shouting, "The voice of a god, and not of a mortal!" And immediately, because he had not given the glory to God, an angel of the Lord struck him down, and he was eaten by worms and died' (Acts 12:21–23). Josephus tells a slightly different story saying that Agrippa appeared in a robe of silver which shone so brightly in the sunlight that the people shouted out that he was a god. In any case Paul would have seen this incident as a rehearsal of the end of time, 'the day of the Lord', when the man of lawlessness 'opposes and exalts himself above every so-called god or object of worship, so that he takes his seat in the temple of God, declaring himself to be God' (Paul's Second Letter to the Thessalonians 2:4). Professor Bruce[5] considers that this part of Paul's picture of the end-time probably reflects Caligula's attempt to be worshipped in the Jewish temple. When Paul visited Jerusalem however, it was only five years after the dramatic death of Agrippa and the coin would have reminded Paul of that event. The day of the Lord was very much part of Paul's thinking during his missionary journeys and he looked forward to a time when 'the Lord himself, with a cry of command, with the archangel's call and with the sound of God's trumpet, will descend from heaven, and the dead in Christ will rise first. Then we who are alive, who are left, will be caught up in the clouds together with them to meet the Lord in the air; and so we will be with the Lord forever' (1 Thessalonians 4:16,17).

15. Troas 49 A.D.

Paul ... went through Syria and Cilicia strengthening the
churches. Paul went on also to Derbe and to Lystra ... went
through the region of Phrygia and Galatia ... passing by
Mysia, they went down to Troas.
Acts 15:41; 16:1a,6a,8

Paul's second missionary journey is usually dated from the second
half of 49 to about 52 A.D. because the Apostolic Council
occurred in 49 A.D. and Paul's visit to Corinth can be precisely
dated from the governorship of Gallio before whom he appeared.
Therefore it seems reasonable to assume that Paul's visit to Troas
occurred in the second half of 49 A.D.

At that time Troas was a busy seaport on the north-west
coast of Asia Minor. It was an important centre in the Roman
system of communications and a regular port of call for vessels
journeying between Macedonia and Asia. The Greek geographer
Strabo (64 B.C.–24 A.D.) wrote that the original settlement was
called Sigia. It was probably founded about the seventh century
B.C. by Aeolians from the adjacent island of Tenedos. In 310 B.C.
a new city was founded on the site by Antigonus I, one of
Alexander's generals, who named it Antigoneia. After Antigonus
was defeated at the battle of Ipsus in 301 B.C. Lysimachus,
another of Alexander's generals, changed the name of the city to
Alexandreia. As there were many cities with this name it became
known as Alexandreia Troas, after the district in which it was
situated. In ancient times the whole of the north-west corner of
Asia Minor was called Troas (genitive case: Troados) or the Troad,
after the city of Troy. Troy was also called Ilion (Latin: Ilium) and
was twenty kilometres north-north-east of Alexandreia Troas.

Ilium was famous as the city before which the Trojan War was fought in about 1200 B.C. This war was the subject of Homer's epic poem *The Iliad*.

The Troad was part of the kingdom of Pergamum which was bequeathed to Rome by Attalus III in 133 B.C. Alexandreia Troas was a free city until Augustus gave it the status of a Roman colony. It was henceforth known as Colonia Augusta Troadensium. It was the only colony founded by Augustus in Western Asia Minor.[1] By Paul's time it had become the wealthiest and most populous city in the Troad.

Nowadays the city is more commonly called Alexandria Troas. Its site is covered by extensive ruins overgrown with shrubbery, the scattered sarcophagi of its great necropolis giving it the appearance of a wrecked city of the dead.[2] For most visitors Alexandria Troas is a mood, a place which, like so many places in Turkey, conjures up that feeling of great antiquity disappearing beneath the slowly grinding wheels of time.[3] The tiny seaside hamlet of Dalyan developed in Ottoman times around the silted-up port where a line of broken monoliths lie in the shallows along a sandy beach. Yet archaeologists have been able to identify the remains of the theatre, the gymnasium, the agora, and the temple of Apollo.[4]

Apollo was important in Alexandria Troas. In fact he was the dominant deity for the whole of the Troad, except for Ilium where his sister Athena held sway. He was worshipped in the form known in ancient times as Apollo Smintheus. Exactly what Smintheus means is unknown today, but Jones[5] says that the word was thought to be derived from 'sminthos', meaning 'mouse' in the Aeolic dialect. His most famous temple was at Chryse near Hamaxitus in the Troad. The ruins of this Smintheum can be seen today near Gulpinar, a village 25 kilometres south of Alexandria Troas. Strabo mentions that the temple had a remarkable wooden cult-statue of Apollo by which the god was represented with a mouse under his foot. The work was carved by the great sculptor Scopas, who was born on the Aegean island of Paros in about 420 B.C. The mouse may point to Apollo's role as protector of crops against the ravages of field mice[6], but more likely the mouse was connected in some way with Apollo's prophetic function.[7] Apollo was the god who communicated to man through prophets and oracles his knowledge of the future and the will of his father, Zeus. Often this communication would come in the form of dreams, and usually the temples of Apollo had places where enquirers could sleep and have their dreams interpreted by priests the next morning.

No coins were minted at Alexandria Troas during the first century A.D. The question therefore arises which coins circulated in the city during this period. *RPC* considers the possible arrangements of coinage[8], but states that at present there is too little information about the patterns of circulation. We know, however, that Ilium was quite productive at this time and some of the bronze coins which Paul handled in Alexandria Troas were probably minted in Ilium. If so, it is likely that Paul saw the large bronze coin issued from Ilium by Caligula (*RPC* 2312). It is no surprise that Caligula chose Ilium, the home of Aeneas, the ancestral hero of the Romans, as the mint for this coin. It is 28 millimetres in diameter and on the obverse it has the bare head of Caligula facing the radiate head of Augustus and the inscription ΓΑΙΟC ΚΑΙCΑΡ ΘΕΟC ΑΥΤΟΚΡΑΤωΡ CΕΒΑCΤΟΙ (Gaius Caesar God Commander Augusti). On the reverse it has the bust of Roma facing the bust of the Senate and between them a statue of Athena, standing, facing, and holding a spear and shield. The inscription on the reverse is ΘΕΑ ΡωΜΗ ΙΕΡΑ CΥΝΚΛΗΤΟC ΙΛΙ (Goddess Roma Sacred Senate Ilium).

Figure 45 – A bronze of Caligula. (*RPC* 2312)

Not enough is known about the circulation of silver coinage in the province of Asia, of which the Troad was part, to say which silver coins Paul would have handled in Alexandria Troas in 49 A.D. There were probably denarii minted in Rome as well as Asia, and cistophori[9] minted in Ephesus under Claudius. Roman gold aurei probably circulated in Alexandria Troas and some of these could have been minted in Asia.

In the second and first centuries B.C. Alexandria Troas issued silver and bronze coins which all honoured Apollo. A series of handsome tetradrachms (Sear 4025) dated from 176 B.C. to 77 B.C. showed the laureate head of Apollo on the obverse, and the standing figure of Apollo Smintheus on the reverse with the inscription ΑΠΟΛΛΩΝΟΣ ΙΜΙΘΕΩΣ[10] and in the exergue ΑΛΕΞΑΝΔΡΕΩΝ ΛΥΣΑΓΟΡΟΥ (of Alexandrians of Lysagoros). It is unlikely that Paul would have seen any of these tetradrachms. Three bronze coins minted at Alexandria Troas are undated but are usually assigned to the second and first centuries B.C. It is possible they might have been seen by Paul as they are common today. The largest (Sear 4031) is 22 millimetres in diameter and has the laureate bust of Apollo three-quarter face to the right on the obverse and on the reverse a lyre within a wreath and the inscription ΑΛΕΞΑΝ. Sear 4033 is only nine millimetres in diameter and has a lyre on the obverse and on the reverse a tripod and ΑΛΕΞ. The lyre was a symbol of Apollo and referred to his function as god of music. The tripod was also associated with the cult of Apolllo and referred to his prophetic power. At Delphi the priestess of Apollo transmitted prophecies from the god while sitting on a tripod, in imitation of Apollo sitting on the navel (omphalos) of the world.

Figure 46 – A bronze with bust of Apollo. (Sear 4031)

So whether through coins or through his surroundings at Alexandria Troas, Paul would have come under the influence of Apollo, who was without doubt a very powerful figure in Greek religion. According to Sir William Smith[11] Apollo had more influence on the Greeks than any other god. Smith goes on to assert that the Greeks would never have become what they were without the worship of Apollo: in him the brightest side of the Grecian mind is reflected.

Among his many functions Apollo was a god of colonization, both in Hellenic and Roman times, and led the emigrants on their voyages.[12] So Apollo, the god of light, was responsible for the spread of higher civilization in the world. It cannot be entirely coincidental that at Alexandria Troas 'during the night Paul had a vision: there stood a man of Macedonia pleading with him saying, "Come over to Macedonia and help us." When he had seen the vision, we immediately tried to cross over to Macedonia, being convinced that God had called us to proclaim the good news to them' (Acts 16:9,10). From Troas Paul embarked on the next step of his mission: the evangelization of Europe.

16. Philippi 50 A.D.

We set sail from Troas and took a straight course to
Samothrace, the following day to Neapolis, and from there to
Philippi, which is a leading city of the district of Macedonia
and a Roman colony.
Acts 16:11,12a

If, as Professor Bruce[1] suggests, Paul reached Corinth in about
October 50 A.D., it is safe to assume that his visit to Philippi and
his subsequent journey through Greece also occurred in 50 A.D.
By this time Claudius had been in power for nine years.

Neapolis was the port for Philippi which was 16 kilometres to
the north-west over a mountain range. Neapolis was situated on
a promontory with a harbour on either side. In the western
harbour the galleys of Brutus and Cassius had been moored
during the battle of Philippi in 42 B.C. when Octavian and
Mark Antony defeated these assassins of Julius Caesar. Although
Neapolis means 'new city' a town had existed on the site for
many centuries before Paul's arrival. The site is now occupied by
the town of Kavala, and there is little to see from Paul's time.
Blaiklock[2] mentions a shrine of Parthenos (the maiden goddess)
from the Classical Greek period and various inscriptions from the
Roman period. The stone aqueduct which dominates the central
part of the town dates from the sixteenth century A.D. Neapolis
produced no coins since the fourth century B.C. when a gorgon's
head featured on the obverse and the head of a maiden on the
reverse.

The first settlement at Philippi was made by people from
the island of Thasos to exploit the gold mines in the area. It was
called Krenides (springs). Philip II, the father of Alexander the

Great, captured the city and renamed it after himself. The city was fortified and contained a theatre which was restored by Marcus Aurelius in the second century A.D. After the battle of Pydna in 168 B.C. the city passed into Roman hands. In 42 B.C. the battle of Philippi was fought on the marshy plains to the south-west of the city, and afterwards it was probably Mark Antony who founded the first Roman colony there because his head appears on some of the first coins (*RPC* 1646–1649). On the obverse these coins have the letters AICVP, which probably stand for Antonii Iussu Colonia Victrix Philippensis (by command of Antony, Victory Colony of Philippi). The largest coin has a man with a veiled head ploughing with two oxen and is clearly a foundation issue. The next size has a seated togate figure with an urn at his feet and *RPC* suggests that this scene represents the giving out of allotments by lot to the Roman veterans.

After the battle of Actium in 31 B.C. when Octavian defeated Antony and Cleopatra many of Antony's followers who had been dispossessed of their Italian properties were settled at Philippi. The colony was then renamed Colonia Iulia Philippensis to honour Julius Caesar, and in 27 B.C. when Octavian was given the title Augustus the name was changed to Colonia Augusta Iulia Philippensis (the Augustan, Julian Colony of Philippi). It is this name, in abbreviated form, which appears on the large coin issued by Augustus (*RPC* 1650). This coin is 26 millimetres in diameter and has the laureate head of Augustus on the obverse with the inscription COL AVG IVL PHIL IVSSV AVG. On the reverse is a statue of Augustus in military dress being crowned by Julius Caesar in a toga. On either side of the base of the statue is probably an altar.[3] This statue would have been erected in the forum of Philippi in gratitude for Augustus' re-establishment of the colony. This coin is of leaded bronze, but the other coin (*RPC* 1651), which is usually attributed to Augustus, is of copper, and *RPC* points out that copper coins were not produced in Macedonia before the reign of Claudius. *RPC* therefore considers that a Claudio-Neronian date is more likely. In this case Paul may well have seen this coin when he visited Philippi. It is 18 millimetres in diameter and on the obverse it has the winged figure of Victory holding a wreath and palm branch. The Victory stands on a base which suggests that there was such a statue at Philippi. The letters VIC and AVG appear on either side of the figure of Victory. What victory or victories this refers to is unknown. Octavian's victory at Actium seems at first unlikely because Actium was a long way from Philippi, but the Roman historian Dio Cassius (51:4) records that Antony's followers were settled at Philippi after the battle of Actium. Perhaps the three standards on the reverse of the coin were the standards of the three praetorian cohorts[4] who had previously guarded Antony. It is possible, of course, that the Victory refers to a victory or victories of Claudius or Nero and that the praetorian cohorts were settled at Philippi during their reigns. The three standards on the reverse of the coin are surrounded by the inscription COHOR PRAE PHIL, which probably expands to Cohortes Praetoriae Philippensis (Praetorian Cohorts of Philippi).

Figure 47 – A copper coin of Claudius or Nero. (*RPC* 1651)

Another coin which Paul probably saw at Philippi was the large copper coin which has the bare head of Claudius on the obverse (*RPC* 1653). It is 26 millimetres in diameter and has the inscription TI CLAVDIVS CAESAR AVG P M TR P IMP (Tiberius Claudius Caesar, Augustus, Pontifex Maximus, Tribunitia Potestate, Imperator) on the obverse. Minor variations occur in the obverse inscription. On the reverse is the same statue of Augustus and Julius Caesar as on the coin of Augustus except that the statue base is inscribed DIVVS AVG (Divine Augustus). Obviously the base of the statue at Philippi had been so inscribed after Augustus had been deified in 14 A.D. It is this inscribed statue that Paul would have seen in the forum. The inscription on the reverse reads COL AVG IVL PHILIP (Colonia Augusta Julia Philippensis).

Figure 48 – A bronze of Tiberius. (*RPC* 1653/1)

These coins with their glorification of war and their adoration of military leaders indicated to Paul that Philippi was a colony of a great military power where the ruling dynasty was in firm control.

From 1914 to 1938 archaeological work was done at Philippi by the French School at Athens. The site was uninhabited and they were able to excavate the forum which was 100 metres long and 50 metres wide and lay about three to five metres below the present ground level. This forum dates to the second century A.D. but was built on the site of the previous forum known to Paul. It would have been a busy place as Philippi lay at the eastern end of the Via Egnatia which was the main thoroughfare crossing the Balkans from west to east and linked Rome to Asia and beyond. As might be expected from its mixed Thracian, Greek and Roman population, religious practices would have been diverse and the temple sites and inscriptions discovered by the archaeologists show the dominant Greco-Roman deities, together with Cybele, Bendis (a Thracian goddess similar to the Greek Artemis), Isis and Serapis.[5] The only coins minted at Philippi before the foundation coins of Mark Antony were gold, silver and bronze coins dated to the period 357–330 B.C. They have Heracles on the obverse and a tripod, the symbol of Apollo, on the reverse; so these gods probably continued to be important in the Philippi of Paul's day.

In the book of Acts Luke relates an interesting episode when a woman who has a spirit of divination (literally a Pythonic spirit) shouts out, 'These men are slaves of the Most High God, who proclaim to you a way of salvation' (Acts 16:17). Python was a serpent killed by Apollo and the use of the term indicated that the woman was inspired by Apollo. So it seems that the god Apollo looked favourably on this small band of wandering Christians even though this attitude was not reciprocated by Paul.

Why should Apollo be supporting this first Christian mission to Europe? The explanation is that Luke was a gentile physician from Antioch in Syria and he would have been a worshipper of Apollo before becoming a Christian. Near Antioch was the grove of Daphne, a major cult centre for the worship of Apollo, one of whose functions was god of medicine. While accepting the Christian god, Luke must have retained respect for the god of his pagan past.

In the account from Acts 16:10 to Acts 16:17, i.e. from Troas to the woman with the Pythonic spirit at Philippi, the first person plural pronouns 'we' and 'us' are used for the first time, indicating that Luke himself was with Paul at this time. These pronouns are not used again until Acts 20:5 when Paul was again in Philippi, suggesting that Luke had stayed in that city. In the first of these so-called 'we' passages, Apollo seems to be in the background trying to help the missionaries. Perhaps when Paul continued his journey, visiting the synagogues in the various cities of Greece, Luke concentrated his efforts on the gentiles attending the pagan temples at Philippi, building on the prophecy of the woman with the Pythonic spirit. Although the woman cried out that they were proclaiming a way of salvation, Paul later wrote to the Christians at Philippi, 'Work out your own salvation with fear and trembling; for it is God who is at work in you, enabling you both to will and to work for his good pleasure' (Philippians 2:12b,13).

17. Amphipolis and Apollonia 50 A.D.

*After Paul and Silas had passed through Amphipolis and
Apollonia ...*
Acts 17:1a

Amphipolis was 45 kilometres from Philippi and one-third of the
distance to Thessalonica. Apollonia was 80 kilometres from
Philippi and two-thirds of the distance to Thessalonica. Professor
Bruce[1] considers that Paul reached Amphipolis in one day and
Apollonia in two days, and that he apparently halted at each
city for one night only. In this case it is unlikely that he saw any
of their coins. On his third missionary journey, however, he probably again passed through these cities on two occasions. All of
these cities were on the Via Egnatia, the great Roman road which
led from the Adriatic Sea to the northern Aegean at Neapolis. It
was one of the main military and commercial highways of the
Roman Empire.

The Romans divided the province of Macedonia into four
districts. The first district included Neapolis and Philippi but its
administrative centre was Amphipolis. Amphipolis was situated
on a terraced hill on the east bank of the Strymon river about five
kilometres from its mouth. According to Herodotus (book VII,
section 114) the place was originally called 'The Nine Ways' and
was in the territory of a Thracian tribe called the Edonians.
When the Persian king Xerxes reached the Strymon river with
his army in 480 B.C. and heard that the place was called 'The
Nine Ways', he took nine pairs of the local youths and maidens
and buried them alive on the spot as an offering to the god who

lives underneath the earth. In 436 B.C. the Athenians drove out the Edonians, and the leader of the Athenian colonists, Hagnon, called the town Amphipolis, which means 'around the city'. Thucydides (book IV, section 102) says that Hagnon called the city by this name 'because the Strymon flows round it on two sides, and he built it so as to be conspicuous from the sea and land alike, running a long wall across from river to river, to complete the circumference'. In Paul's time Amphipolis was an important city on the Egnatian Way and the centre of a fertile district producing oil, wine and figs. In addition there were gold and silver mines in the area. Today there is a village called Amfipolis on the site of the ancient city. There are still traces of a Roman aqueduct and ancient fortifications, and numerous inscriptions from the Roman era have been found there.

Amphipolis preserved its independence until 357 B.C. when it was captured by Philip II, king of Macedon. The independent city produced gold and silver coins from about 410 B.C. and the earliest tetradrachms featured a beautiful facing head of Apollo.[2] After the battle of Pydna in 168 B.C. the Romans allowed the city to continue to mint bronze coins, and in Paul's time its production was fairly prolific. Augustus issued five coins which featured Artemis, the sister of Apollo, either on the obverse or reverse. The city issued two coins in honour of the divine Augustus and one coin in honour of the divine Julia (Livia). The inscription on the latter reads ΙΟΥΛΙΑ ΣΕΒΑΣΤΗ ΘΕΑ (Julia Augusta Goddess) and as Livia was not deified until 42 A.D. by her grandson Claudius, the coin could not have been issued before this date. All three of these coins have Artemis Tauropolis on the reverse. In this form Artemis is depicted riding a bull and holding a veil over her head. The veil is inflated by the wind and forms an arc around her head. The significance of this swirling veil or scarf is not obvious, although Ferguson[3] says that it assimilates Artemis to the sea-goddess. Probably it is meant to represent the firmament.

According to Liddell and Scott's Lexicon[4] tauropolis means 'hunting bulls', but Professor Jones[5] says that the derivation of the title is uncertain and it may be connected with her cult among the Taurians in the Black Sea area, which was brought to

Greece and practised in many places, or it may be connected with tauros, bull, and mean 'bull-hunting' or 'drawn by bulls'. According to Robert Graves (op. cit., 116.3) 'tauropolos' suggests the Cretan bull sacrifice. The coins show the goddess riding on a bull but the significance of this remains unknown.[6]

Artemis riding on a bull was obviously important for the citizens of Amphipolis because the type occurs on the reverse of almost every coin issued by Tiberius, Caligula, Claudius and Nero. Tiberius issued three coins with his laureate head on the obverse and Artemis Tauropolis on the reverse. Caligula issued two leaded bronze coins. One had a bearded head, probably Zeus, on the obverse and on the reverse Caligula on a horse with one arm raised. *RPC*[7] suggests that this reverse may have been derived from an actual statue. It probably stood in a public place at Amphipolis. This coin is rare today, but much more common is a 21 millimetre diameter coin (*RPC* 1637) with Caligula on a horse with one arm raised on the obverse and on the reverse Artemis Tauropolis. The inscription on the obverse is ΚΑΙΣΑΡ ΓΕΡΜΑΝΙΚΟΣ ΘΕΟΣ ΣΕΒΑΣΤΟΣ (Caesar Germanicus God Augustus). This coin is very significant as it is one of the few coins of the Roman Empire which refer to the living emperor as god. If Paul had seen this coin he would have been aghast.

Figure 49 – A bronze of Caligula. (*RPC* 1637)

Tiberius would never have allowed such an inscription, and Claudius did not repeat it. Claudius issued two leaded bronze coins (*RPC* 1639 and 1640). *RPC* 1639 has on the obverse the emperor in military dress, standing left, raising his right hand and holding in his left arm a short staff with an eagle on the end. This type also may have been derived from a statue. The inscription reads ΤΙ ΚΛΑΥΔΙΟΣ ΣΕΒΑΣΤΟΣ (Tiberius Claudius Augustus). On the reverse is Artemis Tauropolis, left, with the inscription ΑΜΦΙΠΟΛΙΤΩΝ (of the Amphipolitans). *RPC* 1640 is similar except that the bull is moving to the right.

Figure 50 – A leaded bronze of Claudius. (*RPC* 1639)

The Praetorian Guard at Rome had brought Claudius to power and although this scholarly and physically disabled man was no soldier, he is here portrayed in military pose. It was a facade designed to impress the numerous Roman legions as well as the average citizen. Nero, even less a soldier, repeated the type on the coins he issued from Amphipolis.

Apollonia was just south of the middle of Lake Volvi which is 20 kilometres long and about five kilometres wide. There is a village called Apollonia in the area today but there are no remains of the ancient city. With the possible exception of a bronze coin minted about 200 B.C., which is mentioned by Head[8], Apollonia issued no coins. It is likely that most of the coins, especially the gold and silver ones that circulated in these cities on the Egnatian Way, and in fact throughout the Roman provinces of Macedonia and Achaia, were minted at Rome and were similar to those which circulated in Italy.[9] Achaia was the ancient name for Greece and in Paul's time it was applied to the region consisting of Thessaly, Epirus and all areas to the south. In 15 A.D. Tiberius removed Achaia and Macedonia from senatorial control and united them with Moesia to the north to form one huge province under the control of an imperial legate. In 41 or 44 A.D. Claudius again made Achaia and Macedonia separate provinces under senatorial control.

The Apollonia that Paul saw in 50 A.D. was neither a large nor important city, and although we know virtually nothing about it, we can be sure that there was a temple of Apollo there. In his Theogony written about 700 B.C. Hesiod explains that Apollo was the son of Zeus and Leto, who was the daughter of

Titans, a race of divine beings. One of Apollo's functions was god of healing and medicine, but his son Ascelpius, whose mother was mortal, was generally considered the god of medicine, having inherited this ability from his father. In Rome a temple to Apollo was built after a plague in 433 B.C. and he was especially honoured by Augustus who built a magnificent temple to him on the Palatine Hill which rivalled that of Jupiter on the Capitoline Hill. Apollo, who had a shrine at Actium on the west coast of Greece, had presided over the decisive battle of Actium in 31 B.C. According to Stapleton[10] Apollo 'represented a level of moral excellence and his cult at Delphi had enormous influence ... From its influence there arose an extension of tolerance: the discouraging of vengeance and blood feud, and the recognition that crime must be expiated, no matter what the power or stature of the guilty person'. There are, of course, many similarities between Apollo and Christ.

18. Thessalonica and Beroea 50 A.D.

After Paul and Silas had passed through Amphipolis and Apollonia, they came to Thessalonica ...
Acts 17:1a
That very night the believers sent Paul and Silas off to Beroea ...
Acts 17:10a

Thessalonica was named after a daughter of Philip II of Macedon. In 352 B.C. Philip allied himself with the Greeks of Thessaly and defeated the Greeks of Phocis in central Greece. When his daughter was born in the same year he called her Thessalonike, meaning Thessalian victory. She was the half-sister of Alexander the Great and married one of his generals, Kassandros. In 316 B.C. Kassandros founded the city and named it after his wife. The city flourished and became the chief city of Macedonia. After the Romans defeated the Macedonian king Perseus in 168 B.C. they divided Macedonia into four districts and Thessalonica was designated the capital of the second district. In 146 B.C. it became the capital of Macedonia when the whole area was made a Roman province. Today it is an important industrial and commercial centre second to Athens in population and to Piraeus as a port.

In Paul's time the Via Egnatia passed through the city from east to west and it is still a main thoroughfare called Egnatia Street. Otherwise there is nothing to see that Paul would have seen. The massive Roman arch on Egnatia Street was built by the emperor Galerius in 303 A.D.

Paul certainly would have handled the coins of Thessalonica because in the two letters he subsequently wrote to the Christians there, he prided himself in not being dependent on others: 'We did not eat anyone's bread without paying for it; but with toil and labour we worked night and day, so that we might not burden any of you' (2 Thessalonians 3:8, c.f. I Thessalonians 2:9). As Thessalonica was the capital of the Roman province of Macedonia it was a fairly prolific source of base-metal coinage, mostly leaded-bronze, although copper coins were produced under Claudius and Nero.[1]

The head of Augustus appears on the obverse of all his coins except for one issue (*RPC* 1563) where the bust of Livia, his wife, appears on the obverse and on the reverse is a horse galloping. The horse was the traditional type of the old Macedonian kingdom and appeared on another coin of Augustus, as well as on coins of Claudius and Nero. Macedonia was famous for its horses, and Philip, whose name means 'fond of horses', paid a large sum of money for the horse called Bucephalos which no one was able to break in except his son Alexander, who subsequently rode the horse through all his campaigns.

Most of the types on the coins of Thessalonica which Paul would have seen honour members of the imperial family. Augustus so honoured his adoptive father, Julius Caesar, his son-in-law Tiberius, and his grandson Gaius Caesar. The only other types issued by Augustus refer to the battle of Actium (a prow or Nike standing on a prow) or simply have ΘΕΣΣΑΛΟΝΙΚΕΩΝ (of Thessalonians) surrounded by a wreath.

Tiberius had the portrait of his mother, Livia, on all his reverses except for one which has the goddess Demeter carrying torches and riding in a serpent car (a chariot with two wheels and two serpents rearing up in front). The reverse inscription on this coin is ΣΕΒΑΣΤΗ ΘΕΣΣΑΛΟΝΙΚΕΩΝ (Augusta, of Thessalonians). Apparently the purpose of this coin was to identify Livia with the goddess. Demeter was another manifestation of the Earth Mother and was sometimes depicted on Greek coins riding in such a car.[2] The snakes may have alluded to her function as a goddess of health or may simply have reflected the fact that she was an earth goddess. The torches probably referred to her searching all over the world for her daughter Persephone, who had been abducted by the god of the underworld. The wheels suggest that this image was led in procession out from her temple. This would have occurred at night when the flaming torches would have highlighted the painted features of the idol and the heads of the serpents. Accompanied by the voices and music of her devotees she would have been an impressive sight. It is easy to see why Livia should have been identified with Demeter because as empress she was in a sense the provider of the fruits of the earth and as the grieving widow of Augustus she was in a way searching for her divine husband.

In one of the Greek myths Demeter changes into a mare to escape (unsuccessfully) the amorous advances of the sea god Poseidon, and this perhaps explains why we find Demeter in Thessalonica where horses were important. This coin (*RPC* 1566) has a diameter of 21 millimetres and was probably equivalent to a Roman as. It has the head of Tiberius on the obverse with the inscription ΤΙ ΚΑΙΣΑΡ ΣΕΒΑΣΤΟΣ (Tiberius Caesar Augustus).

Figure 51 – A bronze of Tiberius. (*RPC* 1566)

Caligula issued five coins, three of which (*RPC* 1573, 1574, 1575) had the veiled head of his grandmother, Antonia, on the reverse with the inscription ΑΝΤΩΝΙΑ [ΣΕΒΑΣΤΗ ΘΕΣΣΑΛΟΝΙΚΕΩΝ] (Antonia Augusta, of Thessalonians). All the coins were 21 millimetres in diameter. The other reverses were a portrait of his father, Germanicus, who died at Antioch in Syria probably of natural causes, and the word ΘΕΣΣΑΛΟΝΙΚΕΩΝ (of Thessalonians) in two lines in a wreath. Antonia was the younger daughter of Mark Antony and Octavia, the sister of Octavian. She was the mother of Claudius and the grandmother of Caligula. Her elder sister was also called Antonia and was the grandmother of Nero. These two sisters are usually referred to as Antonia Senior and Antonia Junior. The situation is further confused by the fact that Antonia Junior's grand-daughter, Claudius' daughter by his second wife Aelia Paetina, was also called Antonia. According to Stevenson[3] Antonia Junior was 'spoken of, by historians, as a sensible, amiable woman; of a handsome countenance and of graceful manners; a noble exemplar of conjugal fidelity, and of honourable widowhood'. She died in 38 A.D. at the age of about 74, in the second year of the reign of Caligula. Caligula at first conferred honours on her, investing her with the title Augusta, but she soon fell out of favour and Suetonius[4] records that, according to some people, he poisoned her.

Figure 52 – A bronze of Caligula. (*RPC* 1573/1)

Claudius issued thirteen coins (*RPC* 1577–1589). His head appears on the obverse of only six. The rest all have the bust of his mother Antonia with the inscription **ANTONIA** or **MAPKIA**. Although *RPC* considers the latter word puzzling, as it is not used elsewhere as a name of Antonia, it is the feminine form of Marcus and was probably a prenomen referring to her famous father Markus Antonius. Mark Antony would have been popular in Thessalonica. He and Octavian were welcomed there in 42 B.C. after the battle of Philippi and they made Thessalonica a free city in gratitude for its support. Magistrates (politarchs) were elected from the people to govern the independent city which then issued three leaded-bronze coins with Mark Antony and Octavian on the obverse and on the reverse the bust of Eleutheria (Freedom), the head of Agonothesia (Athletic Games – probably held regularly to celebrate the victory at Philippi), or the bust of Homonoia (Unity – referring to the relationship between Thessalonica and Rome). This popularity of Mark Antony explains why Antonia, his daughter, features so prominently on the coins of Thessalonica. The coins indicated to the people that, through Antonia, the blood of the hero found its way into the veins of the reigning emperor Claudius.

The reverses of Claudius' coins feature Nike on a globe; a horse galloping or walking; ΘΕΣΣΑΛΟΝΙΚΕΩΝ in a wreath; a bust of Claudius' son Britannicus; the head of the divine Augustus; and a veiled head with the inscription ΘΕΣΣΑΛΟΝΙΚΗ (Thessalonike). Whether the veiled head is the city goddess or the daughter of Philip II or some other woman is not apparent. The coins in honour of Augustus (*RPC* 1578, 1579 1580) have the laureate head of Claudius with the inscription ΤΙ ΚΛΑΥ ΚΑΙΣΑΡ ΣΕΒΑΣΤΟΣ [ΓΕΡΜ] (Tiberius Claudius Caesar Augustus Germanicus) on the obverse, and on the reverse the radiate and laureate head of Augustus with the inscription ΘΕΟΣ ΣΕΒΑΣΤΟΣ ΘΕΣΣΑΛΟΝΙΚΕΩΝ (God Augustus, of Thessalonians).

Figure 53 – A bronze of Claudius honouring Augustus. (*RPC* 1578)

All these coins of Thessalonica promote the Roman emperor, his family, and their divine pretensions.[5] Although Paul respected the Roman authorities, his agenda, of course, was quite different. He was promoting the kingdom of God: 'urging and encouraging you and pleading that you lead a life worthy of God, who calls you into his own kingdom and glory' (1 Thessalonians 2:12), and proclaiming Jesus Christ: 'explaining and proving that it was necessary for the Messiah to suffer and to rise from the dead, and saying, "This is the Messiah, Jesus whom I am proclaiming to you"' (Acts 17:3).

Paul's preaching resulted in a disturbance in the city and some of his followers were brought before the politarchs[6] on the charge that 'they were all acting contrary to the decrees of the emperor, saying that there is another king called Jesus' (Acts 17:6). So the Christians of Thessalonica immediately sent

Paul away to Beroea, a city 65 kilometres west-south-west of Thessalonica. It was situated at the foot of Mount Bermios on a tributary of the Haliacmon river. It was not on the Egnatian Way and Paul was able to start preaching again. Beroea is the modern town of Veria, and the only remains of the ancient city are a large number of inscriptions. No coins were minted at Beroea, so the bronze coins which Paul saw there would have been minted at Thessalonica, the provincial capital, or at Rome. The silver and gold coins, of course, would have been similar to those which circulated in Italy.

During his time in Macedonia it is likely that Paul handled coins issued by the Macedonian koinon or federation of Macedonian cities. *RPC*[7] considers that these coins were probably minted in Thessalonica. Some have the head and name of Claudius (or Nero) but many have no head and only the inscription ΜΑΚΕΔΟΝΩΝ (of Macedonians). Of these 'headless' coins, the commonest type is a Macedonian shield, which was a round shield decorated with oval patterns around the edge. Of the Claudian coins by far the commonest today is *RPC* 1612. It is 23 millimetres in diameter and has the head of Claudius on the obverse with the inscription ΤΙ ΚΛΑΥΔΙΟΣ ΚΑΙCΑΡ (Tiberius Claudius Caesar). On the reverse it has a Macedonian shield and the inscription ΣΕΒΑΣΤΟΣ ΜΑΚΕΔΟΝΩΝ (Augustus, of Macedonians).

Figure 54 – A bronze of Claudius. (*RPC* 1612)

The shield had appeared on coins of Macedonia from the pre-Roman period and it was an appropriate type because the Macedonians were a war-like people. In his first letter to the Thessalonians Paul speaks of military weapons in an unprecedented way, saying, 'Let us be sober, and put on the breastplate of hope and love, and for a helmet the hope of salvation' (1 Thess. 5:8). He later wrote, 'In all circumstances take the shield of faith, with which you will be able to quench all the flaming arrows of the evil one' (Eph. 6:16). What reminded the Macedonians of their war-like past inspired Paul to think of the power of faith.

19. Athens 50 A.D.

Those who conducted Paul brought him as far as Athens.
Acts 17:15a

When Paul visited Athens it was still considered the cultural centre of Greece and wealthy Romans sent their sons there for further education, but its great creative spirit was almost exhausted and it had produced no major artists or thinkers for many years. Yet physically it had not changed since classical times. Its beautiful temples and public buildings were still standing, all crowned by the glorious temple of Athena on the Acropolis, the flat-topped rocky mountain which dominated the city.

In the temple of Athena was a wonderful ivory and gold statue of the goddess made by Phidias in the fifth century B.C. In this form she was known as Athena Parthenos, the maiden or virgin, and hence the temple was called the Parthenon. In front of the Parthenon was another colossal statue of Athena also made by Phidias. It was of bronze and represented Athena in fighting pose about to hurl a spear. In this form she was known as Athena Promachos, the front warrior. When travellers approached Athens from the sea, as Paul probably did, their first glimpse of the city was the sunlight glinting on the tip of Athena's spear.

Paul, like other visitors to Athens before and since, would have been impressed by the Acropolis. H.V. Morton[1] describes what he saw when he visited the city in 1936, 'Lifted high above Athens, with nothing behind it but the blue sky of summer, far larger than I had ever imagined it to be, yet looking queerly weightless, the Parthenon, even in ruin, looks as if it has just alighted from heaven upon the summit of the Acropolis'. Morton points out that Athens was different from all other cities that Paul had visited because he was 'the first Christian missionary in the intellectual stronghold of the Roman world. I think there are few moments in the history of early Christianity more dramatic, or in their sequel more notable, than the moment when the eyes of St Paul first saw the Acropolis'.

North-west of the Acropolis was the Agora, a large public square and market place, partly surrounded by colonnaded walkways called stoas. South of the Agora was a rocky hill called the Areopagus or Hill of Ares.[2] The hill's name was given to a council of Athenians who met on the top of the hill. The council was still called the Areopagus even when it was transferred to one of the stoas called the Royal Stoa. In Paul's time the Areopagus was concerned with cases of forgery, maintaining correct standards of measure, supervision of buildings, and matters of religion and education.[3] Its responsibility probably extended to the city's coinage. Although Achaia was a Roman province the Romans made Athens a free city, in deference to its glorious past, allowing it to manage its own affairs.

When Paul preached 'the good news about Jesus and the resurrection' (Acts 17:18) in the Agora, some of the philosophers who frequented the area brought him before a meeting of the Areopagus. Paul then delivered his famous speech which began with reference to an altar he had seen dedicated to an unknown god. One of the members of the Areopagus, whose name was Dionysius, became a follower of Paul.

Apart from the Acropolis there are today many ruins in Athens relevant to Paul's visit. The Agora has been excavated by the American School of Classical Studies.[4] Along the east side of the Agora the stoa built by Attalus II, king of Pergamum, in the second century B.C., has been rebuilt and it is now possible to imagine the area as Paul saw it.

The coins of Athens which Paul saw did not have the emperor's head on them because the city had been exempted from the obligation of placing the head of the reigning emperor upon the obverses of any of its coins.[5] As a result it is not easy to determine which period these bronze coins belong to. No silver coins were issued by Athens probably because the city simply could not afford it. In more prosperous times the city had produced its well-known silver tetradrachms which dominated the Greek coinage for centuries. According to *RPC* the precise date of the cessation of Athenian silver is uncertain, but it seems to lie in the decade 50–40 B.C. They add that during the first century B.C. Roman denarii had come to play an increasing role. The last issues of Athenian silver are known as 'new-style tetradrachms': they have broad flans with the head of Athena Parthenos on the obverse and the owl, the symbol of Athena, on the reverse. The head of Athena Parthenos was not an exact copy of the statue by Phidias because Pausanias[6,] who visited Athens in the second century A.D., described it as having a sphinx on the top of the helmet and a griffin on either side, whereas on the tetradrachms there is no sphinx and the griffin is replaced by Pegasus, the flying horse.

The bronze coins minted at Athens during the reign of Augustus all have the helmeted head of Athena Parthenos, facing right, on the obverse. Paul, of course, had already met Athena on the coins of Attalia in Pamphylia. Concerning the reverse types on these bronze coins Kroll[7] attributes the sphinx type (*RPC* 1311) to the 20s B.C. As well as being on the helmet of Athena Parthenos the sphinx, a winged lion with a human head, was the signet of Augustus.[8] On the coin the sphinx wears a modius (a vessel for measuring grain) on its head. The significance of this modius is unknown. The only inscription on the coin is AΘE on the reverse.

Figure 55 – A bronze from the time of Augustus. (*RPC* 1311)

RPC divides the bronze coins of Athens under Augustus into three periods: Period 1 (c. 31 B.C. to early 20s B.C.); Period 2 (c. mid to late 20s B.C.); Period 3 (c. 10s B.C.). *RPC* states that the issues of Period 2 were on a very large scale. This probably explains why no bronze coins were minted at Athens under Tiberius, Caligula or Claudius. Whether the Augustan coins were still in circulation in Athens in 50 A.D. or had been displaced by coins minted elsewhere is debatable.

The reverse types of the first period had all been seen by Paul in other cities: Demeter, Nike, Zeus. The reverse types of the second period were: Athena advancing, owl standing on prow, and sphinx. The third period is represented by only one coin (*RPC* 1312), and as the most recent, it is the most likely of all the bronze coins of Athens to have been seen by Paul. It is 18 millimetres in diameter and of leaded bronze. On the obverse is the helmeted head of Athena Parthenos. On the reverse is an owl standing on an amphora with a coiled snake or cicada in the field to the right, all within a wreath. The inscription on the reverse is AΘE. The coin was like a small bronze copy of the earlier new-style tetradrachms.

Figure 56 – A leaded bronze from the time of Augustus.
(*RPC* 1312A)

The serpent and the cicada were sacred to Athena and probably relate to her origins as an earth goddess. The amphora probably referred to the Panathenaic Games which were held annually at Athens. They included races, athletic contests and regattas, as well as contests of music, singing and dancing. A laurel wreath and an amphora full of olive oil were awarded to the winners. These amphoras were of a particular shape[9], being more pointed towards the base than usual. It is this amphora on which the owl stands on the reverse of the coins. Paul felt that in a way he too was in a race, 'Do you not know that in a race the runners all compete, but only one receives the prize? Run in such a way that you may win it. Athletes exercise self-control in all things; they do it to receive a perishable wreath, but we an imperishable one' (1 Corinthians 9:24,25).

The owl was the symbol of Athena, the goddess of wisdom, and if Paul saw this coin it may have prompted him to think about wisdom: 'Where is the one who is wise? . . . Has not God made foolish the wisdom of the world?' (1 Corinthians 1:20)

20. Corinth October 50 A.D. to April 52 A.D.

After this Paul left Athens and went to Corinth.
Acts 18:1

According to Acts 18:11 Paul stayed in Corinth a year and six months. We know fairly precisely when this was because during his stay he was brought before the governor of Achaia, Gallio, whose period in office can be determined from an inscription found at Delphi.[1] On the basis of this information Bruce[2] estimates that Paul was in Corinth from the autumn of 50 A.D. to the spring of 52 A.D. These dates are supported by another piece of information given in Acts, that Claudius had recently expelled the Jews from Rome. According to Bruce this expulsion order is probably to be dated in 49 A.D. Murphy-O'Connor[3], however, questions whether there was any real relationship between the edict of Claudius and the move to Corinth of Aquila and Priscilla which preceded Paul's visit there.

When Paul visited Corinth it was the administrative centre of the Roman province of Achaia. It was a busy commercial city situated only 12 kilometres west-south-west of the centre of the isthmus that joins the Peloponnesos to the rest of Greece. It had a seaport at the eastern end of the isthmus, Cenchreae, and a seaport near the western end, Lechaeum. As goods were transported from one seaport to the other there was no need for the long and perilous journey around the southern tip of Greece. So Corinth was in a very favourable position and flourished as a trading centre.

In 146 B.C., because of an anti-Roman revolt, Corinth was almost completely destroyed by the Roman general L. Mummius. He spared the temple of Apollo which stood just north-west of the central market place, or Agora. The site lay derelict for 100 years until Julius Caesar founded a Roman colony there in 44 B.C. It was called Colonia Laus Julia Corinthiensis (Colony Corinth, the praise of Julius). The city soon became very prosperous with a mixed population, mostly Greeks, but with seamen and adventurers from many parts of the empire. Like busy seaports through the ages, it gained a reputation as an immoral city which catered to the base desires of its citizens. In fact the Greek term 'Corinthian girl' was a synonym for a prostitute, and 'Corinthianise' meant to fornicate. Its reputation was well deserved as the temple of Aphrodite, which stood on the summit of the Acrocorinth, the rocky mountain overlooking the city, provided large numbers of women for such purposes.

Although the temple of Aphrodite has disappeared there are extensive ruins which date from the Corinth that Paul knew. Seven columns of the temple of Apollo are still standing and one can walk in the Agora where Paul would have walked. These ruins are preserved because in 1858 an earthquake levelled the old city forcing its citizens to leave and build a new city, modern Corinth, a few kilometres to the north-east, on the coast.

Since 1896 excavations at old Corinth have been carried out by the American School of Classical Studies. They have shown that the Agora was surrounded by shops and various municipal buildings. At its eastern end stood a hall known as the Julian Basilica. Nearby, the remains of a triumphal arch have been found. This gateway was described by Pausanias when he visited the city in the second century A.D.: 'The gateway from the Agora on the road to Lechaeum is surmounted by two gilded chariots. In one stands Phaethon, son of Helios, and in the other Helios himself'. The gateway features on a coin of Hadrian (117–138 A.D.)[4], and Helios in his chariot features on a coin of Nero (*RPC* 1195 – see figure 79). Near the north-east corner of the Agora was a spring called the Fountain of Peirene[5] after the nymph who lived there. Today the courtyard, adjacent arcade, and stone steps leading down to the dry floor of the pool can be seen. Price[6], using coins of Corinth issued by Septimius Severus (193–211 A.D.), has been able to show that a statue of the sea monster Scylla stood in front of the fountain facade and that water probably cascaded down either side of it. From such coins Price has been able to describe several of the architectural features of the city.

The Fountain of Peirene was famous in antiquity because legend related how Bellerophon, a young man of Corinth, was able to catch Pegasos, the wonderful winged horse, when it came to drink at the fountain. Bellerophon tamed Pegasos using a golden bridle given to him by Athena, and was able to kill the Chimaera, a fire-breathing monster with the head of a lion and the body of a goat and the tail of a serpent, by dropping lumps of lead into its mouth. The lead was melted by the Chimaera's breath and ran down its throat killing it.

The American School of Classical Studies has also excavated the site of the Sanctuary of Poseidon which was on the isthmus some distance from Corinth but still under its control. Pausanias described the temple of Poseidon as having statues of Tritons[7] on its roof, and coins of Corinth issued by Geta (198–211 A.D.) show a temple with this feature, indicating that it is the temple of Poseidon. The famous Isthmian Games were held at this sanctuary every two years. They began with a sacrifice to Poseidon and lasted several days with athletic, equestrian, and musical competitions. The athletic events included footracing and boxing. The winners were awarded wreaths of pine leaves. Professor Vos[8] considers that Paul probably attended the Isthmian Games.

It is not surprising that Poseidon, the god of the sea, was an important deity in this area. He was generally represented in mythology as cruel and uncaring[9], an appropriate persona for the sea. In Greek religion he was associated with horses[10], having created the first horse. In the isthmian region his cult was connected with veneration for a legendary character called Melicertes. Melicertes was the son of Athamas, the king of Orchomenos in Boeotia, and Ino, the daughter of Cadmus[11], the Phoenician hero who brought the Greek alphabet from Phoenicia. Ino incurred the wrath of the goddess Hera, who caused Athamas to become mad and kill his son Learchos. Ino, in order to save their other son

Melicertes, jumped with the child into the sea where she became a goddess. The dead body of Melicertes was carried by a dolphin to the coast. Although venerated throughout the isthmian region there was a shrine to Melicertes in a pine grove by the shore at Cromyon, a town of Megara, along the coast north of Cenchreae. Price[12] illustrates two coins which show this shrine: a coin of Corinth issued by Marcus Aurelius (161–180 A.D.) where the body of Melicertes lies on a dolphin in a small temple with an ornately tiled domed roof; and a Corinthian coin of Septimius Severus (193–211 A.D.) which shows the same temple empty but an ox prominent in the left field.

Why such a fuss about this minor mythological character, Melicertes? To answer this question we must delve a little deeper. The first aspect that is revealed is that Ino is not simply an innocent woman, but a very nasty person indeed. In another myth she and her sister Agave, while in a religious frenzy, tear to pieces Agave's son Pentheus[13] because he was spying on them in their Bacchic revels. In yet another story, at the beginning of the epic about Jason and the Argonauts, Ino hates her stepchildren so much that through trickery she organises for her husband, Athamas, to sacrifice them to the gods but at the last minute Hera sends a ram with fleece of gold to carry the children away on its back. So it seems that Ino is not a safe person to have around children.

Delving deeper, it is interesting to consider the derivation of the names 'Ino' and 'Melicertes'. Ino, if a Greek word, may derive from 'inos' meaning strength. Melicertes does not seem to be a Greek word as its possible derivations, e.g. honey-cutter, do not make much sense. It has been suggested[14] that it is derived from Melqart, the Phoenician god of Tyre. This certainly makes sense as Melqart was the Phoenician sea-god portrayed on coins as riding on a hippocamp, a winged horse with the tail of a dolphin. The Phoenicians were a sea-faring people who traded widely in the Mediterranean forming colonies all over its coast, including Carthage, about the eighth century B.C. They would also have had an influence on the Corinthian isthmus, an important area for this trading and seafaring people.

It is difficult to avoid the conclusion that the religion of

Phoenicia had a profound influence on the religion of the isthmus. A feature of Phoenician religion was child sacrifice[15] and the cult of Melicertes was probably concerned with this. It seems that unwanted infants were, through drowning, made sacred to the god of the sea (Poseidon or Melqart), and that their mothers were able to endure this, and the priests or priestesses able to do it, by means of religious trance or ecstasy. In Paul's time it is unlikely that child sacrifice was actually performed, as the Roman authorities would not have allowed it. The cult probably continued with the substitution of an ox, or perhaps a dolphin, for the sacrificial child. In any case it was still influential in Paul's time as its symbols and associations appear on the coins that he saw in Corinth.

As Corinth was the provincial capital it issued large numbers of bronze coins during the reigns of Augustus, Tiberius, Caligula, and Claudius.[16] It is debatable whether the bronze coins of Augustus were still in circulation when Paul stayed in Corinth, but Paul would certainly have handled the coins that were, because he worked with his friends Aquila and Priscilla who were also tent-makers.[17]

The most notable feature on the bronze coinage of Corinth was the appearance on the coins of the names of the two annual magistrates, or duoviri (Latin: two men), who were responsible for the coins. Both names, or either one of the names, appear on nearly every coin issued at Corinth. Being originally a Roman colony, all the inscriptions are in Latin. According to RPC[18] the coins were of bronze or leaded bronze, except for one issue of brass (RPC 1133). The principal denomination was an as which was about 20 millimetres in diameter and about seven grams in weight.[19] Corinthian denominations were probably compatible with Roman denominations which no doubt circulated in the colony after its foundation in 44 B.C.

Under Augustus the obverses featured most commonly the head of Augustus and members of his family.[20] In addition there was the head of Poseidon, Pegasos flying, an athlete running or walking with a palm on his shoulder, a dolphin, a bucranium (ox's skull), and a table with a wreath on it. The last three obverses referred to the cult of Poseidon and Melicertes. The table is also found on certain later coins of Corinth where it is supporting the prostrate body of Melicertes stretched out on a dolphin.[21] The reverses on these three coins show a trident (the symbol of Poseidon) corresponding to the dolphin reverse, and a praeferculum (a jug used in sacrificial ceremonies) corresponding to the other two obverses.

The most common reverse of Augustus was the names of the duovirs within a wreath. Other reverses showed members of Augustus' family[22], and a lighted race torch which corresponded to the obverse with the athlete running or walking. This last coin (*RPC* 1135) celebrated the Isthmian Games. It has the inscription **IIVIR CORINT** on the obverse and the names of the two duovirs[23] on the reverse.

Figure 57 – A bronze of Augustus. (*RPC* 1135)

Under Tiberius the most common obverse was the laureate head of Tiberius or the head (or bust) of a member of his family.[24] Other obverses were Pegasos flying, Isthmos naked standing with a rudder in each hand, or Melicertes with a thyrsus[25] over his shoulder riding a dolphin. Isthmos was the personification of the isthmus and the rudders represented Lechaeum and Cenchreae.

The reverses of Tiberius showed Pegasos, Melicertes lying on a dolphin, Isthmos, Victory on a globe, members of Tiberius' family[26] or the names of the duovirs[27] in a wreath; but the most common reverse was a hexastyle temple inscribed **GENT IVLI** (to or of the Julian clan). The gens or clan of Julius Caesar was an important group of Roman families. The name Caesar was originally just a surname, but it became a title of the emperor. The building shown on the coin was probably the Julian Basilica which stood at the eastern end of the Agora. *RPC* 1157 has this building on the reverse with the name of a duovir[28], and on the obverse the radiate head of Augustus with the name of the other duovir.[29]

Figure 58 – A bronze of Tiberius. (*RPC* 1157)

Caligula also featured Pegasos on the reverse, as well as facing busts of Nero and Drusus[30], two cornucopias, or a rudder with a globe. The obverse had the head of Caligula or a member of his family.[31] Pegasos had featured on the silver staters of Corinth when it first began to mint coins about the middle of the sixth century B.C. and for another 150 years. It is good to see Pegasos still flying during the reign of Caligula. *RPC* 1172–3 (Sear 384) has the bare head of Caligula on the obverse with the inscription C(AIVS) CAESAR AVG(VSTV), and on the reverse Pegasos flying left or right with the name of one of the duovirs.[32]

Figure 59 – A bronze of Caligula. (*RPC* 1172)

Claudius also minted bronze coins at Corinth. His last issue was in 50/51 A.D. so Paul would have noticed these bright new coins during his stay. The obverses of Claudius' coins show the laureate head of Claudius or the bust of his niece-wife Agrippina, as well as the radiate bust of Helios or Melicertes lying on one or two dolphins. The reverses show Agrippina's son Nero, and Claudius' son Britannicus, standing face to face; Poseidon naked holding a dolphin and trident; Pegasos on rocks; or a hexastyle temple on the Acrocorinth.

Helios, the sun god, was usually considered a manifestation of Apollo, the god of light. At Corinth there was a temple of Apollo as well as the statues of Helios and Phaethon on the triumphal arch. Paul would have seen these sights and noticed that the sun god's bust appeared on the obverse of one of these new coins. The reverse of this coin (*RPC* 1185) featured Poseidon naked standing left and holding a dolphin and trident. The inscription on the obverse was the names of the duovirs[33] while the inscription on the reverse was COR SE (Corinth, semis). The semis was a Roman denomination equivalent to half an as. This was one of the few coins in the Roman empire which had an indication of its value on it. This coin also points to the great rivalry between Helios (Apollo) and Poseidon. According to the myth related by Pausanias a dispute arose between these two gods concerning who possessed Corinth and the Isthmus. The giant Briareus was chosen to arbitrate and awarded Corinth to Helios and the Isthmus to Poseidon. Helios later relinquished the Acrocorinth to Aphrodite.

Figure 60 – A bronze of Claudius. (*RPC* 1185)

The great temple of Aphrodite on the Acrocorinth features on the reverse of a coin of Claudius. It appears as a hexastyle temple on the top of a rocky mountain. The reverse inscription is the name of the duovirs.[34] On the obverse of this coin (*RPC* 1180) is the laureate head of Claudius with the inscription TI CLAVDIVS CAESAR.

Figure 61 – A bronze of Claudius. (*RPC* 1180)

Paul would have seen the temple of Aphrodite standing on the Acrocorinth, as well as the temple of Apollo and the temple of Gens Julia in the city, and he probably saw the great temple of

Poseidon on the Isthmus. All of these temples, of course, contained the idol of the god. With these in mind he later wrote to the Christians of Corinth, 'What agreement has the temple of God with idols? For we are the temple of the living God; as God said, "I will live in them and walk among them, and I will be their God, and they shall be my people"' (2 Corinthians 6:16). Aware of the licentiousness of the city he wrote, 'Shun fornication! Every sin that a person commits is outside the body; but the fornicator sins against the body itself. Or do you not know that your body is a temple of the Holy Spirit within you?' (1 Corinthians 6:18,19a). Whether or not Paul attended the Isthmian Games, he used the metaphor of running and boxing when he encouraged the Corinthian Christians to lead moral lives, 'I do not run aimlessly, nor do I box as though beating the air; but I punish my body and enslave it, so that after proclaiming to others I myself should not be disqualified' (1 Corinthians 9:26,27). The coins of Corinth reflected aspects of the city which Paul later referred to in his letters to the Christians there.

21. Cenchreae, Ephesus, Jerusalem, Antioch 52 A.D.

Paul ... sailed for Syria, accompanied by Priscilla and Aquila. At Cenchreae he had his hair cut, for he was under a vow. When they reached Ephesus, he left them there ... When he had landed at Caesarea, he went up to Jerusalem and greeted the church, and then went down to Antioch.
Acts 18:18b,19a,22

Cenchreae was the port for Corinth at the eastern end of the Isthmus. According to Pausanias (Book 2,2:3) the name derives from Cenchreas, one of the two sons of Poseidon and the nymph Peirene. It was because of the deaths of these children that Peirene wept so inconsolably that her tears produced the famous fountain in Corinth. In Paul's day a bronze statue of Poseidon stood on a mole extending out into the sea. On one side of the harbour was a temple of Aphrodite and on the other were the sanctuaries of Asclepios and Isis, a goddess originally from Egypt but becoming more widely popular in Paul's time. Today much of the old city of Cenchreae is below the sea but there are still some ruins to see on the shore. Cenchreae produced no coins and presumably the bronze coins which circulated there came from Corinth. It was such a busy port that the moneychangers would have been busy there.

Paul stayed only briefly in Ephesus and it will be dealt with in the next chapter. He stayed there two years on his third missionary journey. Similarly Caesarea will be dealt with in a later chapter.

Jerusalem had not changed in Paul's absence except that work continued on the temple. A new governor, Felix, was appointed in 52 A.D. Antioch was just the same. Claudius issued silver coinage from Antioch to honour Agrippina Junior, whom he had married in 49 A.D., and her son, Nero, the future emperor. So Paul probably would have seen these coins in 52 A.D. There were three issues: *RPC* 4169; 4170; and 4171. *RPC* 4169 was a tetradrachm and had the laureate head of Claudius on the obverse and the draped bust of the young Nero on the reverse. *RPC* 4171 was a didrachm and had the young Nero on the obverse and on the reverse a lituus[1] and a simpulum[2] with the inscription ΔΙΔΡΑΧΜΟΝ (didrachm). This was one of the few coins of the empire that had its value inscribed on it. *RPC* 4170 was also a didrachm and had the draped bust of Agrippina Junior on the obverse with the inscription ΑΓΡΙΠΠΕΙΝΗϹ ϹΕΒΑϹΤΗϹ (of Agrippina Augusta). On the reverse was the draped bust of the young Nero with the inscription ΝΕΡWΝΟϹ ΚΑΙϹΑΡΟϹ ΓΕΡΜΑΝΙΚΟΥ (of Nero Caesar Germanicus).

Figure 62 – A didrachm of Agrippina and Nero. (*RPC* 4170)

Paul was probably interested to see the face of Nero on this coin. Little did he realise that this innocent-looking youth would one day order his execution.[3] Nor could he foresee that the beautiful Agrippina would poison her husband, Claudius, and that she in turn would be murdered by Nero.

The only new bronze coins that Paul saw at Antioch in 52 A.D. were SC and legate issues of Claudius struck in 47/48 A.D. (*RPC* 4278, 4279, 4280) and probably two undated SC issues of Claudius (*RPC* 4281, 4282). The legate coin refers to the legate Cassius and carries the date 96. This number refers to the Caesarean era which began in 47 B.C. when Julius Caesar made Antioch a free city. Although nominally a free city it would have been very much under the thumb of the Roman governor of the province. Paul thought a lot about the concept of freedom because he discusses it often in his letters, but it was freedom from sin and the law that he was concerned about. For example, in his second letter to the Corinthians he writes, 'Now the Lord is the Spirit, and where the Spirit of the Lord is, there is freedom' (2 Corinthians 3:17).

22. Ephesus 53–54 A.D.

After spending some time there he departed and went from
place to place through the region of Galatia and Phrygia,
strengthening the disciples ... Paul passed through the interior
regions and came to Ephesus.
Acts 18:23; 19:1b

Acts 19:10 tells us that Paul spent two years in Ephesus and as we
have precise chronological information about his stay in Corinth,
we can be fairly confident that Paul was in Ephesus in 53 and
54 A.D. Ephesus was an important city and seaport near the
mouth of the Cayster river in Asia Minor. It was situated south of
the river about five kilometres upstream from where it enters the
Aegean Sea. Its harbour was reached by a canal which was constantly in danger of silting up. The canal and harbour were kept
deep enough for ocean-going vessels by dredging. With dwin-
dling fortunes in the third century A.D. and the sacking of the
city in 262 A.D. by the Goths it became impossible to maintain
the harbour, and Ephesus gradually became an isolated inland
town. By the tenth century the prosperous city of Roman times
was completely deserted, its buildings crumbling and its harbour
a marsh.

Ephesus was an ancient city even in Paul's time. By the
middle of the second millennium B.C. settlers of Asiatic origin
inhabited the site.[1] According to legend the Amazons[2], a mythical race of warrior women, built the city because it was near the
birthplace of the Earth Goddess; but according to Strabo (Geog.
XIV. 1:4; 1:21) Androclus, a king of Athens, conquered the local
people in the eleventh century B.C. and established the city
as one of the twelve cities of the Ionian Confederation. In about

560 B.C. the Lydians under King Croesus captured Ephesus but were in turn defeated by the Persians under Cyrus in 546 B.C. After Alexander the Great defeated the Persians in 334 B.C. the city was in the hands of his successors, eventually passing to the Seleucid ruler Antiochus II. In 190 B.C. Antiochus was defeated by the Romans who gave Ephesus to the king of Pergamum. The last Pergamene king, Attalus III, bequeathed his kingdom to the Romans in 133 B.C. Although Pergamum remained the capital Ephesus flourished under Augustus and became the chief city of Asia. In fact, it was, with Rome, Alexandria and Antioch, one of the four great cities of the Roman Empire. It has been estimated that when Paul visited the city it had a population of 250,000.[3]

The city prospered because of trade but also because of the great temple of Artemis, which attracted tourists and pilgrims from all over the known world. It was one of the Seven Wonders of the World. It was 110 metres long and 55 metres wide, and it stood on a platform 127 metres long and 73 metres wide.[4] Its roof was supported by 117 columns 18 metres high and nearly two metres in diameter. Thirty-six of the columns were sculptured at the base with life size figures.[5] There were eight columns on the main facade. Today only a solitary (reconstructed) column stands among the marble fragments at the site. Originally a shrine to the Asian mother goddess must have stood on the site, but with the coming of the Greeks she was assimilated with the Greek goddess Artemis, known to the Romans as Diana.

This temple of Artemis, or Artemision, was three kilometres north-east of the centre of the Roman city. Although devastated by the Goths in 262 A.D. it was finally demolished in the fourth century A.D., its stones and columns being used for the construction of the basilica of Saint Sophia in Constantinople and the church of St John in Ephesus. The site became a marsh until 1869 when British archaeologist J.T. Wood was excavating the theatre and found an inscription of the emperor Trajan which indicated the direction of the Artemision. Wood discovered the ruins of the Artemision at a depth of six metres below the present surface level. His excavations revealed the remains of the last temple built about 350 B.C., as well as the platform of an earlier temple of identical plan built in the sixth century. The Lydian king Croesus (560–546 B.C.) contributed to the earlier building and Strabo (Geog. XIV. 1:22) relates how it was burnt down in 356 B.C. by a man called Herostratus who wanted to make a name for himself. In 1904 another British archaeologist D.G. Hogarth, discovered beneath the centre of the earlier temple the remains of three even earlier structures as well as a number of primitive coins and other objects. These coins are of great importance to the history of coinage.[6]

Excavations have continued at Ephesus by the Austrian Archaeological Institute, and in 1965 the Austrian excavators found the foundations of a large altar[7] facing the western facade of the Artemision. They discovered that a U-shaped wall was interposed between the altar and the temple with the open side to the sea. Apparently the priest made his offering while facing south towards a cult statue. Price and Trell[8] have shown from the study of coins that there were three windows in the west pediment[9] of the temple. At the central window the goddess probably appeared in some form. This epiphany could be seen by the worshippers standing before the outside altar. Price and Trell have also shown that there were four statues in the pediment and they suggest these were the Amazons which decorated the altar of the earlier temple and were moved to the pediment when the temple was rebuilt after 350 B.C.

We know what the idol in the Artemision looked like because several replicas[10] have survived. It was a strangely ornamented mummiform figure. On the chest were rows of bulbous objects which have been assumed to be breasts but various other interpretations have been proposed. W.M. Ramsay suggested they were bees' eggs because the symbol of Artemis was a bee.[11] Other suggestions were dates, grapes, and bulls' testicles.

In the account of Paul's visit in Acts 19 the town clerk says that the city of the Ephesians was the temple keeper[12] of the great Artemis and of the statue that fell from heaven. What this statue was is unknown, but it could well have been an idol made from a meteorite. Perhaps this was the cult statue which was worshipped at the outside altar.

When Paul visited Ephesus it was a different city from what

we can imagine from the present ruins, because most of the ruins we see today are of structures built after Paul's visit. The theatre which was built into the side of the hill in Hellenistic times still dominates the site as it did in Paul's time, although the two-storey stage building was erected by Nero (54–68 A.D.) and a third storey added in the second century A.D. The theatre was enlarged by Claudius as well as Nero and Trajan, and could hold 24,000 people. As Paul's preaching had reduced the business of the artisans who made small silver shrines of Artemis, a riot occurred and the people rushed to the theatre, shouting 'Great is Artemis of the Ephesians'. Eventually the town clerk was able to quieten the people and they dispersed.

Near the theatre are the ruins of the commercial agora, or market place, which existed in Paul's time. It was built in Hellenistic times but enlarged by Augustus, Nero and Caracalla. The surrounding stoas date from Septimius Severus (193–211 A.D.). The silversmiths who rioted probably had their shops in this agora. A thoroughfare would have led from the harbour to the agora and the theatre, but the impressive one we see today dates from the time of Arcadius (383–408 A.D.). The stadium in which Paul may have had to fight wild animals (1 Corinthians 15:32a) was extensively modified by Nero. The library of Celsus, which is the most impressive building to see today, was built in the second century A.D. and has recently been restored by the Austrians. According to Acts 19:9b Paul spoke in the lecture hall of Tyrannus but unfortunately we have no idea where it was.

Before Paul's visit Ephesus had been producing coins of electrum, gold, silver and bronze almost continuously since the seventh century B.C. The question therefore arises how long these coins remained in circulation. Silver coins tended to circulate longer than bronze[13], and we know that silver coins of Augustus were still in circulation during the reign of Vespasian because examples exist of cistophori of Augustus minted in Ephesus with countermarks of Vespasian.[14] Presumably the countermark identified them as still being acceptable. In view of such evidence C.H.V. Sutherland[15] states that the full life-span of silver, until it was entirely worn out, might be as long as a century, with that of bronze not more than about half as much.

Paul, therefore, would have seen in Ephesus silver and bronze coins dating from the reign of Augustus (27 B.C.–14 A.D.). Moreover, as Ephesus was the commercial centre of Asia, coins from neighbouring cities, especially Pergamum, would have circulated in Ephesus in Paul's time.

Paul would have been impressed with the beautiful silver coins which were called cistophori. The name means 'basket bearer' and the first issues of this coin under the kings of Pergamum always featured an open basket with a snake sliding out of it. The basket was called a cista mystica and was used in the mystic rites of Dionysus. The first issue under Augustus (*RPC* 2203) featured Pax (Peace) on the reverse but it still had a small cista mystica in the right field on the reverse. This was omitted in subsequent issues.

Figure 63 – A Cistophorus of Augustus. (*RPC* 2203)

The cistophorus circulated widely in the province of Asia. It weighed about 12 grams and was equivalent to three Roman denarii. Denarii circulated in Asia along with the cistophori. According to *RPC*[16] denarii were produced in Asia from 49 B.C. Under Augustus denarii and aurei were struck at Pergamum in conjunction with an issue of cistophori made in 19–18 B.C., but no more denarii were struck until an issue of denarii and aurei from Ephesus under Vespasian.

The cistophori of Augustus have been studied by C.H.V. Sutherland.[17] He divided them into seven groups. The first group consisted only of the Pax coin already mentioned (*RPC* 2203). It was minted at Ephesus probably to commemorate the peace which followed the battle of Actium in 31 B.C. Group II also consisted of only one coin (*RPC* 2204), issued soon after 27 B.C. from an uncertain mint in Asia. It has the bare head of Augustus on the obverse with the inscription IMP CAESAR. On the reverse is a seated sphinx with the inscription AVGVSTVS. The sphinx was the signet of Augustus with which he sealed official papers and private letters. According to Jones[18] he is said to have changed the sphinx on his signet to a head of Alexander the Great because of the unpleasant associations which it had (since the sphinx was associated with dark, riddling prophecies and perhaps with Cleopatra).

Figure 64 – A cistophorus of Augustus. (*RPC* 2204)

Groups III and IV (*RPC* 2205–2212) were issued in 27–26 B.C. probably from Pergamum. They are divided into three phases: Phase I has Augustus' head, left, with a lituus on the obverse; Phase II has his head, right, with a lituus; and Phase III has his head, right, without a lituus. The types on the reverses are a sphinx, a capricorn, and a bunch of six ears of corn.

Groups V and VI (*RPC* 2213–2215) were issued in about 25–20 B.C. from Ephesus. The obverses all have the head of Augustus, right, with the inscription IMP CAESAR, but without the lituus. The types on the reverses are a capricorn (*RPC* 2213), a bunch of six ears of corn (*RPC* 2214), and a garlanded altar decorated with two hinds (*RPC* 2215). The inscription on the reverse is AVGVSTVS. The capricorn was a sign of the zodiac in the form of a goat with the tail of a fish from whose back a cornucopia grows. Augustus was born under the zodiacal sign of Capricorn.[19]

Figure 65 – A cistophorus of Augustus. (*RPC* 2213)

The significance of the bunch of six ears of corn is unknown. It is usually assumed that it is simply a symbol of plenty under the regime of Augustus, but it is more likely it had some religious significance, perhaps relating to the cult of the Earth Mother who was assimilated to the Greek Artemis.

Figure 66 – A cistophorus of Augustus. (*RPC* 2214)

The altar was obviously an altar of Artemis because the hind was the animal which accompanied this goddess. It is unknown where in the Artemision this altar stood, whether it was part of the outdoor complex or an altar inside the actual temple.

Figure 67 – A cistophorus of Augustus. (*RPC* 2215)

Group VII (*RPC* 2216–2220) was issued in 19–18 B.C. from Pergamum and has three different types on the reverse. The first

The obverse of a tetradrachm of Tyre showing the god, Heracles.
Two Jewish men could pay the Temple tax with one of these coins
(Matthew 17:27).

The reverse of a tetradrachm of Tyre showing an eagle, the symbol
of Zeus. In front of the eagle is a club, the symbol of Heracles.

The obverse of a tetradrachm minted at Antioch by Tiberius.
It shows the laureate head of Tiberius. This is the coin held by
Jesus in Mark 12:16.

The reverse of a tetradrachm minted at Antioch by Tiberius.
It shows the radiate head of Augustus.

A lepton of the Hasmonean king, Alexander Jannaeus, showing a star. This coin was probably the 'widow's mite' of Mark 12:42

A prutah of Herod the Great showing an anchor.

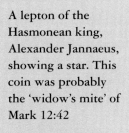

A copper coin of Herod Antipas minted in 39 A.D. showing a palm branch.

A prutah issued by Pontius Pilate showing a libation ladle (simpulum).

A tetradrachm
minted at Antioch in
5 B.C., showing the
emperor, Augustus.

An as minted at
Rome showing the
emperor, Caligula.

An as minted at
Rome showing the
emperor, Claudius.
The blue spots
indicate 'bronze
disease', an
accumulation of
copper salts on the
surface of a coin.

An aureus minted at
Rome showing the
emperor, Nero.

type is a triumphal arch surmounted by a charioteer in a quadriga with S P R SIGNIS RECEPTIS (for the standards taken back by the Senate and Roman People) in the opening of the arch. In 20 B.C. Phraates, the king of Parthia, returned the standards which the Romans had lost at the battle of Carrhae in 53 B.C. and on other occasions, and this triumphal arch was built in Rome to celebrate the event. The second type is a temple with six columns and with the inscription ROM ET AVGVST (Rome and Augustus) on the entablature, as well as COM ASIAE (Commune of Asia) in the field on either side of the temple. This temple was authorised by Augustus in 29 B.C.[20] It stood in Pergamum and served the imperial cult which presumably was the responsibility of the Commune Asiae. The exact significance of the term 'Commune Asiae' is unknown, but it may have referred to the union of Asian cities under the cult of Rome and Augustus.[21] According to Jones[22] it showed that the coins were issued on behalf of the Roman administrative area of Asia. The third type was a circular temple with four columns containing a military standard and with MART VLTO (Martis Ultoris = of Mars the Avenger) in the field. The standards returned by the Parthians were kept in this temple. Jones[23] says that two temples were dedicated to this god during the reign of Augustus, the first in 20 B.C. and the second in 2 B.C. The earlier one, built on the Capitol, was used to house the military standards recovered from the Parthians and is the one which is represented on coins of Augustus, in the form of a round building with four or six columns visible. The later one, which was vowed during the battle of Philippi in 42 B.C. as a memorial to Julius Caesar, does not appear on coins.

The cistophori of Augustus were produced in enormous numbers and Paul would certainly have seen them. Sutherland[24] states that although there are today a total of about 700 specimens, they were struck from a minimum of 355 obverse dies and 568 reverse dies, and he estimates that originally between three and four million coins were produced.

Neither Tiberius nor Caligula issued cistophori and therefore when Claudius produced two issues they must have caused considerable interest. The later issue is dated to 51 A.D. and Paul would have noticed these bright new coins. The earlier issue consisted of two coins (*RPC* 2221 and 2222) and these have the head of Claudius on the obverse with the inscription TI CLAVD CAES AVG. On the reverse *RPC* 2221 features a temple with two columns inscribed ROM ET AVG and enclosing the figure of Augustus being crowned by a female figure with a cornucopia, and in the field is COM ASI. This is obviously the temple of Rome and Augustus at Pergamum but the coin has die links with *RPC* 2222 which features the Artemision at Ephesus and therefore Mattingly[25] attributed both coins to Ephesus. *RPC* 2222 shows a temple with four columns enclosing the cult statue of Artemis, and in the field is DIAN EPH (Diana Ephesia = the Ephesian Diana). All of these coins have Latin inscriptions and the Roman name for Artemis is used. It is interesting to note that the Artemision on this coin has only four columns yet we know that there were eight columns in the western facade and ten in the eastern facade.

Figure 68 – A cistophorus of Claudius. (*RPC* 2222)

The later issue consisted of three coins (*RPC* 2223,4,5). On the obverse *RPC* 2223 has the laureate head of Claudius and the inscription TI CLAVD CAESAR AVG P M TR P X IMP XIIX which dates it to 50–51 A.D. On the reverse it has the draped bust of his niece-wife Agrippina II. *RPC* 2224 has on the obverse the jugate head of Claudius and bust of Agrippina with the inscription TI CLAVD CAES AVG AGRIPP AVGVSTA. On the reverse it has the facing cult statue of Artemis with the inscription DIANA EPHESIA.

Figure 69 – A cistophorus of Claudius and Agrippina. (*RPC* 2224)

RPC 2225 has the draped bust of Nero on the obverse with the inscription NERONI CLAVD CAES DRVSO GERM (to Nero Claudius Caesar Drusus Germanicus). On the reverse it has a wreath enclosing a shield inscribed COS DES PRINC IVVENT (Consul Designatus Princeps Iuuentutis = Consul Designate, Leader of the Youth). In March 51 A.D. the title 'Leader of the Youth' was given to Nero whose mother Claudius had married in 49 A.D. This title had first been given to Lucius and Gaius, the grandsons of Augustus, but eventually it was given routinely to the heir of the current emperor.

Figure 70 – A cistophorus of Nero. (*RPC* 2225)

Concerning the bronze coins Paul would have seen in Ephesus, the CA coinage[26] can be excluded because it was produced from about 27 to 23 B.C., which was more than 75 years before Paul's visit. Also it is unlikely that Paul saw much of the ordinary bronze coinage issued by Augustus, although it seems to have been produced in large quantities. This bronze coinage is undated but bears the names of magistrates in Greek. It was issued in four sizes: 15, 16, 19, and 21 millimetres. The types are: the bare head of Augustus; jugate busts of Augustus and Livia; a stag standing; the forepart of a stag; and the facing cult statue of

Artemis with supports. The last three types, of course, celebrate the cult of Artemis of Ephesus.

The bronze coinage of Tiberius was issued in one size, 16 millimetres, except for *RPC* 2619, which was 15 millimetres in diameter. For the common size (*RPC* 2613–2618) the laureate head of Tiberius was on the obverse and a facing cult statue of Artemis with supports was on the reverse. *RPC* 2619 has on the obverse a stag standing, with the inscription ΑΡΧΙ ΑΛΕΞ (ΑΡΧΙΕΡΕΩΣ ΑΛΕΞΑΝΔΡΟΥ = of High Priest Alexander), and on the reverse a hen with a palm branch and ΓΡΑ ΕΦΕ (ΓΡΑΜΜΑΤΕΥΣ ΕΦΕΣΙΩΝ = Scribe of the Ephesians). The significance of the hen with the palm branch is unknown except that Artemis was the protectress of animals and the young, and the date palm was one of her symbols. A similar type (a cock with a palm branch) occurs on the reverse of a coin (Sear 4412) minted at Ephesus in the period 48–27 B.C. Also one of the earliest electrum coins (Sear 3437) shows a cock and a hen. The stag was associated with Artemis and may allude to the story of Actaeon who, like Artemis, was a hunter. One day he was chasing a stag when he came upon Artemis bathing. Enraged that he should see her nakedness, Artemis changed Actaeon into a stag and his dogs tore him to pieces.

Figure 71 – A bronze issued under Tiberius. (*RPC* 2619)

All the 16 millimetre coins of Tiberius struck at Ephesus have the name 'Alexander' with his various titles on the reverse. Alexander's name is usually associated with the name of another magistrate which varies with each coin. The titles of Alexander are Grammateus (literally scribe, but in this context usually translated town clerk) and Archiereus (high priest). It is obvious that Alexander was an important man well-known in Ephesus.

This Alexander may be the Alexander who occurs in the book of Acts trying to quieten the riotous Ephesians who had gathered in the theatre. 'Some of the crowd gave instructions to Alexander, whom the Jews had pushed forward. And Alexander motioned for silence and tried to make a defence before the people. But when they recognised that he was a Jew, for about two hours all of them shouted in unison, "Great is Artemis of the Ephesians!"' (Acts 19:33,34). In the account in Acts Alexander is suddenly introduced without any explanation, the author assuming that his readers would know who Alexander is. Professor Bruce[27] says, 'Alexander is introduced as though readers might be expected to recognise his name, but nothing more is known of him'. Similarly Professor Walls[28] says Alexander is introduced 'as if well known'. However, the fact that the Alexander of Acts was a Jew would be against identification with the numismatic Alexander who holds the title of high priest. This high-priestly office was probably concerned with the imperial cult and not the worship of Artemis; for it was apparently from the ranks of the leading citizens of the major cities in the province that the annually elected high priest of the imperial cult was drawn.[29] Nevertheless, Alexander held this high-priestly office many years before Paul's visit to Ephesus and he could well have converted to Judaism in the meantime.

It is interesting to note that the word 'grammateus' (town-clerk), which occurs on these coins of Ephesus also occurs in the account in Acts (Acts 19:35), showing that the author of Acts was aware of the correct term. Such evidence confirms the historicity of the book of Acts. As Bruce[30] states, Luke 'sets his narrative in the framework of contemporary history; his pages are full of references to city magistrates, provincial governors, client kings and the like, and these references time after time prove to be just right for the place and time in question'.

The bronze coins of Claudius (*RPC* 2620–2625) are the coins which Paul is most likely to have actually handled. With one exception, *RPC* 2625, which has the head of the young Nero, they all have the head of Claudius and the bust of Agrippina II on the obverse, and were issued to celebrate their marriage which occurred in 49 A.D. The largest coin, *RPC* 2620, which is 23 millimetres in diameter, has ΘΕΟΓΑΜ[ΙΑ] (divine wedding) with the head of Claudius facing the draped bust of Agrippina on the obverse, and on the reverse a facing cult statue of Artemis with supports and the inscription ΕΦΕΣΙΑ. All of these coins are dated to 49–50 A.D.

Figure 72 – A bronze of Claudius and Agrippina II. (*RPC* 2620)

It is important for numismatists to recognise which coins Paul probably touched because anything that touched Paul's skin has miraculous healing powers. This is stated quite clearly in Acts: 'God did extraordinary miracles through Paul, so that when the handkerchiefs or aprons that had touched his skin were brought to the sick, their diseases left them, and the evil spirits came out of them' (Acts 19:11,12). Therefore all of these Claudian bronzes will be described. Of course the more worn the specimen, the more likely it is to have come in contact with Paul.

RPC 2621 is 20 millimetres in diameter and has the jugate laureate head of Claudius and draped bust of Agrippina II on the obverse, and on the reverse a facing cult statue of Artemis with supports and the inscription ΕΦΕΣΙΑ. *RPC* 2622 is similar but on the reverse it has a stag standing and the inscription ΕΦΕΣΙΩΝ. *RPC* 2623 is 21 millimetres in diameter and is similar to *RPC* 2622 except that ΕΦΕ occurs on the obverse and the reverse inscription is Π ΜΕΜΜΙΟΥ [ΡΗΓ]ΟΥΛΟΥ ΑΝΘΥΠΑΤΟΥ, ΚΟΥΣΙΝΙΟΣ ΕΠΙΣΚΟΠΟΣ ΤΟ Δ (of P. Memmius Regulus Proconsul, Kousinios Supervisor for the fourth time). There is some doubt about the first letter of this inscription. P. Memmius Regulus was proconsul of Asia from 47 to 54 A.D. *RPC* 2624 is similar except that it is 20 millimetres and the reverse inscription is ΚΟΥΣΙΝΙΟΣ ΤΟ Δ, ΕΦΕ. ΤΟ has a bar above it indicating that it is an abbreviation for ΤΟΣΟΣ (so many times). *RPC* 2625 is 16 millimetres and has ΕΦΕ and a bust of Nero on the obverse, while the reverse has a

facing cult figure of Artemis with supports and the inscription
ΚΟΥΣΙΝΙΟΣ ΤΟ Δ.

Figure 73 – A bronze of Claudius and Agrippina II. (*RPC* 2623)

According to *RPC* the title ΕΠΙΣΚΟΠΟΣ given to
Kousinios seems unknown elsewhere. Literally it means supervisor or overseer, and in the early church it was the term used for
a bishop.[31] On *RPC* 2623 it probably refers to an official with
some organizational responsibility in the city, like a manager. The
use of the title for the leader of a Christian community may have
originated in Ephesus where it was already well known. If this is
so, it would support the argument that the original role of a
bishop was managerial rather than monarchical, and suggests
that Paul's use of the term, even in his early writings[32], had a
specific rather than a general sense.

Paul was two years in Ephesus and nearly every coin that he
handled would have referred to the goddess Artemis. Not only
did Artemis dominate the life of the city, she dominated its
coinage. Yet Paul never refers to her in his writings. However, in
a letter he later wrote to the Ephesians he insists, 'You must live
no longer as the Gentiles live, in the futility of their minds.
They are darkened in their understanding, alienated from the life
of God because of their ignorance and hardness of heart'
(Ephesians 4:17,18).

23. Macedonia, Greece, Troas
55–57 A.D.

He left for Macedonia. When he had gone through those regions and had given the believers much encouragement, he came to Greece, where he stayed three months ... He decided to return through Macedonia ... We joined them in Troas, where we stayed for seven days.
Acts 20:1b,2,3a,3c,6b

In this part of his third missionary journey Paul revisits Macedonia and Greece. He probably visits some new cities in these provinces as well as the ones he visited earlier. Also it has been suggested that during this period he travelled through Illyricum, the large province between the Adriatic sea and the Danube river, because in the letter he wrote to the Romans probably from Corinth in 57 A.D.[1] he says, 'From Jerusalem and as far around as Illyricum I have fully proclaimed the good news of Christ' (Romans 15:19b), and there would have been no other opportunity for him to visit Illyricum. According to Bruce[2], 'We must understand that he travelled west along the Egnatian Way, perhaps as far as its termination at Dyrrhachium (modern Durrës) on the Adriatic, and then turned north in the direction of Illyricum. The period between his departure from Ephesus and his leaving Macedonia for "Greece" (i.e. the province of Achaia) ... may well have covered about a year and a half – say, from the summer of A.D. 55 to the late part of 56'.

If Paul did spend so much time in Macedonia and Illyricum, then major problems arise concerning the chronology of his career, because the fourth century church historian Eusebius states that Festus, who sent Paul to Rome soon after his appointment as governor of Judaea, was appointed in 55 A.D. As Paul was already two years in prison in Caesarea before Festus was appointed, the time for Paul's career becomes impossibly short.

As Eusebius was also bishop of Caesarea, many scholars[3] bow to his authority and compress Paul's career in the period from 51 A.D. (when he appeared before Gallio) to 55 A.D. (when Festus sent him to Rome). Ramsay[4], however, considered that the evidence supplied by Eusebius, if properly understood, actually supported the date 59 A.D. for Festus' appointment. According to Carson et al[5] there is a growing consensus among scholars that Festus replaced Felix as governor of Judaea in 59 A.D. Bruce[6] also favours this date. Therefore a chronology based on Festus being appointed in 59 A.D. will be followed here.

In the five years since Paul had previously visited Macedonia, there had been a few new issues of coins. Nero succeeded Claudius in 54 A.D. and some cities had already minted coins in his honour. The Macedonian koinon or federation of Macedonian cities issued two bronze coins, which *RPC*[7] considers were minted early in Nero's reign, so Paul may have seen them. The first (*RPC* 1613) is 30 millimetres in diameter and has Nero's head on the obverse with the inscription ΝΕΡΩΝ ΚΑΙΣΑΡ. On the reverse there is the standing figure of Mars holding a wreath and spear, with a Macedonian shield in the right field and the inscription ΜΑΚΕΔΟΝΩΝ (of the Macedonians). The shield was a symbol of Macedonia and the Mars type may allude to the vow Augustus made during the battle of Philippi in 42 B.C. to build a temple to Mars in Rome. It took a while to build as it was not dedicated until 2 B.C.

Figure 74 – A bronze of Nero. (*RPC* 1613)

The second (*RPC* 1614) is 23 millimetres in diameter and has Nero's head on the obverse and a Macedonian shield on the reverse. It is similar to the coin of Claudius (*RPC* 1612 – see figure 54) except that the obverse inscription reads ΝΕΡΩΝ ΚΑΙΣΑΡ.

Philippi issued a bronze coin in 57 A.D. (*RPC* 1655). It is similar to the coin of Claudius (*RPC* 1653 – see figure 48) except that the obverse inscription reads **NERO CAES AVG P M TR P COS II** (Nero Caesar Augustus, Pontifex Maximus, with tribunician power, Consul for the second time). On the reverse it has two statues (Julius crowning Augustus) and on the base is inscribed **ΔIVVS AVG** (Divine Augustus). The type was common to the coins of Augustus, Claudius and Nero, indicating that Nero was of the Julio-Claudian dynasty and intended making no changes in the way his ancestors were regarded. Paul may have seen this coin just before he finally left Macedonia (see Acts 20:6).

Amphipolis issued two undated bronze coins honouring Nero and they too were similar to a coin of Claudius (*RPC* 1640 – see figure 50) with a standing figure of the emperor in military dress on the obverse, and on the reverse Artemis Tauropolis on a bull.

Thessalonica produced a number of undated bronze coins under Nero (*RPC* 1590–1603) as well as four coins of Agrippina II, Nero's mother (*RPC* 1604–1606A). For the Neronian coins, the reverse types are a horse trotting, a bust of Agrippina II, an eagle in a wreath, Nike on a globe, Roma standing, and Apollo playing a lyre. The last type may refer to Nero's visit to Greece in 67 A.D. when he took part in musical contests, and won them all, of course. As Nero expelled his mother from the imperial palace in 55 A.D. and had her killed in 59 A.D. the coins which bear her name would have been minted early in his reign and might have been seen by Paul. They have her bust on the obverse with the inscription ΑΓΡΙΠΠΙΝΑ ΣΕΒΑΣΤΗ (Agrippina Augusta) or ΣΕΒΑΣΤΗ, and on the reverse either Nike on a globe or a horse trotting with a star and crescent above.

Figure 75 – A bronze of Agrippina II. (*RPC* 1605/1)

Athens issued no coins during this period, but Corinth continued its prolific output. The coins of Corinth can be dated
quite precisely because the names of the duovirs occur on the
reverses. We can be sure, therefore, that in 56 A.D. Paul would
have seen the coins issued under the duovirs M. Acilius Candidus
and Q. Fulvius Flaccus in 54/5 A.D. (*RPC* 1189–1200). The
obverses of these bronze coins feature Nero, his mother Agrippina
II, and his first wife, Octavia. Octavia was the daughter of
Claudius by his third wife Messalina. Nero married Octavia in
53 A.D. In 58 A.D. he began to have an adulterous affair with
Poppaea Sabina, the wife of Otho, his friend and a future
emperor, but he did not feel secure enough to divorce Octavia
until 62 A.D. Octavia was then imprisoned on the island of
Pandateria and killed later in the year. According to Tacitus[8],
'Octavia was bound, and all her veins were opened. However, her
terror retarded the flow of blood. So she was put into an exceed-
ingly hot vapour-bath and suffocated. An even crueller atrocity
followed. Her head was cut off and taken to Rome for Poppaea to
see'. By then Nero had already killed his mother and his step-
brother Britannicus.

The reverses of these coins have the name of one of the duovirs
and features the Genius of the Colony, Poseidon in a biga drawn
by hippocamps, Aphrodite holding a mirror in a biga of Tritons,
Helios in a quadriga, or a bust of Aphrodite (beneath which is
a galley inscribed CENCHREAE or a dolphin inscribed
LECHAVM). Apart from the Genius of the Colony Paul was
acquainted with all of these gods from his previous visit to Corinth.

RPC 1189 has the laureate head of Nero with the inscription
NERO CLAV CAES AVG (Nero Claudius Caesar Augustus) on
the obverse, and on the reverse the standing figure of the Genius

of the Colony holding a patera and a cornucopia, with the name of one or other of the duovirs, **GEN COL** (Genius Coloniae) in the field, and **COR** (Corinthus) in the exergue. Genius is a Latin word which is generally translated 'spirit' and referred to the life force or supernatural essence of a person, group of persons or a place. Rome had her Genius, represented as a goddess to whom a statue was erected in the city, and Corinth could well have had a statue of its Genius, a representation of which occurs on this coin. The influential presence of these unseen beings was held in such high veneration by the Romans that when they entered any place for the first time they invariably paid a salutation to the Genius Loci, the Spirit of the Place.[9] In the east the Greek cities had their Tyches.

On this coin the Genius of Corinth appears as a man[10] wearing a toga pulled over his head like a priest and holding a patera in his right hand. A patera was a shallow bowl used for pouring libations to the gods, and it often had a boss in the centre. As the gods themselves are often shown holding them it has been suggested[11] that the divinity or personification who holds it is the one to whom libations might properly be poured.

Figure 76 – A bronze of Nero. (*RPC* 1189)

RPC 1193 has a bust of Agrippina II on the obverse with the inscription **AGRIPPIN(A) AVGV(STA)**. On the reverse it has Poseidon in a biga drawn by hippocamps, with the name of one or other of the duovirs. Hippocamps featured on coins of Tyre minted in the fifth and fourth centuries B.C. before its conquest by Alexander the Great and suggest a link between the Corinthian isthmus and Phoenicia.

Figure 77 – A bronze of Agrippina II. (*RPC* 1193)

RPC 1199 has a bust of Octavia on the obverse with the inscription **OCTAVIAE NERONIS AVG** (for Octavia Nero Augusta). On the reverse it has Aphrodite holding a mirror and riding in a biga drawn by two Tritons, with the name of one or other of the duovirs. Tritons were usually associated with Poseidon, and their appearance here may refer to the myth of Aphrodite arising from the sea or to the fact that Poseidon had two sons by Aphrodite, Rhodius and Herophilus. In any case the type points to a link between the two main Corinthian cults. Corinth was dominated by the temple of Aphrodite on the acropolis, and the great temple of Poseidon stood on the nearby isthmus.

Figure 78 – A bronze of Octavia. (*RPC* 1199)

The reverse of *RPC* 1195 features Helios, the sun god, driving a quadriga. This may be a representation of one of the quadrigas which stood on the gateway from the Corinthian Agora to the road to Lechaeum, described by Pausanias in the second century A.D.

Figure 79 – A bronze of Nero. (*RPC* 1195)

The reverse of *RPC* 1200 features a bust of Aphrodite beneath which is a galley inscribed CENCHREAE or a dolphin inscribed LECHAVM. Cenchreae and Lechaeum were the eastern and western harbours of Corinth, and the galley and dolphin may have been their respective symbols.

Figure 80 – A bronze of Nero. (*RPC* 1200)

Although Paul revisited Troas for only seven days, an interesting incident occurred there (Acts 20:7–12). On the Sunday (Bruce[12] suggests 24 April 57 A.D.) Paul spoke at a meeting of the Christians. He talked on and on beyond midnight and a young man called Eutyches fell asleep. He was sitting in a window and fell to the ground three floors below, but Paul was able to revive him.

Although Troas was a busy seaport and commercial centre it produced no coins in the first century A.D. The bronze coins of Ilium probably circulated there because Ilium was the nearest mint to Troas. Under Nero Ilium produced one coin (*RPC* 2316). It had the head of Nero facing the bust of his mother, Agrippina II, on the obverse, so it must have been struck before 59 A.D. and Paul may have seen it in 57 A.D. On the reverse it has a statue of Athena within a wreath. Athena supported the Greeks in the Trojan War and was the goddess of Ilium. She was well-known to Paul from her appearance on other coins. Neither she nor all the gods of Olympus could prevent the spread of the new religion which Paul propounded so enthusiastically.

24. Assos 57 A.D.

He met us in Assos.

Acts 20:14a

In Luke's account in the book of the Acts of the Apostles, he mentions that Paul had arranged to go by land to Assos while he went by ship. Why Paul made this arrangement is not explained, but it may have had something to do with the fact that Paul was probably carrying on his person a considerable sum of money. In his letter to the Romans, Paul writes, 'At present, however, I am going to Jerusalem in a ministry to the saints; for Macedonia and Achaia have been pleased to share their resources with the poor amongst the saints at Jerusalem. They were pleased to do this, and indeed they owe it to them; for if the Gentiles have come to share in their spiritual blessings, they ought also to be of service to them in material things. So, when I have completed this, and have delivered to them what has been collected, I will set out by way of you to Spain' (Romans 15:25–28). Perhaps certain dealings had occurred with the moneychangers in the important commercial centre of Troas, and Paul decided it was safer to travel overland to Assos. Such a change of plan would confuse any possible robbers. In any case, if Paul was carrying this money, any bronze coins would have been exchanged for silver and gold ones. As the money was intended for the poor Christians in Jerusalem we can speculate that the silver coins were tetradrachms of Tyre or Antioch, and the gold coins[1] were aurei minted in Rome or Asia. Burnett[2] points out that the aureus was

164

'the sole gold coin in circulation, and it circulated freely every-where, even in the otherwise closed province of Egypt'. In the ancient world, according to Casson[3], money and valuables were carried in a purse on a belt around the waist or in a little bag on a cord around the neck. Murphy-O'Connor[4] says that in addition to the usual moneybelt or neck-bag, each member of Paul's party 'had a number of gold coins sewn into his or her garments in such a way that they would not chink. Since gold is heavy for its volume, the danger of distorting the shape of the garment would have limited the number of coins that any one individual could carry. In consequence, the number of Paul's companions was con-ditioned by the amount of money that had to be transported'. Although Murphy-O'Connor's logic is sound, he is probably overestimating the amount of money that Paul had been given. The number of aurei that even a small leather purse could hold would have been a veritable fortune in first-century Judaea.

Assos stood on a volcanic hill about 235 metres high on the southern coastline of the Troad where it faces towards the island of Lesbos. It was founded about 900 B.C. by Aeolian Greeks from Lesbos. It is a spectacular site where steep cliffs rise from the sea, and terraces, both natural and man-made, cover the less steep parts of the hill. Although not a major Greek city, it had a long and varied history before Paul visited it. Aristotle taught there from 348 to 345 B.C. and the Stoic philosopher Cleanthes[5] was born there about 330 B.C. So it was appropriate that the principal goddess of Assos was Athena, the goddess of wisdom. Her temple stood on the summit of the hill. It was built about 530 B.C. and was originally Doric in style but embellished with Ionic elements. It had thirteen columns on the sides and six at the ends.[6] Reliefs from the temple may be seen in the museums of Istanbul, Boston, and Paris.

The agora of Assos was on a slope further down the hill. It was roughly rectangular with a two-storey north stoa and a three-storey south stoa, but because of the slope, the top floor of the south stoa was level with the first floor of the north stoa. At the east end of the agora stood the council chamber and at the west end a Hellenistic temple. The area was explored and excavated by an American Archaeological Institute team from 1881 to 1883.

Around the base of the hill stood a wall built in the fourth century B.C. It was over three kilometres in length and nine metres high, and one of the towers of the gate still stands to a height of fourteen metres. The harbour from which Paul and Luke sailed has silted up and is now covered with gardens. A small artificial harbour has been constructed in modern times. The Turkish town of Behramkale now occupies the site, but the temple of Athena has been partly reconstructed and there are still some remains of the ancient city to be seen.[7]

Since the fifth century B.C., coins were minted at Assos.[8] Under Augustus Assos issued a bronze coin 16 millimetres in diameter (*RPC* 2320). On the obverse it has the bare head of Augustus with the inscription ΣΕΒΑΣΤΟΣ (Augustus), and on the reverse it has a reclining griffin and the inscription ΑΣΣΙ (abbreviation of ΑΣΣΙΩΝ = of the people of Assos). A griffin was a mythical creature with the head and wings of an eagle and the body of a lion.

Claudius issued three bronze coins (*RPC* 2322–2324). The first (*RPC* 2322) is 30 millimetres in diameter and has the facing heads of Claudius and Agrippina II with the inscription ΚΛΑΥΔΙΟΣ ΑΓΡΙΠ[(Claudius Agrippina) on the obverse, and on the reverse a reclining griffin with the inscription ΑΣΣΙΩΝ. The second (*RPC* 2323) is 17 millimetres in diameter and has the laureate head of Claudius with the inscription ΤΙ ΚΛΑΥΔΙΟΣ ΣΕΒΑΣΤΟΣ (Tiberius Claudius Augustus) on the obverse, and on the reverse, a reclining griffin and the inscription ΑΣΣΙ.

Figure 81 – A bronze of Claudius. (*RPC* 2323)

The third coin of Claudius (*RPC* 2324) is similar to *RPC* 2323 except that it has the helmeted head of Athena on the reverse.

Figure 82 – A bronze of Claudius. (*RPC* 2324)

The griffin and the helmeted head of Athena were traditional types on the coins of Assos. A griffin appears on the obverse of the first coins of Assos minted about 450 B.C. About 400 B.C. Assos produced a beautiful silver tetradrachm (Sear 4045) with the head of Athena on the obverse, and on the reverse an archaic statue of Athena Polias (guardian of the city) holding a spear and fillets. This statue probably stood in the temple of Athena at Assos. The head of Athena on the obverse of this coin wears a crested helmet ornamented with a griffin. This indicates that the griffin was associated with Athena in her capacity as protector of the city.

Athena Polias was the form of the goddess in her earliest temple on the acropolis of Athens, and this form is to be distinguished from Athena Parthenos (maiden) and Athena Promachos (fighting in front). The statue of Athena by Pheidias which stood in the Parthenon at Athens from the fifth century B.C. was described by Pausanias[9] as having a griffin on each side of the helmet. So the griffin on Athena's helmet at Athens probably referred to this ancient aspect of the goddess as protector of the city, and the griffin on the coins of Assos would have had a similar function, pointing to the goddess as Athena Polias. According to Stapleton[10], Athena was a goddess of many aspects, and as Athena Polias she has been identified with the goddess of Mycenaean Greece, which points to her origins in the original mother goddess. He explains that it would have been many centuries before one particular function of a universal goddess emerged as the preference of any community.

Griffins were mythical beasts whose function was to guard or protect. Herodotus[11], the fifth century B.C. historian, mentions that the gold which existed in the land between the Arimaspi (men with one eye) and the Hyperboreans (beyond the north wind) was guarded by griffins, and the Arimaspi were continually stealing it. Griffins also appear in association with Apollo, who presumably owned the gold that the griffins guarded. They are sometimes depicted pulling the chariots of Zeus and Nemesis, the personification of vengeance; and this suggests that griffins could play a more aggressive role, as the destroying power of the gods.

The griffin was a popular decorative motif in the ancient Near East and Greece. It probably originated in the Levant in the second millennium B.C. and spread to Greece by the fourteenth century B.C.[12] It is usually depicted with long pricked ears indicating vigilance, and a peculiar knob growing from the top of its head. The griffins on the coins of Assos probably have these features although the details on these small bronze coins are not clear.

If Paul saw the griffins on the coins of Assos he might have thought of the cherubim which guarded the Tree of Life in the Garden of Eden and the Ark of the Covenant in the holiest part of the temple in Jerusalem. These cherubim are not described in the Old Testament but they were probably composite creatures similar to griffins or winged sphinxes. Like the griffins of Greek legend their role was to guard nearby treasure.

Paul would have been surprised to know that the griffin became a symbol of Christ. According to Mercatante[13], the griffin could symbolise the devil flying away with souls, as in an Italian medieval bestiary, but in general the griffin is a symbol of Christ who was like a lion because he reigned as king and like an eagle because of the Resurrection. Most scholars see the griffin as a symbol of Christ in Dante's Divine Comedy (Purgatory, canto 29), where it may represent the two natures of Christ: human and divine.

25. Miletus 57 A.D.

*When he met us in Assos, we took him on board and went to
Mitylene. We sailed from there, and on the following day we
arrived opposite Chios. The next day we touched at Samos,
and the day after that we came to Miletus.*
Acts 20:14–16

Miletus was situated on a promontory which extended out from
the southern shore of the gulf of Latmos. On the northern shore
of the gulf was the estuary of the Meander river, and over the
centuries the silt deposited by the river slowly filled in the gulf so
that Miletus is now ten kilometres from the sea, and the eastern
end of the gulf is a lake.

German archaeologists have been studying the site on and off
for a century. Their research has shown that a Minoan colony was
superseded by Mycenaeans about the thirteenth century B.C.[1]
This suggests that there is some truth in the legend[2] which
relates how Miletus was founded by a hero called Miletus who
was the grandson of King Minos of Crete and the son of Apollo.
Ionian Greeks migrating from Greece in the eleventh century
B.C. took over the city and it became an important Ionian centre.
In the archaic period from the eighth to sixth centuries B.C. the
Milesians founded about sixty colonies on the shore of the Black
Sea and the Hellespont, including Abydos, Cyzicus, Sinope,
Olbia and Panticapaeum.

Miletus became a busy trading centre acting as the seaport for
the Meander valley which extended well into Anatolia. It was
notable not only as a commercial centre and coloniser, but for its
intellectual achievements. The philosophers Thales, Anaximander,

and Anaximenes were leading figures in the flowering of Greek culture which began in the sixth century B.C.

Before 500 B.C. Miletus was the greatest Greek city in the east. In 499 B.C. the Milesians led the Ionic Revolt which began the Greco-Persian wars, and the city was sacked by the Persians in 494 B.C. After its conquest by Alexander the Great in 334 B.C. various Hellenistic rulers competed for control of Miletus, which continued to be an important commercial centre. However, the Meander river was slowly depositing more silt and by the sixth century A.D. the harbours of Miletus were unusable and the city was eventually abandoned.

Paul probably arrived at the main harbour of Miletus known as the Lion Harbour. This was a deep indentation in the western side of the peninsula, and on either side of its entrance stood a large stone lion. These lions still guard the harbour though they are largely worn away and the harbour is full of earth. They date from the Hellenistic period so Paul would have noticed them as he, Luke, and their companions floated into the busy harbour.

The lions may have been simply guardians of the harbour without any particular religious significance, but lions feature on some of the earliest (600–550 B.C.) electrum coins of Miletus and on all the subsequent coins issued by the city before the Roman era. On these coins the lion is usually shown looking back at a star; and as Apollo, the principal god of Miletus, was a god of light it is likely that this type was connected with Apollo. According to Head[3], the emblems of Apollo worshipped at Didyma, twenty kilometres south of Miletus, were the lion and the sun. He suggests that the earliest coins of Miletus which bore these sacred symbols may have been issued under the auspices of the priests of Didymean Apollo.

For Paul, who was well versed in the Hebrew scriptures, the sight of the lions of Miletus might have reminded him of Daniel entering the lions' den (Daniel 6:16) or perhaps that the lion was the symbol of Judah (Genesis 49:9). In the book of Revelation, written after Paul's time, Jesus is called the Lion of the tribe of Judah (Revelation 5:5) and in later Christian iconography the lion is the symbol of the Gospel written by Saint Mark.

After leaving his ship in the Lion Harbour Paul would have

entered the city through the Harbour Gate which stood near the innermost part of the harbour. The remains of this impressive sixteen-columned gate[4] can still be seen. Just east of the Harbour Gate was the most important sanctuary in Miletus, the shrine of Apollo Delphinios, that is, the Apollo associated with delphis (dolphin). According to Greek legend dolphins guided the Greeks when they migrated to foreign lands. The original temple was destroyed when the Persians levelled Miletus in 494 B.C. but in Paul's time it enclosed an area 50 by 60 metres with a central altar. The oldest temple in Miletus was that of Athena which stood in the south-west part of the city. Archaeologists have uncovered its seventh century B.C. outline.[5]

After entering through the Harbour Gate Paul would have walked south down the Processional Way, a grand boulevard 100 metres long and 28 metres wide, with pavements 5.75 metres wide on either side. On Paul's left was an Ionic stoa with arcaded shops. Behind this stoa were the Baths of Capito, who was the governor of Asia in the reign of Claudius. In 57 A.D. the citizens would have been proud of this splendid new bathing complex. South of the baths was a gymnasium donated to the city by the Pergamene king Eumenes II (197–160 B.C.). The magnificent four-columned entrance to the gymnasium has recently been restored and re-erected.

On Paul's right, as he walked south along the Processional Way, was the market place called the North Agora, and south of this was the Bouleuterion, or council chamber, where the city council met. It was a stately building, established by Antiochus IV (175–164 B.C.). At the end of the Processional Way Paul would have passed through an impressive gateway into the South Agora, which was the largest of all Greek markets, measuring 164 by 196 metres and covering over three hectares. It was surrounded by a Doric colonnade and would have been a hive of commercial activity in 57 A.D. The two-storeyed gate through which Paul entered the South Agora was built in 165 B.C. and has been rebuilt in the Pergamene Museum in Berlin.

If Paul had continued walking south he would have come to the southern wall of the city where the Sacred Gate marked the beginning of the Sacred Way which led to the great temple of

Apollo at Didyma 20 kilometres to the south. This temple was a massive structure, the third-largest building in the Hellenistic world after the Artemision in Ephesus and the temple of Hera on the island of Samos. While hardly anything remains of the Artemision today, there are extensive remains of the Didymaion, with three of the original 122 Ionic columns still standing 20 metres high.

There was a famous oracle of Apollo at Didyma, equivalent to the oracle of Apollo at Delphi in Greece. As at Delphi, the priestess of Apollo put herself into a trance-like state during which the god entered her body and uttered the prophecies in her voice. The statue of Apollo at Didyma was of bronze, made by the sculptor Canachus. When the Persians suppressed the Ionian revolt in 494 B.C. they destroyed the temple at Didyma and carried off the statue to Ecbatana, a city in the hill country midway between modern Baghdad and Tehran, which the Persian kings used as a summer residence. The statue resided at Ecbatana until about 300 B.C. when Seleucus I, one of the generals of Alexander the Great, gained control of the city and returned it to Didyma.

Paul would not have visited Didyma because he was carrying money to Jerusalem and according to Luke (Acts 20:16) he was eager to be in Jerusalem on the day of Pentecost. Luke says that Paul decided to sail past Ephesus so that he did not have to spend time in Asia, but it seems more likely that Paul changed his plans in order to confuse any possible robbers. Luke apparently wants to down-play the matter of the collection, as it became a cause of embarrassment when Paul reached Jerusalem.

When he arrived in Miletus he sent a message to Ephesus, asking the elders of the church to come to Miletus. In his address (Acts 20:18–35) he told them that he had been declaring to both Jews and Greeks that they must turn to God and have faith in the Lord Jesus Christ, that he had been preaching the kingdom of God, and that now they must guard the church as he was going to Jerusalem and would not return.

Paul was probably no more than a few days in Miletus and he may not have seen any of the local coins. These coins would have been in good condition as Miletus did not produce coins in the imperial era until Caligula (37–41 A.D.). The coins of Caligula and Claudius were of brass and all 20 millimetres, but those of Nero were of bronze and in three sizes: 26, 20, and 16 millimetres.

The coins of Caligula (*RPC* 2702–2707) all have the laureate head of Caligula (Gaius) on the obverse. The reverse types are the bust of Apollo Didymeus, the cult statue of Apollo Didymeus, a bust of Drusilla (Caligula's sister), a bust of the personified Senate, and a temple of six columns. In front of the emperor's face on all the coins of Caligula and Claudius is a star, the significance of which is unknown. It may be a symbol of Apollo, or perhaps it implies that the emperor himself is divine.

RPC 2702 has the laureate head of Caligula with a star and the inscription ΓΑΙΟΣ ΚΑΙΣΑΡ ΓΕΡΜΑΝΙΚΟΣ ΣΕΒΑΣΤΟΣ (Gaius Caesar Germanicus Augustus) on the obverse. On the reverse it has the laureate bust of Apollo Didymeus (i.e. Apollo worshipped at Didyma) with a laurel branch and the inscription ΜΙΛΗΣΙΩΝ ΔΙΔΥΜΕΥΣ (of the Milesians, Didymeus[6]). The laurel tree was sacred to Apollo and the leaf was chewed by the priestess during her prophetic trance. Laurel wreaths were awarded to winners at athletic contests and laurel crowns were worn by the Roman emperors. The Greek term for laurel was daphne.[7]

Figure 83 – A bronze of Caligula. (*RPC* 2702)

RPC 2707 has the same obverse as *RPC* 2702. The reverse has a temple with six columns and the inscription ΜΙΛΗΣΙΩΝ (of the Milesians). *RPC* suggests that the temple is the temple of Apollo Didymeus rather than the provincial temple of Caligula which was at Miletus, because it also appears on a coin of Claudius.

Figure 84 – A bronze of Caligula. (*RPC* 2707)

The coins of Claudius (*RPC* 2708–2711) all have the laureate head of Claudius with a star and the inscription ΣΕΒΑΣΤΟΣ (Augustus) on the obverse. The reverse types are the cult statue of Apollo Didymeus, a temple with six columns, a lion standing with a star above, and a bust of a woman[8] who is either Messalina or Agrippina II. *RPC* 2708 has the inscription ΜΙΛΗΣΙΩΝ ΔΙΔΥΜΕΥΣ (of the Milesians, Didymeus) on the reverse with the cult statue of Apollo Didymeus holding a stag in his right hand and a bow in the left.

Figure 85 – A bronze of Claudius. (*RPC* 2708)

RPC 2710 has the inscription ΜΙΛΗΣΙΩΝ (of the Milesians) on the reverse with a lion standing right and looking back at a star above. The type is similar to that which occurred on the pre-imperial coins.

Figure 86 – A bronze of Claudius. (*RPC* 2710)

The coins of Nero (*RPC* 2712–2717) are undated and it is unlikely that they were issued before 57 A.D. They all have the laureate head of Nero on the obverse except for *RPC* 2717 which has the laureate head of Apollo. The reverses all bear the name of the magistrate Tiberius Damas[9], with a variety of types: Apollo Delphinios; the hero Miletus[10]; the cult statue of Apollo Didymeus; the cult statue of Apollo's sister Artemis with a stag behind; a lion looking back at a star above.

RPC 2712 has the laureate head of Nero with the inscription ΝΕΡΩΝ ΣΕΒΑΣΤΟΣ (Nero Augustus) on the obverse, and on the reverse Apollo Delphinios seated on a rock, holding a bow with the inscription ΕΠΙ ΤΙ ΔΑΜΑ ΜΙΛΗΣΙΩΝ (in the time of Tiberius Damas, of the Milesians). This statue probably stood in the temple of Apollo in Miletus.

Figure 87 – A bronze of Nero. (*RPC* 2712)

It was appropriate that Paul should have said goodbye to the Christians of Asia in this city of Apollo. More than any other figure in Greek religion Apollo embodied the spirit of Greek civilization, and when Paul sailed away from Miletus, that civilization would never be the same again. Apollo would fade away, but the wonderful Greek spirit would be infused into the new Christian world that eventually became modern western civilization.

26. Patara, Tyre, Ptolemais, Caesarea 57 A.D.

We came by a straight course to Cos, and the next day to Rhodes, and from there to Patara. When we found a ship bound for Phoenicia, we went on board and set sail . . .
We landed at Tyre . . . and stayed there for seven days . . .
We arrived at Ptolemais . . . The next day we left and came to Caesarea . . . staying there for several days.
Acts 21:1b,2,3b,4b,7b,8a,10a

Paul was travelling to Jerusalem and changed ships at Patara, a city of Lycia in south-west Asia Minor. As Patara was a busy port, he may have spent no more than a few hours there. It was one of the cities of the Lycian League, a federation of independent, self-governing cities which was formed in the second century B.C. after the Romans freed the Lycians from Rhodian rule in 168 B.C. When Claudius incorporated Lycia into the Roman Empire in 43 A.D. the Lycian League continued to exist, at least nominally.

The Lycians were not Greeks but a people related to the Hittites. The 'lu' element in Lycia, Lycaonia and Lydia suggests a common background. The Lycians had their own language and alphabet and inscriptions were written in this language from about 500 B.C. to 200 B.C. The first coin produced by Patara (Sear 5321) dates from about 400 B.C. and has the name of the city in Lycian letters. By Paul's time, however, Hellenistic culture had pervaded Lycian life and Patara probably looked like a Greek city.

Patara had one of the best harbours on the Lycian coast. It was protected by a headland with a lighthouse. Its entrance was 250 metres wide and it extended inland for one kilometre. Today the entrance is covered with sand and marshes cover the harbour area. There are still some ruins[1] to be seen near the modern village of Gelemish: a triple-arched gate, parts of the city wall, and a fine theatre dating from the time of Tiberius.

Patara was famous for an oracle of Apollo. The people believed that he spent the winter months there while absent from his more famous sanctuary on the island of Delos. Some authorities[2] consider that Apollo was originally a god of Lycia. The Apollo of Patara was given the epithet 'Patroös' meaning paternal. The significance of this epithet is unknown. In this form he was portrayed standing and holding a branch, bow or arrow.

In the first century B.C. the Lycian League issued silver and bronze coins. It is uncertain which Lycian cities actually minted the coins, but they mostly feature Apollo, his symbol of a cithara (a type of lyre), and his sister Artemis. Under Claudius the League issued silver and bronze coins which have the head of Claudius on the obverse and a variety of types on the reverse, mostly referring to Apollo and Artemis. Apollo Patroös appears on the reverse of *RPC* 3340, a bronze coin 29 millimetres in diameter. It has the bare head of Claudius with the inscription ΤΙΒΕΡΙΟΣ ΚΛΑΥΔΙΟΣ ΚΑΙΣΑΡ ΣΕΒΑΣΤΟΣ (Tiberius Claudius Caesar Augustus) on the obverse, and on the reverse it has Apollo Patroös facing and holding a branch in his right hand and a bow in the left. The reverse inscription is ΠΑΤΗΡ ΠΑΤΡΙΔΟΣ ΓΕΡΜΑΝΙΚΟΣ ΑΥΤΟΚΡΑΤΩΡ (Father of the Nation, Germanicus, Commander). The title 'Father of the Nation' was given to Claudius by the Roman Senate in 41 A.D., but was not adopted by him till 42 A.D. Troxell[3] considers that these coins of Claudius were probably minted in 43 A.D. when Lycia was joined with Pamphylia to form the province of Lycia-and-Pamphylia. The title 'Germanicus' had been inherited by Claudius from his father.

Figure 88 – A bronze of Claudius. (*RPC* 3340)

When Paul arrived at Tyre it too was a busy seaport. His ship unloaded its cargo there. It was an important Phoenician city with a long history. It is mentioned in Egyptian texts of the nineteenth century B.C., and by the time of King Hiram I in the tenth century it had become a wealthy commercial centre. According to Josephus[4] Hiram constructed a temple to Melqart at Tyre as well as the temple at Jerusalem for King Solomon. The name 'Melqart' simply means 'Lord of the city' and was applied to the god of Tyre, who at some early period was identified with the Greek god Heracles, known to the Romans as Hercules. When Herodotus[5] visited Tyre in the fifth century B.C. he found a highly venerated temple of Heracles there: 'I visited the temple and found it richly adorned with a number of offerings, among which were two pillars, one of pure gold, the other of emerald, shining with great brilliance at night'. The priests told him that the temple was built when the city was founded 2300 years before their time. Herodotus found this information confusing, as Heracles, the hero of the Greek legend, could not have been born as early as that. He concluded that there were two Heracles: an ancient god and a Greek hero. This makes sense, as it is difficult to understand why the Greek Heracles should be worshipped by the Phoenicians at Tyre long before the coming of Alexander the Great in 332 B.C. The ancient god Heracles may well have had origins in Phoenician religion and this Heracles must have influenced the religion of the Greeks.

Tyre was originally an island but when Alexander the Great besieged the city in 332 B.C. he built a causeway to the island. This causeway has slowly expanded to become a wide isthmus converting Tyre into a peninsula. When Alexander captured Tyre

10,000 inhabitants were put to death and 30,000 were sold into slavery, and the city became a centre of Hellenistic influence in the region. Before this the coins of Tyre had shown Melqart as a bearded figure holding a bow and riding on a hippocamp (a winged horse with a fish's tail), indicating that the god of Tyre was a god of the sea. After Alexander, when Tyre became autonomous in 126 B.C., it issued coins showing the typical head of Heracles with a lion's skin knotted around his neck. Alexander thought of himself as the incarnation of Heracles and the tetradrachms issued by many cities in his empire for many years after his death showed the head of Heracles wearing a lion's skin with a lion's head as a helmet. Between 323 and 126 B.C. Tyre was under the control of the Ptolemies of Egypt until 198 B.C. and then the Seleucids of Syria, and its coins were similar to those minted elsewhere by those kings except that they bore the name or monogram of Tyre.

After 126 B.C. Tyre was a self-governing independent city. In 64 B.C. it was annexed to the Roman province of Syria, but it was allowed to continue to mint its tetradrachms and didrachms well into the first century A.D.[6] These coins retained their high silver content (over 90 per cent) and were needed by the Jews to pay the temple tax in Jerusalem. Paul would have seen these coins on many occasions because, like all Jews, he would have had to pay the temple tax, which was a half shekel (didrachm) for the upkeep of the temple in Jerusalem. Ya'akov Meshorer[7] has suggested that the Romans allowed Tyre to continue issuing this silver coinage because Herod the Great was friendly with Augustus and was able to convince him of the necessity for this high-quality Tyrian silver. Moreover, Meshorer noticed that the tetradrachms minted on or after 18/17 B.C. had the letters **KP** on the reverse in the right field and he surmised that these letters stood for 'kratos' (power). He also noticed a change in style after this date, and concluded that these KP coins were minted in Jerusalem. Hendin[8] points out that there is an interesting section in the Talmud, a Jewish scholarly work from the period 200 to 500 A.D., which states, 'Silver, whenever mentioned in the Pentateuch, is Tyrian silver. What is a Tyrian silver [coin]? It is a Jerusalemite'.[9] However, Brooks Levy[10] disputes Meshorer's conclusion and suggests that KP stands for KAISAP (Caesar). She considers there is no perceptible change in style at the point Meshorer posits a transfer of the mint from Tyre to Jerusalem, although she does concede that some of the later, crude tetra-drachms, which were still of high-quality silver, may have been imitations informally produced in Jerusalem or Judaea.

Tyre also produced bronze coinage throughout the Augustan period and right through the first century A.D. These issues were intermittent and consisted of three denominations. The smallest is 15 millimetres in diameter and has the veiled head of Tyche on the obverse and on the reverse, a palm tree, an impor-tant symbol in Phoenician and Carthaginian religion. The next denomination is 19 millimetres in diameter and has a similar obverse but on the reverse, a galley, symbolising Tyre's mercantile greatness. The largest (*RPC* 4707–4719) is 21 millimetres in diameter and has on the obverse the laureate head of Hercules (Melqart) with a lion skin knotted around his neck, and on the reverse a club, the symbol of Heracles, surmounted by a mono-gram of **TYP**. In the field on the reverse are the Phoenician letters l t s r (of Tyre) and the date.[11]

Figure 89 – A Tyrian bronze of first century BC/AD. (*RPC* 4719)

When Paul arrived in Tyre he contacted the Christian com-munity there and stayed with them for a week. This community must have been successful because there is evidence that a Christian church had been built near the site of Heracles' temple by the third century A.D. However, this church was destroyed during the great persecution of Christians under Diocletian (284–305 A.D.). In the twelfth century the Crusaders built a large stone cathedral on the site, using material from the nearby temple of Heracles. Today the area of the cathedral and the temple of Heracles contains extensive ruins, although the adjacent hippodrome, which dates from the Roman period, is one of the best preserved, and largest, hippodromes in existence. The hippodrome and the temple of Heracles had been built on the mainland of Tyre. On the island area there is also an extensive area of ruins, some lying beneath the houses of the modern town. Archaeologists have been working at Tyre since the nineteenth century but only systematically since 1947 when the Lebanese Department of Antiquities[12] began excavations there. On the island area the main thoroughfare has been exposed. It is eleven metres wide, paved in marble, and flanked by two colonnaded pavements each five metres wide. It dates from the Byzantine era but lies on top of a marble road built in the fourth century A.D. The street on which Paul would have walked lies even deeper. According to Vos[13] 'neither the Roman city of Paul's day nor the old Phoenician city have been recovered at Tyre. Nor are they likely to be. Archaeology is very destructive. It would be necessary to obliterate the structures now excavated to get at the lower levels'.

The next city on Paul's journey was Ptolemais. He spent a day with the Christians there and set out for Caesarea the next day. It is not clear from the account in Acts whether he travelled to Caesarea by ship or by road.

Ptolemais was the most southerly of the Phoenician ports. It was the terminus of an important land route which crossed the mountains via the Valley of Esdraelon and it was an ancient city even in Paul's time. Egyptian texts of about 1900 B.C. mention the city and in the Amarna letters of the fourteenth century B.C. it is referred to as Akka. It was subsequently known as Akko until Ptolemy II named it Ptolemais after himself when he took it from Seleucus I in 281 B.C. It was regained by Antiochus III in 219 B.C. and from the time of Antiochus IV (175–164 B.C.) it was called Antiocheia in Ptolemais. When Julius Caesar visited the city in 47 B.C. it resumed the name Ptolemais, but in 6/5 B.C. the original name ΑΚΗ (Ake) appears on a coin of Augustus.

Under Claudius it seems that the name was changed to Germanicia in Ptolemais because the inscription ΓΕΡΜΑΝΙΕΩΝ ΤΩΝ ΕΝ ΠΤΟΛΕΜΑΙΔΙ (of the Germanicians[14] in Ptolemais) occurs on all the coins of Claudius minted in Akko. According to *RPC*, sometime between 50/51 A.D. and the end of Claudius' reign, it became a Roman colony, Colonia Claudia Stabilis Germani(cia?) Felix Ptolemais (the Claudian Colony, Steadfast Germanicia, Fortunate Ptolemais). The name Germanicia was probably introduced to honour Claudius, one of whose titles was Germanicus, which he inherited from his father, Nero Claudius Drusus, who campaigned successfully in Germany but died after falling from a horse in 9 B.C. Also Claudius' popular brother who died in Antioch in 19 A.D. was called Germanicus.

So when Paul arrived in Ptolemais in 57 A.D. it was a Roman colony and Paul would have noticed veterans of the various legions[15] which served in the Middle East. During the First Jewish War (66–70 A.D.) Ptolemais became the principal base of the Roman forces. In the twelfth century A.D. the city was again teeming with soldiers when the Crusaders captured the city and made it their chief port. The Crusaders gave the name 'Akko' a French form, calling it Acre. As the Knights of St John were the Crusaders in charge of Acre they expanded the name to St Jean d'Acre. The name Acre is still often used to refer to the city, although its most ancient name, Akko, is also used.

Paul would have been disappointed to know that as a result of his mission to the Gentiles, great armies would come from the west and pass through Ptolemais in order to capture the place where Jesus was crucified and buried; for Paul, and Jesus, were advocates of non-violence. In his letter to the Romans, Paul wrote, 'Love does no harm to its neighbour' (Romans 13:10a). In the Garden of Gethsemane Jesus said, 'All who draw the sword will die by the sword' (Matthew 26:52b). This was to come horribly true when nearly 100,000 Crusaders died in the violent struggle for Acre between 1189 and 1191 A.D. In 1291 A.D. the Crusaders finally lost Acre, their last stronghold in Palestine.

Today Akko still stands on a rocky promontory which juts out in a southerly direction into the Bay of Haifa. The town of solid stone buildings which occupies the promontory is known as Old Akko, and there is still a small harbour on its south-eastern corner, but the harbour has largely silted up and it is now a haven only for small fishing vessels. The Jews have tended to leave Old Akko to the Arabs and have developed a new town to the north-east. A great wall and a moat built by Ahmed Pasha

Al-Jazzar in 1799 separate the old and new towns. Actually the Old Akko which we see today has largely been shaped by Al-Jazzar, and the present street level of the city is some eight metres above that of Crusader times. Even the great Citadel of Akko dates only from the late eighteenth century, having been built on thirteenth century Crusader foundations. The strong sea wall which surrounds most of the promontory was re-faced with stone by Al-Jazzar on a twelfth century Crusader wall. There is very little to see of the Ptolemais that Paul knew, although in 1976 archaeologists working in the harbour area uncovered the foundations of a large tower and defensive wall of the Hellenistic town. The original city which was known to the ancient Israelites as Akko and is mentioned in the Book of Judges (1:31) is now a mound called Tell-el-Fukhar (Mound of Potsherds) about 1.5 kilometres east of the present city.

The first coins of Akko were issued soon after it was captured by Alexander the Great in 332 B.C. They were of gold and silver, the latter having a bust of Heracles on the obverse, and on the reverse Zeus seated on a backless throne. Under the Ptolemies a silver tetradrachm was minted in Ptolemais with the head of Ptolemy I on the obverse and on the reverse an eagle with a monogram of ΠΤ. The Seleucid rulers issued silver and bronze coins with the monogram of the city. Mark Antony and Cleopatra also minted coins there. Under Augustus bronze coins were minted in 27/26 B.C., 9/8 B.C., and 6/5 B.C. The first two issues featured a head of Zeus on the obverse and the standing figure of Tyche on the reverse. The last issue had the head of Tyche on the obverse, and on the reverse Perseus advancing to the left, with the inscription ΑΚΗ (Ake). Under Claudius three issues were minted. These issues can be dated to 50/51 A.D. because they carry two date numbers: year 11 in the Claudian era (from 40/41 A.D.) and year 99 in the Caesarian era (from 47 B.C.). The largest coin (*RPC* 4746) is 22 millimetres in diameter and has the laureate head of Claudius with an inscription (too worn to read) on the obverse, and on the reverse Tyche standing with a rudder and a cornucopia, and the inscription ΓΕΡΜΑΝΙΕΩΝ ΤΩΝ ΕΝ ΠΤΟΛΕΜΑΙΔΙ (of the Germanicians in Ptolemais) with ΑΙ L (year 11) and ΘϞL (year 99) in the field.

Figure 90 – A bronze of Claudius. (*RPC* 4746)

RPC 4747 is similar except that it is 19 millimetres in diameter and has Zeus standing with a sceptre on the reverse. *RPC* 4748 is 15 millimetres in diameter and has the laureate head of Claudius on the obverse, and on the reverse, Perseus holding the head of Medusa and the harpa[16], with LOϘ (year 99) in the field.

Figure 91 – A bronze of Claudius. (*RPC* 4748)

Apparently Perseus was important to the citizens of Ptolemais during the early imperial period. Perseus had been very important to the people of Joppa, a port city 100 kilometres to the south, but about 140 B.C. the inhabitants of Joppa were driven out by Simon Maccabeus (1 Maccabees 13:11) so that the newly independent Jewish kingdom would have a port on the Mediterranean coast. The Greek inhabitants of Joppa probably fled to the nearest Seleucid-controlled city, which was Ptolemais.

Perseus was particularly venerated at Joppa because, according to Greek legend, it was near Joppa that he saved Andromeda, the daughter of King Cepheus of Ethiopia. Cepheus' wife, Cassiopeia, boasted that she was more beautiful than the sea nymphs. This aroused the anger of Poseidon the sea god, who sent a monster to ravage the country. Only the sacrifice of Andromeda could stop the destruction, and so she was chained to a rock on the seashore. Perseus, returning from his exploit of beheading Medusa, noticed Andromeda and flew down, just in time to save her from the sea monster whom he killed. All the characters in the story became constellations in the night sky, even the sea monster (Cetus), and according to Pliny the Elder[17], the people of Joppa could point out the very rock where Andromeda had been chained. It was even said that Pompey's general, Marcus Scaurus, had taken the bones of a 12-metre monster back to Rome!

So there must have been a shrine or temple of Perseus and his father, Zeus, at Ptolemais when Paul visited the city. The legend of Perseus would have been known to the Christians there, even the strange story of his birth, how his mother, Danae, had been imprisoned in a bronze chamber by her father and in order to impregnate her Zeus descended in the form of a shower of golden droplets which filtered through chinks in the roof, thus mocking the precautions of her father. Perhaps this story influenced the account of the virgin birth of Jesus.

The cult of Perseus would have been respected by the Roman colonists in Ptolemais. In Pompeii, near Naples, wall paintings showing Perseus rescuing Andromeda have been found. Also Perseus may have been linked to the worship of Mithras, a sun god who was popular with Roman soldiers at the time. The first coin (*RPC* 4750) that Nero minted at Ptolemais, however, shows a typical foundation scene on the reverse. Here a togate man is ploughing a furrow with two oxen, and behind him are four standards inscribed III, VI, X, and XI. The inscription on the reverse is DIVOS CLAVD STAB GER FELIX P (Divine Claudius, Steadfast Germanicia, Fortunate Ptolemais). On the obverse there is the laureate head of Nero with a star and crescent, and the inscription IMP NER CLA CAES AVG GER PM TR POT (Imperator Nero Claudius Caesar Augustus Germanicus Pontifex Maximus Tribunicia Potestate). It is 25 millimetres in diameter. A later coin of Nero (*RPC* 4749) is similar but the inscription includes COS IIII[18] which indicates that the coin was minted between 60 and 67 A.D., so that Paul would not have seen it in 57 A.D.

Figure 92 – A bronze of Nero. (*RPC* 4750)

Paul left Ptolemais and went to Caesarea where he stayed with a Christian called Phillip who was one of the seven officers appointed by the early church to supervise the distribution of food. Perhaps Paul was anxious to reach Phillip in order to give him the money that he had been carrying. In any case Caesarea would have been a safe place to keep money because it was the seat of the Roman governor. The coins of Caesarea will be dealt with in a later chapter.

27. Jerusalem May 57 A.D.

After these days we got ready and started to go up
to Jerusalem.

Acts 21:15

Since Paul last visited Jerusalem the governor of Judaea had
issued two coins (Hendin 651 and 652). This governor, Felix, had
been appointed in 52 A.D., and the coins were minted in 54 A.D.
Felix had been a slave like his brother Pallas, but they were freed
by their owners and Pallas became the financial secretary of the
emperor Claudius and thereby one of the most powerful men in
Rome. Felix probably owed his appointment as governor[1] to his
brother. When Pallas proposed that Claudius marry Agrippina,
on the grounds that the son she would bring with her was the
grandson of Germanicus, Claudius' brother, he became even more
influential. However, his relationship with Agrippina led to his
undoing because when she fell out with her son Nero, Pallas
was dismissed from his position in 55 A.D. Pallas still retained
some influence until 62 A.D. when Nero executed him in order
to seize his wealth.

The wife of Felix was Drusilla, a Jewess. She was born in
32 A.D., the youngest daughter of King Herod Agrippa I. She
was the sister of King Herod Agrippa II, whose realm was extensive but did not include Judaea. In 54 A.D. Nero added some
territories to the kingdom of Agrippa, and as a compliment to
Nero, Agrippa changed the name of his capital from Caesarea
Philippi to Neronias. Since 48 A.D. Agrippa had been given
the prerogative of appointing the high priest in Jerusalem.

187

Drusilla had been given in marriage by her brother to Azizus, king of Emesa in Syria. She must have been an attractive woman because Felix wanted to marry her and he persuaded her to desert Azizus and marry him. Felix's previous wife, who died in 38 A.D., was also called Drusilla. She was the daughter of Agrippina I and Germanicus, the brother of Claudius, and so Felix was related by marriage to the emperor Claudius himself.

In view of all these connections it is no surprise that the coins of Felix carry more names than those of any of the other governors: Claudius, his wife, Agrippina, his step-son Nero, and his son Britannicus. Hendin 651 is a bronze prutah with IOY/ ΛIAAΓ/ PIΠΠI/ NA (Julia Agrippina) within a wreath on the obverse, and on the reverse two crossed palm branches with TI KΛAVΔIOC KAICAP GERM (Tiberius Claudius Caesar Germanicus) around, and the date LIΔ (year 14, of the reign of Claudius, i.e. 54 A.D.). Palm branches were used in religious ceremonies and as a symbol of royalty and victory. The palm tree was also a symbol of abundance and became the symbol of Judaea.[2]

Figure 93 – A bronze prutah of Felix. (Hendin 651)

Hendin 652 is also a bronze prutah. On the obverse it features two crossed shields with two crossed spears behind, and the inscription NEPW KΛAV KAICAP (Nero Claudius Caesar). On the reverse is a six-branched palm tree bearing two bunches of dates, with BRIT (Britannicus) above and LIΔ (year 14) and KAI (Caesar) below. The shields were the oblong ones known as scuta and were the ordinary shields carried by the Roman soldiers. The legionaries based in Judaea would have had these shields as well as the spears shown on the coin. Paul would have seen Roman soldiers with these weapons on many occasions.

Grant[3] points out that:

... on his coins issued in Jerusalem Felix tactfully (though with some risk to Jewish sentiment) copies a design of two shields and two spears which Claudius' coins had depicted in honour of his father, Antonia's husband, Drusus the elder. And the coinage of Felix looks ahead as well. Faced, like all Romans, with the delicate task of deciding which of two possible heirs to the throne to commemorate, the emperor's own son Britannicus (by a former marriage), or Nero the son of Claudius' present wife, Agrippina (likewise by a former marriage), Felix discreetly names both. It was fortunate for him that he did not omit to name Nero, since it was Nero who shortly afterwards succeeded to the throne (54 A.D.), whereupon Felix gave Sepphoris, now the Roman capital of Galilee, the name of Neronias.

Britannicus was the son of Claudius and Messalina. He was born in 42 A.D. and was originally called Germanicus, but his name was changed to Britannicus to celebrate Claudius' conquest of Britain. Nero poisoned him in 55 A.D.

Figure 94 – A bronze prutah of Felix. (Hendin 652)

Paul spent only about ten days in Jerusalem but his time there was very eventful. According to the account in Acts Paul's small band stayed at the home of Mnason, a Christian from Cyprus. Paul and his group went to see James, the brother of Jesus, and the elders of the church in Jerusalem, but they pointed out to Paul that all the Jewish Christians there were devoted to the Mosaic Law. They had heard that Paul was teaching the Jews who lived among the Gentiles not to follow the Law. To show that this was not so, they told him to pay the expenses of four men who had made a vow and to join in their purification rites according to Mosaic custom. Paul agreed to this; but after about a week when he was in the temple the crowd tried to kill him, shouting, 'He has actually brought Greeks into the temple and

has defiled this holy place' (Acts 21:28). The news of the disturbance reached the tribune of the Roman cohort in Jerusalem
and he took Paul to the barracks. The next day the tribune
brought Paul before the Jewish Council, but they began to argue
amongst themselves. Hearing that there would be a conspiracy to
kill Paul, and knowing that he was a Roman citizen, the tribune
sent Paul to Caesarea to be dealt with by Felix himself.

Some scholars have felt that there are aspects of Luke's account
which are rather odd. For example, why is there no mention of
the money which Paul brought as a gift from the Gentile
churches? Presumably this was the reason for Paul's visit to
Jerusalem, but there is not a word about it. Perhaps Luke's
account has been sanitised for later Christian readers and one
needs to delve deeper in order to discover what really happened.

Reading between the lines there are a number of possible
scenarios. The first scenario to consider is that James and the
elders were hostile to Paul and his mission to the Gentiles and
would accept the money only on the condition that Paul pay for
the four Jewish Christians to make a vow and accompany them to
the temple. Paul would then walk into an ambush and be dis-
posed of. They did not expect the conscientious Roman tribune
to immediately run from the Antonia Fortress and save Paul at
the last minute. The evidence for this set-up of Paul is that in the
account in Acts there is no mention of any effort on the part of
the Jewish Christians to plead for Paul before the Roman and
Jewish authorities. Also, according to Romans 15:31, Paul
himself was afraid that the money would not be acceptable to the
Jewish Christians. Mattill[4] suggests that the Jerusalem church
refused to accept Paul's collection, thereby symbolising their
break with the Pauline mission.

According to another scenario Gentile Christians accompany
Paul to Jerusalem as mentioned in 1 Corinthians 16:3–4, but four
of these men make a vow to cross the barrier which separates Jews
and Gentiles in the temple. This symbolic act would have been in
keeping with Paul's teaching (e.g. Ephesians 2:11–22) that there
is no barrier between Jew and Gentile in Christ. These men,
including Paul, intended to become martyrs and expected to be
resurrected (hence Paul's harping on resurrection in Acts 23:6 and

24:15). Whether or not they were able to follow Paul across the barrier is unknown[5], but any possibility of Paul becoming a martyr was thwarted by the prompt arrival of the Roman tribune. The evidence to support this scenario is that the high priest accused Paul of trying to desecrate the temple (Acts 24:6). Also an analogy can be drawn between Jesus setting his face to go to Jerusalem (Luke 9:51) where he would be crucified, and Paul making his final journey to Jerusalem, despite warnings from the Holy Spirit, to face possible martyrdom.

Conservative scholars accept that the account in Acts is a true account of what happened and maintain that it is misleading to try to read between the lines. They point out that Paul would have been prepared to demonstrate his Jewishness. His position in regard to the Mosaic Law was clear from his letters. He was happy to conform to Jewish customs when he found himself in Jewish society (Romans 14:1–8), but he believed that such conformity made no difference to one's status before God: 'In Christ Jesus neither circumcision nor uncircumcision counts for anything; the only thing that counts is faith working through love' (Galatians 5:6).

All are agreed that there was a disturbance in the temple and that Paul was saved by the prompt action of the Roman tribune. Whatever actually happened, Paul was shielded by the Roman military, and therefore it is particularly appropriate that the coins which circulated in Jerusalem at the time of Paul's visit should bear crossed Roman shields and spears.

28. Caesarea 57–59 A.D.

When they came to Caesarea and delivered the letter to the governor, they presented Paul also before him ... Then he ordered that he be kept under guard in Herod's headquarters.
Acts 23:33,35b

Today archaeologists can point to the site where King Herod's headquarters stood in Caesarea. Josephus describes it as 'a most splendid palace'. Herod the Great, of course, died in 4 B.C. but the palace was subsequently used by the Roman governors. Paul would have been kept in one of the less pleasant areas, although according to Acts 24:23 he was allowed some freedom and his friends were permitted to take care of his needs.

Herod the Great spent twelve years building the harbour and city of Caesarea virtually from nothing. There had been only the decaying remains of a Phoenician town called Strato's Tower.[1] He started building in 22 B.C. and used huge concrete blocks to construct massive breakwaters extending well out into the sea. Towers bearing enormous statues of Augustus marked the entrance and there was a lighthouse fuelled by oil. There is little to see of Herod's harbour today, but the submerged breakwaters are discernible by aerial photography on a calm day.

The city itself was built on a grand scale. On rising ground opposite the harbour-mouth stood a temple to Augustus.[2] Josephus says that it was of exceptional size and beauty and that it contained a colossal statue of Augustus, no less inferior to the Olympian Zeus. The city was designed on a grid pattern around a main street more than fifteen metres wide. The street was paved with mosaics and bordered by columns.[3] There was a theatre with 4000 seats, the earliest of its kind in Judaea. There were aqueducts, temples, a hippodrome with 38,000 seats and an amphitheatre (the probable site of the death of King Herod Agrippa I). Herod named this impressive Greco-Roman city, Caesarea, after Augustus. It became known as Caesarea Maritima (on the sea-coast) to distinguish it from other cities called Caesarea. The actual harbour was called Sebastos (Augustus).

The city remained impressive until 640 A.D. when it was captured by the Arabs and allowed to fall into disrepair. In 1101 A.D. the Crusaders took the city and discovered a green glass bowl which they believed to be the Holy Grail, the vessel from which Jesus drank at the Last Supper. The bowl is now kept in the cathedral of Saint Lorenzo in Genoa. The city changed hands between Arabs and Crusaders until King Louis XI of France captured it in 1251 A.D. when he added most of the walls and fortifications which are visible today. The Crusaders built a church on the site of the temple of Augustus. Ten years later, however, Sultan Baybars broke through the walls and destroyed the city. Over the centuries the ruins gradually became submerged under the sand dunes. Only with the formation of modern Israel and the development of a nearby kibbutz (Sdot Yam) has ancient Caesarea begun to emerge from the sand and become an increasingly popular tourist destination.[4]

Paul remained in detention in Caesarea for two years (Acts 24:27) until Felix was replaced by Porcius Festus. This fact is of great importance to the chronology of Paul's career, but unfortunately there is doubt about when Festus replaced Felix. Some scholars place considerable weight on the fact that a new coin (Hendin 653) was issued by the Roman governor of Judaea in year 5 (58/59 A.D.) of Nero's reign. E.M. Smallwood[5] made the suggestion that the issue of this coin is 'more likely to be the work of a new procurator than of an outgoing one who had already minted a large issue'. The change of procurators is therefore dated to 59 A.D. This argument is very tenuous. A counter argument can be made that the coin was issued by Felix to curry favour with Nero as the influence of his brother Pallas began to wane in Rome. Pallas, as the former financial secretary to the emperor, may have suggested, or even arranged, such an issue, especially as no other governor of Judaea had issued coinage since 31 A.D. The coin lauds Nero without, of course, showing his portrait. In any case, Josephus[6] records that Felix was deposed by Nero, and was only saved from punishment by the entreaties of his brother Pallas.

The coin at the centre of this controversy has on the obverse NEPWNOC (Nero) in a wreath which is tied at the bottom with an X. On the reverse it has a palm branch surrounded by KAICAPOC (Caesar) and the date LE (year 5). The palm branch was a symbol of victory and royalty. The wreath around Nero's name was also a symbol of victory. The coin is common today.

Figure 95 – A bronze prutah attributed to Festus. (Hendin 653)

Festus died in office after about two years. Strangely nothing is known of his life before his appointment. Soon after his arrival in Caesarea King Agrippa II and his sister Berenice visited him and he brought Paul before them. Luke says that Festus did this so that he 'may have something to write' to the emperor about Paul. Luke's reason for Agrippa's interrogation of Paul does not ring true. It seems much more likely that it was part of Agrippa's responsibilities to look into matters affecting the temple, but he had waited until Felix and Drusilla left the country before proceeding to Caesarea. According to Josephus[7] Berenice hated Drusilla because she was jealous of her beauty. Another reason for Agrippa's procrastination might have been that he had not forgiven Drusilla for breaking the Jewish law by marrying Felix. In any case Paul must have known that as soon as Felix and Drusilla left the country Agrippa, who was both pro-Jewish and pro-Roman, would arrive. He therefore appealed to Caesar via Festus. Festus and Agrippa could do nothing but concur, and arrangements were made to send Paul to Rome.

In the account in Acts, Luke puts Agrippa in a very favourable light, and there must have been a reason for him to do this.

Agrippa was still a very influential figure when Luke was writing Acts in the latter part of the first century, probably after the First Jewish War (66–70 A.D.).[8] Perhaps at the time of Luke's writing efforts were being made to convert Agrippa to Christianity. This would explain Agrippa's remark to Paul: 'Are you so quickly persuading me to become a Christian?' (Acts 26:28) and Paul's reply: 'Whether quickly or not, I pray to God that not only you but also all who are listening to me today might become such as I am – except for these chains' (Acts 26:29).

In his defence speech before Agrippa Paul described the circumstances of his conversion, how the risen Christ appeared to him on the road to Damascus and told him, 'I will rescue you from your people and from the Gentiles – to whom I am sending you to open their eyes so that they may turn from darkness to light' (Acts 26:17,18a). Paul emphasised to Agrippa that he was 'saying nothing but what the prophets and Moses said would take place: that the Messiah must suffer, and that, by being the first to rise from the dead, he would proclaim light both to our people and to the Gentiles' (Acts 26:22b,23).

The kingdom of Agrippa extended over a wide area, including the area around the sea of Galilee, but it did not include Judaea with its administrative capital of Caesarea. The father of Agrippa II, Agrippa I (37–44 A.D.), had been king of Judaea as well as other territories, and he issued an innocuous coin for circulation in areas largely populated by Jews.[9] This was Hendin 553 which has an umbrella-like canopy on the obverse and three ears of barley on the reverse (see figure 44). For non-Jewish areas Agrippa I issued a series of coins (Hendin 545–559) with a variety of types, mostly portraits of himself, members of his family, or the emperor. These coins would have circulated in Caesarea where there was a large non-Jewish population. One of these coins (Hendin 555) has the name of the city on the reverse, indicating that it was minted there. This coin is 20 millimetres in diameter and on the obverse it has the diademed, draped bust of Agrippa I and the inscription ΒΑCΙΛΕΥC ΜΕΓΑC ΑΓΡΙΠΠΑC ΦΙΛΟΚΑΙ (Great King Agrippa, Friend of Caesar). The title 'Great' probably resulted from Claudius' adding Judaea to Agrippa's kingdom in 41 A.D. On the reverse the coin has Tyche standing with her right hand on a rudder and her left hand holding a palm branch. In the field on the reverse is the date LZ (year 7, from the time of Agrippa's appointment by Caligula in 37 A.D., i.e. 43 A.D.). A similar coin (Hendin 559) has LH (year 8). The inscription on the reverse is ΚΑΙCΑΡΙΑ Η ΠΡΟC ΤΩ CΕΒΑCΤΩ ΛΙΜΕΝΙ (Caesarea, beside Sebastos Harbour). Like many cities in the Middle East there was probably a temple to Tyche (Fortuna) at Caesarea.

Figure 96 – A bronze of Agrippa I. (Hendin 555, *RPC* 4985)

After the death of Agrippa I in 44 A.D. Caesarea again came under the authority of a Roman governor of Judaea. According to *RPC* two coins were minted at Caesarea Maritima during the reign of Claudius: *RPC* 4858 and *RPC* 4859. Hendin considers that these coins, which he lists as 572 and 573, were pre-royal coinage of Agrippa II, i.e. minted at Caesarea Maritima under his authority during the period from 48 A.D. (when he took control of Chalcis) to 66 A.D. (when he issued his first dated coin with his official title). Apparently the Romans wanted Agrippa II to develop his powers gradually, since he was only 17 when his father died in 44 A.D.

Hendin 572 (*RPC* 4858) is a bronze coin 24 millimetres in diameter. On the obverse is the laureate head of Claudius. Although the name ΚΛΑΥΔΙΟC can be discerned the full legend is not visible. On the reverse there are the letters OB C S in a wreath. These letters are an abbreviation for the Latin OB CIVES SERVATOS (for saving citizens). The oak wreath is the corona civica or civic crown, which was originally awarded to a man who had saved the life of a fellow citizen in battle or by a heroic action that had somehow saved the life of citizens. It was the equivalent of the modern Victoria Cross or George Cross. The Roman Senate awarded the corona civica to Claudius soon after his accession in 41 A.D. because they considered he had saved the lives of Roman citizens by ending the reign of Caligula; but Stevenson[10], referring to a Roman sestertius of Claudius with a similar reverse, comments, 'The words EX S.C. OB CIVES SERVATOS inscribed within a laurel crown, forms the legend of the reverse on a first brass coin of Claudius, as if that most indolent and apathetic, if not most stupid, of Emperors, ever did an heroic or humane action to merit the eulogy conveyed in this senatus consultum'. Hendin 572 was presumably minted after the death of Agrippa I in 44 A.D. *RPC* knows of only two specimens, one of which was found on the beach at Caesarea Maritima.

Figure 97 – A pre-royal bronze of Agrippa II under Claudius.
(*RPC* 4858/1 (Hendin 572))

Hendin 573 (*RPC* 4859) is a bronze coin 24 millimetres in diameter. On the obverse there is the laureate head of Claudius with apparently the same legend as on the obverse of Hendin 572. On the reverse is Agrippina II, the niece-wife of Claudius. She is veiled and holds a branch and cornucopia. Above her head is a crescent, which suggests that Agrippina is here being identified with Diana, the Roman form of Artemis, the sister of Apollo. The reverse inscription is ΑΓΡΙΠΠΕΙΝΗΣ ΣΕΒΑΣΤΗΣ (Agrippina Augusta). As Agrippina married Claudius in 48 A.D. the coin must have been minted between 48 and 54 A.D.

Figure 98 – A pre-royal bronze of Agrippa II under Claudius.
(*RPC* 4859 (Hendin 573))

There are Latin-legend coins of Claudius with reverses of a rudder (Hendin 570) or an anchor (Hendin 571) which Hendin lists as pre-royal coinage of Agrippa II minted at Caesarea Maritima. *RPC* considers that there are problems in attributing these coins to Caesarea Maritima rather than Caesarea Philippi, Agrippa's capital.

Hendin also lists two coins of Nero as pre-royal coinage of Agrippa II minted at Caesarea Maritima. They are Hendin 579 which is 23 millimetres in diameter and Hendin 580 which is 19 millimetres in diameter. They both have a bust of Nero on the obverse. On the reverse the larger coin has the veiled, seated figure of Agrippina II, while the smaller one has her draped bust. The inscriptions are in Greek. As Agrippina fell out of favour with her son Nero in 55 A.D. these two coins must have been issued very early in his reign.

Paul was allowed a degree of freedom during his two years in Caesarea. During this time he probably wrote his letters to the Ephesians, the Colossians, and to Philemon[11], and he would have handled all the coins minted at Caesarea. Paul may not have understood the significance of the coin with the corona civica and OB/CS on it, as he probably did not know Latin; but he would have been curious enough to ask, and there would have been plenty of Roman soldiers there to explain it to him. Perhaps this coin gave him the idea of appealing to Caesar. In any case it is interesting to surmise that of the many occasions when the Roman emperors were honoured with the award of the corona civica the time when Paul appealed to Caesar was the only time they really deserved it; for if Paul had remained any longer in Judaea he would almost certainly have been killed by the Jews. The emperor granted Roman citizens the right of direct appeal to him. So, in a way, the emperor saved Paul's life.

29. Sidon 59 A.D.

The next day we put in at Sidon; and Julius treated Paul
kindly, and allowed him to go to his friends to be cared for
Acts 27:3

Sidon was traditionally the mother city of Phoenicia. A Sidonian coin of about 174–150 B.C. (Sear 5958) bears the Phoenician inscription, 'of the people of Sidon, the metropolis of Cambe, Hippo, Kition, Tyre'. In the book of Genesis Sidon is called the firstborn of Canaan (Genesis 10:15).

The city is mentioned in the Amarna Letters from about 1400 B.C. At that time it was submissive to Egypt. It later came under the control of the Assyrians, the Babylonians, and the Persians. It submitted without resistance to Alexander the Great in 332 B.C. and was part of the Ptolemaic kingdom of Egypt from 307 to 197 B.C. Thereafter it was part of the Seleucid kingdom until 111 B.C. when it became autonomous and began to issue silver and bronze coinage dated from 111 B.C. Previously Sidon had issued characteristic tetrashekels, shekels and lesser denominations, from about 425 B.C. These shekels mostly have a war galley on the obverse, and on the reverse, a horse-drawn, two-wheeled cart bearing a driver and a crowned, bearded figure who may be a god, but is more likely to be the king of Persia. According to Diodorus[1] the king of Persia had a residence with a park at Sidon. Behind the cart walks a figure in what looks like an Egyptian royal costume. He is probably the king of Sidon.

When Paul arrived in Sidon it was a busy port. It manufactured glass and was a centre of the purple dye industry. The dye was extracted from the Murex mollusc which grew in abundance in the costal waters off Tyre and Sidon. The production of the dye involved various processes including heating in large lead vessels. It was a very smelly business, and this may explain why ancient Sidon consisted of two parts: a maritime city and an upper city built on the lower spurs of the Lebanon mountain range.

The maritime city was built on a promontory which was protected from the sea by a line of rocks.[2] North of the promontory was the harbour which was protected to the north by a small island joined to the shore by a causeway. On the island Paul would have seen a Phoenician temple to Melqart (Lord of the city), but today a Crusader castle, called the Sea Castle, stands on the site. This castle was built hastily by the Franks in the twelfth century A.D. when they heard that the emperor of Germany, Frederick II, would arrive there. They used stones and columns from previous structures on the site.

On a small hill just to the south of the maritime city probably stood the acropolis, or fortress, of Sidon. Today the site is covered by the ruins of a Crusader castle built by the Franks. At one time the French king Louis IX stayed there. Louis was captured by the Muslims, but was later released and made a saint after his death. The castle is called the Castle of St Louis.

About two kilometres north-east of Sidon was the Phoenician temple of Eshmun. Eshmun was the Phoenician god of healing, equivalent to the Greek god, Asklepios (Roman Aesculapius). The building of the temple complex began in the seventh century B.C. but it was demolished by an earthquake in the fourth century B.C. It was not rebuilt, but remained a place of pilgrimage up to the third century A.D. Additions to the complex, such as a stairway and colonnade, were made in the Roman period. The ruins of the extensive temple complex can be visited today. It is unlikely that Paul visited it on this occasion although he may have on a previous visit (Acts 15:3). He probably knew the Phoenician legend of Eshmun. It was similar to the Greek legend of Adonis and Aphrodite, and to the Babylonian legend of Tammuz and Ishtar. Eshmun was a handsome young man with whom the goddess Ashtoreth (Greek Astarte) fell in love. When he died she was inconsolable and eventually she brought him back to life as a god with the power to heal. His name is a Semitic word meaning 'he whom we invoke'.[3]

Like Apollo Smintheus in the Troad, Eshmun had a curative mouse for his emblem.[4] Also, like the Greek god Asklepios, snakes were used in his cult, as a gold plaque showing a snake coiled around a staff was found at the temple of Eshmun.[5] Perhaps the idea of snakes eating mice was significant for the Greek and Phoenician religions in their healing aspects. The idea of a snake coiled around a staff was certainly significant to the ancient Israelites; for according to the Book of Numbers, 'Moses made a serpent of bronze, and put it upon a pole; and whenever a serpent bit someone, that person would look at the serpent of bronze and live' (Numbers 21:9), although we read in the Book of Kings that Hezekiah, the king of Judah, 'broke in pieces the bronze serpent that Moses had made, for until those days the people of Israel had made offerings to it; it was called Nehushtan' (2 Kings 18:4b).

Ashtoreth was the supreme female divinity of the Phoenicians. She was the Great Mother goddess who controlled nature and fertility. She was equivalent to the Greek Artemis, and Selene, the moon goddess. At the temple of Eshmun there is a large stone throne called the Throne of Astarte.[6] It is carved from a solid block of granite in the Egyptian style and is flanked by two sphinxes.[7] Its precise significance is unknown but it may have signified Astarte as the Queen of Heaven. In Judah in the time of Jeremiah (about 600 B.C.) the Queen of Heaven was worshipped by ordinary Jewish families (Jeremiah 7:17,18). According to the Book of Kings, Solomon (tenth century B.C.) 'followed Ashtoreth the goddess of the Sidonians' (1 Kings 11:4,5) and built 'high places' for her east of Jerusalem (2 Kings 23:13).

Although Astarte was the goddess of the Sidonians she does not feature prominently on Sidon's extensive coinage before Paul's time. She is shown on a war galley on a bronze coin (Sear 5964) of the first century B.C. This was appropriate as she was also the Phoenician goddess of war. On the reverse of a coin of Augustus there is the car of Astarte. This was a two-wheeled cart which was used to transport the baetyl[8] of the goddess. It may have been used to transport the baetyl in religious procession from the goddess's temple in the city to her throne at the temple of Eshmun. In later centuries the cart of Astarte became a common type on the coins of Sidon. In fact, Kevin Butcher[9] says, 'The mark of Sidon was its portable shrine of the moon goddess Astarte a strange contraption with wheels'.

Much more prominent on Sidon's coins were Tyche and Europa. The turreted, veiled, draped bust of Tyche featured on the obverse of a long series of silver shekels and half shekels which Sidon issued from 111 B.C., the beginning of its autonomy. The coins are dated from this time, and have an eagle, the symbol of Zeus, on the reverse. According to *RPC*[10] the production of shekels continued till 30/29 B.C. Production of half shekels continued even longer and issues are known for 31/30 B.C., 6/5 B.C., 18/19 A.D. and 43/44 A.D., the coins of the last three issues being common today. Thereafter the production of silver coinage at Sidon ceased. *RPC* 4561 is a typical half shekel, which Paul might have seen. It is 20 millimetres in diameter and on the reverse it has the inscription ΣΙΔΩΝΙΩΝ ΤΗΣ ΙΕΡΑΣ ΚΑΙ ΑΣΥΛΟΥ (of the people of Sidon, holy and secure).

Figure 99 – A silver half shekel. (*RPC* 4561)

The Sidonians may have considered Tyche more appropriate than Astarte to feature on their coins because she was the goddess of fortune which, no doubt, included business activity. Also Sidon was very much under Hellenistic (Greek) influence at this time. How Tyche related to Astarte is unknown; perhaps Tyche was the aspect of Astarte which was concerned with municipal activities.

Europa featured very prominently on the coins of Sidon at this time, both on the 'autonomous' coins which did not have the head of the Roman emperor and on the coins which did. The former consisted of an extensive series of dated bronze coins.

Their obverse types are Zeus, Dionysus, Tyche, a temple, or an eagle. The reverse types are Europa riding a bull, a cista mystica (similar to the reverses of Asian cistophori), a galley, Nike on a prow, a galley with Astarte, a prow, or a temple.

The coins of Sidon with the head of the emperor were issued by Augustus, Caligula, Claudius and Nero. Except for three coins of Augustus which feature the car of Astarte, Nike on a prow, or a standing goddess, they all have on the reverse Europa riding a bull. *RPC* 4617 is typical. It is 22 millimetres in diameter and has the laureate head of Claudius on the obverse, and on the reverse Europa is riding a galloping bull. She holds one of his small horns with her left hand while the other hand holds the end of a veil or scarf which forms a circle around her head. The inscription on the reverse is ΣΙΔΩΝΟΣ ΘΕΑΣ (of divine Sidon).

Figure 100 – A bronze of Claudius. (*RPC* 4617/4)

According to the Greek legend Europa, the daughter of Agenor, the king of Phoenicia, was abducted by Zeus in the form of a bull. He carried her across the sea to Crete where in the form of an eagle he seduced her and they had three sons: Minos, king of Crete, Rhadamanthus, king of the Cyclades Islands, and Sarpedon, king of Lycia. Agenor sent his sons in search of Europa. Cadmus founded the city of Thebes and brought the alphabet to the Greeks. Phoenix travelled to North Africa and gave his name to the Punic nation there, but he later returned to his homeland which was called Phoenicia in his honour. Celix went to the land which was later called Cilicia. Thasos colonised the island which was named after him.

The name 'Europa' probably means 'broad face',[11] which was a synonym for the full moon. According to Matsson[12] she was at first regarded as a human personality, but in later times she came to be regarded as a divinity, and to some extent was identified with Astarte. Actually the reverse may have been the case: the motif of the moon goddess riding on the sun-bull probably developed in the Middle East and Crete in the second millennium B.C. and with the coming of the Greeks this was interpreted in terms of an historical event: the abduction and rape of the Phoenician maiden Europa. Graves[13] suggests that the rape of Europa commemorated an early Hellenic occupation of Crete; or possibly a raid on Phoenicia by Hellenes from Crete. Such a raid is recorded by Herodotus[14]: 'At a later period, certain Greeks, with whose name they are unacquainted, but who would probably be Cretans, made a landing at Tyre, on the Phoenician coast, and bore off the king's daughter, Europé'. It is more likely, however, that the Greek legend of Europa simply reflected the Greeks bringing the cult of the moon goddess from the east via Crete.

If Paul saw any of these coins of Sidon he would have been reminded of the story of Europa, how she was taken forcibly to the west and how the alphabet was brought to the Greeks as a result. It was appropriate that Paul should finally leave the Middle East from Sidon, because he too was being taken as a prisoner to the west. The continent which bears Europa's name would be profoundly changed as a result.

30. Myra 59 A.D.

After we had sailed across the sea that is off Cilicia and Pamphylia, we came to Myra in Lycia. There the centurion found an Alexandrian ship bound for Italy and put us on board.

Acts 27:5,6

Myra was one of the chief cities of Lycia. It was a few kilometres from the coast and was served by a port called Andriake. Paul probably did not visit Myra but simply transferred from one vessel to another in Andriake harbour. The harbour has now silted up, but a large granary built by the Roman emperor Hadrian (117–138 A.D.) still stands, indicating that Andriake was an important storage depot for grain on the sea route to Rome. Paul was put on one of the grain ships which carried wheat from Alexandria to Rome, and the crew had to throw the cargo of wheat overboard during bad weather.

The ruins of Myra are a few kilometres north of the modern town of Demre, which is also called Kale. The ruins include a well-preserved Roman theatre built in the second century A.D. Many inscriptions have been found at Myra. Some of these inscriptions are in the Lycian language and attest the importance of the city in the Persian period. Inscriptions from the Roman period showed that Myra bestowed on Augustus and Tiberius the generous title, 'Imperator of land and sea, Benefactor and Saviour of the whole universe'.[1] On the rock faces of the nearby cliffs tombs have been cut into the rock. These tombs were carved to resemble Lycian houses and sometimes show the deceased and his family in sculptured relief.

Myra was one of the cities of the Lycian League, the federation of cities formed after the Romans freed the Lycian cities from Rhodian rule in 168 B.C. During the period of the League Myra minted silver and bronze coins. These coins celebrate Apollo and his sister Artemis, and have MY, or sometimes MYPA (Myra), on the reverse. Myra was also the principal mint for the district of Masikytes, a mountainous region of Lycia east of the Xanthus river. These coins also celebrate Apollo and Artemis, but have MA (for Masikytes) on the reverse. One coin (Sear 5310) has MA on the obverse and MY on the reverse.

In 43 A.D. Claudius incorporated Lycia into the Roman Empire, and silver and bronze coinage was issued with his head and the inscription ΤΙΒΕΡΙΟC ΚΛΑΥΔΙΟC ΚΑΙCΑΡ CΕΒΑCΤΟC (Tiberius Claudius Caesar Augustus) on the obverse. On the reverse the types mostly celebrate Apollo and Artemis. The reverse inscription is ΓΕΡΜΑΝΙΚΟC ΑΥΤΟΚΡΑΤWΡ (Germanicus Commander) on the silver, and ΠΑΤΗΡ ΠΑΤΡΙΔΟΣ ΓΕΡΜΑΝΙΚΟΣ ΑΥΤΟΚΡΑΤΩΡ (Father of the Nation, Germanicus Commander) on the bronze. According to RPC[2] there is no clear indication of mints, as the silver and bronze may perhaps have been produced at different places. Apollo Patroös of Patara is shown on both the silver and bronze coins but this does not mean they were minted at Patara since other bronzes show Artemis Eleuthera of Myra.

The Artemis of Myra was given the epithet Eleuthera, meaning 'free'. The significance of this epithet is unknown, but Jones[3] suggests that it is possible that since the goddess is occasionally spoken of as one whose help can be obtained in the freeing of slaves and the purifying of criminals, the name may refer to these aspects of her activities. However, this Greek adjective, like its English equivalent, can be taken in two senses: 'liberated' or 'available to all'[4], and it may be the latter sense which is meant here.

RPC 3342 is one of the bronze coins of Claudius. It is 29 millimetres in diameter and has the head of Claudius on the obverse, and on the reverse the cult statue of Artemis Eleuthera in a temple with two columns.

Figure 101 – A bronze of Claudius. (*RPC* 3342/1)

Paul was probably at Andriake for too short a time to see Myra or any of the local coins. In any case Myra produced a Christian celebrity far more famous than Paul. In fact, in modern times, he has become more widely known than Jesus himself. This celebrity is Santa Claus, whose name is derived from the Dutch dialect form, Sinte Klaas, meaning Saint Nicholas. St Nicholas[5] was the bishop of Myra in the fourth century A.D. Little is known of his life, but there is the story that he saved three girls from prostitution by throwing three bags of gold as dowry into their window at night.[6] Although we know little about Bishop Nicholas he must have been a kind and generous man. Paul would have approved of him. As Paul said to the Philippians, 'Whatever is true, whatever is honourable, whatever is just, whatever is pure, whatever is pleasing, whatever is commendable, if there is any excellence and if there is anything worthy of praise, think on these things' (Philippians 4:8). Paul would not approve of the modern cult of commercialism which has developed around Santa Claus. Instead of celebrating the birth of Christ, Christmas has become a festival for merchants and pawn-brokers.

31. Malta 59 A.D.

He ordered those who could swim to jump overboard first and make for the land, and the rest to follow, some on planks and others on pieces of the ship. And so it was that all were brought safely to land. After we had reached safety, we learned that the island was called Malta.

Acts 27:43b,44;28:1

Paul was shipwrecked on the island of Malta. His ship had been driven by gale-force winds from the east for fourteen days and ran aground in a bay[1] on Malta. The island was called Melita, which was a Phoenician word meaning 'refuge', an appropriate name as far as Paul was concerned.

The ship should have avoided the stormy winter season, but for various reasons it had been delayed. As Luke explains, 'Much time had been lost and sailing was now dangerous, because even the Fast had already gone by' (Acts 27:9). It has been suggested that Luke's mention of the Fast (the Jewish Day of Atonement, which occurred at a variable time according to the Jewish calendar) indicated that it occurred later than usual in that particular year. If this is so, then Luke has given a valuable clue to the chronology of Paul's life. W.P. Workman[2] has calculated that in 59 A.D. the Fast fell on 5 October, but in all the neighbouring years from 57 to 62 A.D. it fell earlier. So the three months that Paul spent in Malta were from November 59 A.D. to January 60 A.D.

People have been living on Malta for thousands of years. The earliest archaeological remains date from about 3800 A.D. when Neolithic farmers lived in caves. In Paul's time the Maltese were mostly of Phoenician stock and spoke a dialect of the Phoenician language. The Phoenician influence on the island dates from about the eighth century B.C. while there is evidence of Carthaginian influence from the sixth century B.C. In 218 B.C., towards the end of the Punic war, Malta was taken by the Romans and came under the control of the Roman governor of the province of Sicily.

Head[3] states that Malta issued bronze coins from 218 B.C. to the end of the first century B.C. However, some of these coins have Punic inscriptions which suggests that they were produced under Carthaginian control. On the other hand, the veiled female head on the obverse of one of the Punic inscription coins is similar to that on coins with Greek and Latin inscriptions, which suggests they are all part of the same series. *RPC*[4] considers that there is little certainty about the chronology except that coins with Greek inscriptions are probably earlier than those with Latin inscriptions. One coin (*RPC* 672, Sear 6592) has a Greek inscription **ΜΕΛΙΤΑΙΩΝ** (of the people of Melita) with a veiled female head on the obverse, and a Latin inscription, **C ARRVNTANVS BALB PROPR** (C. Arruntanus Balbus, Propraetor) with a curule chair on the reverse. *RPC* suggests that this coin belongs to the Triumviral period in the first century B.C. Arruntanus must have been propraetor of Sicily as propraetors or proconsuls were appointed as governors of that province. The curule chair was used by important Roman magistrates, and here indicates Arruntanus' office.

Only one coin, *RPC* 673 (Sear 6591)[5], has only a Latin inscription. It is 20 millimetres in diameter and has a veiled female head on the obverse. On the reverse it has **MELITAS** (of Melita[6]) and a tripod. The tripod also appears on one of the coins which has a Punic inscription, suggesting that it was used in a cult which had its roots in Phoenician religion and was not something recently imposed by the Romans. The cult was probably that of the female divinity shown on the obverse.

Figure 102 – A bronze with Latin inscription only. (*RPC* 673)

Who is the female whose head is featured on the obverse of these coins? *RPC* suggests that she is Astarte. It is very likely that some local form of the great Phoenician goddess Astarte was worshipped by the Maltese at this time.

The Maltese welcomed Paul and looked after him during the winter months. Unfortunately, soon after his arrival, Paul was bitten on the hand by a snake. When the natives saw the snake hanging from his hand they said to one another, 'This man must be a murderer; though he has escaped from the sea, justice has not allowed him to live' (Acts 28:4). The Greek word used here for justice, δικη (dike), is the usual word for justice, but it is unlikely that the native Maltese would have been referring simply to personified justice, or to the goddess Nemesis, a rather vague and uncommon figure in Greek mythology. More likely they were referring to the Astarte worshipped on Malta. So, in their own language, the natives would have said, 'He has escaped from the sea god[7] but Astarte has not allowed him to live'.

Paul was not affected by the bite of the snake which the locals considered to be venomous.[8] Perhaps this was one of the signs which Jesus said would accompany those who believe (Mark 16:17,18).[9] In any case the Maltese became devout Christians, as they still are to this day.

32. Syracuse, Rhegium, Puteoli 60 A.D.

We put in at Syracuse and stayed there for three days; then we weighed anchor and came to Rhegium. After one day there a south wind sprang up, and on the second day we came to Puteoli. There we found believers and were invited to stay with them for seven days.
Acts 28:12, 13, 14a

Syracuse was a port city on the east coast of Sicily. It had been founded in 734 B.C. by colonists from Corinth and became the dominant Greek city in Sicily. During the Classical Age of Greece (fifth century B.C.) it was an important centre of Greek culture: wonderful statues adorned the temples of the city and the coins that were minted there are considered to be masterpieces of Greek art. Some numismatists feel that these coins of Syracuse are the most beautiful ever made. Unfortunately, after the Romans captured the city in 212 B.C. they plundered it and carried off its art treasures to Rome. This greatly increased the appreciation of the Roman people for Classical Greek art. Under Roman rule, however, the city declined and never recovered its former glory.

One particularly notorious governor was Verres, who was proconsul of Sicily from 73 to 71 B.C. He plundered Syracuse and Sicily for his own enrichment, but it was to the credit of the Roman justice system at the time that Cicero, a Roman lawyer, was able to successfully prosecute Verres on behalf of the people of Sicily. When Paul saw Syracuse he would have been reminded of this episode in its past, and his faith in Roman justice would have been strengthened. We know that he already respected the Roman authorities; for when he was in Corinth he wrote to the Christians in Rome, 'Let every person be subject to the governing authorities; for there is no authority except from God, and those authorities that exist have been instituted by God' (Romans 13:1).

Syracuse was originally on an island called Ortygia but in the sixth century B.C. it was joined to the mainland by a causeway. There were harbours north and south of the causeway and these made Syracuse one of the principal ports in the western Mediterranean. On Ortygia there was a fresh-water spring dedicated to the nymph, Arethusa[1], who had featured on many of the early coins of Syracuse. This spring was flowing in Paul's time and is still flowing today. On the highest part of Ortygia stood a great Doric temple to Athena. During the subsequent Christian centuries this temple became incorporated into the structure of the modern cathedral, but it is not difficult to disentangle it from the later structures and alterations, since so much of the original building remains.[2] Paul could not have avoided seeing this impressive temple during his three days at Syracuse. Today on the steps of the cathedral is a wonderful marble statue of St Paul by the eighteenth-century sculptor Marabitti.

On Ortygia near its northern end Paul would have noticed a Doric temple to Apollo, but only fragments of this temple, incorporated into later buildings, can be discerned today. Apollo was popular at Rome since the battle of Actium which Augustus claimed to have won with Apollo's help. Apollo was particularly popular with Nero who was a lover of Greek culture, especially the theatre. In 60 A.D. Nero instituted the Neronia, a festival in honour of Apollo. It was intended to be held every five years and to rival the Olympic Games of the Greeks. In Rome bronze coins were minted to celebrate the festival.[3] As Paul's visit to Syracuse probably occurred in February in the year 60 A.D. these events were still to occur.

Under Roman rule Syracuse was at first allowed to mint bronze coins. The types on these coins honoured the usual Greek gods: Zeus[4], Athena, Apollo, Artemis, Demeter, Persephone, and Nike. One coin (Sear 1231) showed Serapis on the obverse and Isis on the reverse, indicating that these Egyptian gods were becoming popular in other parts of the Roman empire.

By the first century B.C. the production of coins at Syracuse had ceased. It seems that it was a deliberate policy of Rome not to allow the striking of local city coins in the western provinces of the empire, including Sicily. According to Butcher[5] the western coinage began to dwindle in the reign of Tiberius (14–37 A.D.) and had died out altogether early in the reign of Claudius (41–54 A.D.). The only mint left producing coins in the west was at Rome. As far as Sicily was concerned, the last city issues were under Tiberius, mostly from Panormus (modern Palermo) in the north west of the island. So in 60 A.D. the coins circulating in Syracuse had come from Rome. Probably the bulk of these coins were common asses of Claudius, such as Sear 639 which has the laureate head of Claudius and the inscription TI CLAVDIVS CAESAR AVG P M TR P IMP (Tiberius Claudius Caesar, Augustus, Pontifex Maximus, Tribunicia Potestate, Imperator) on the obverse, and on the reverse the standing figure of Minerva advancing to the right, holding a shield and brandishing a javelin. In the field on the reverse are the letters SC (Senatus Consulto = by decree of the Senate). Minerva was the Roman equivalent of the Greek goddess Athena. She was worshipped on the Capitoline hill in Rome where she formed a triad with Jupiter and Juno. She was the Roman goddess of handicrafts and the arts, and as a goddess of war she encroached on the domain of Mars. Jones[6] suggests that she appears on coins of Claudius because this bookish emperor sought her patronage as a goddess of learning.

Figure 103 – An as of Claudius. (Sear 639)

When Paul's ship left Syracuse it probably intended sailing through the strait of Messina which separates Sicily from Italy, but because of adverse winds it had to put in at Rhegium until a favourable south wind blew. Rhegium was a city on the eastern shore of the strait of Messina. On the western shore was the city of Messana, modern Messina, which had originally been called Zankle by the Greek colonists who had founded it in about 725 B.C. Rhegium had in turn been founded by Greeks from Messana in about 720 B.C. It flourished at first but in 387 B.C. it was destroyed by Dionysius I, the ruler of Syracuse. In 280 B.C. the people of Rhegium allied themselves with Rome against the Greek general Pyrrhus. Rome sent mercenaries to Rhegium but they turned on the people killing the men. The city was not restored to its former inhabitants till 270 B.C. During the Second Punic War (218–201 B.C.), when Hannibal invaded Italy, Rhegium again sided with Rome. During the Social War (91–87 B.C.) Rhegium became a municipium, which was an Italian city-state where the inhabitants were granted Roman citizenship but continued as a self-governing community.

In Paul's day the coinage in circulation at Rhegium would have been Roman, as Rhegium had not minted its own coins since the period 203–89 B.C. During that period a variety of Greek gods featured on the coins, including Asklepios (Aesculapius), Apollo, Artemis, Athena, and the Dioskouroi (Dioscuri).[7] The prominence of Asklepios suggests that there was a sanctuary to him at Rhegium. Today the city's name is Reggio di Calabria. There is little to see from Paul's time because the city has been demolished several times by earthquakes. After a major earthquake in 1908 it was rebuilt with wide streets and low, reinforced concrete buildings.

Paul's ship sailed up the coast of Italy, passed the high cliffs of the island of Capri and across the wide bay of Naples to Puteoli, which was a busy seaport in the northern end of the bay. Paul may have seen the palace of Tiberius on the north-east tip of Capri, overlooking the bay. He would have seen Mount Vesuvius, probably with smoke billowing from its summit, and the towns of Herculaneum and Pompeii on the shore of the bay near the mountain. Further north he would have seen the town of Neapolis, which has become the modern city of Naples with a population of over a million. In 79 A.D. Herculaneum and Pompeii were buried by a tremendous eruption of Vesuvius. The cities remained buried until excavation began in 1709.

The name 'Puteoli' is derived from the Greek, potioloi, meaning 'sulphur springs', and there are still sulphurous hot-water springs near the city which is now called Pozzuoli. The volcanic ash from the area was mixed with lime to form a very durable cement which resisted seawater. It was produced even in Paul's time and is called Pozzolana, after the city.

Puteoli was founded by Greek settlers in about 529 B.C. and they called it Dicaearchia (City of Justice). These Greeks probably came from the city of Cumae which was about eight kilometres to the north-west on the coast. They in turn came from the nearby island of Ischia, which was first settled by colonists from Euboea in about 770 B.C. The Greek settlement on Ischia was called Pithekoussai and was the first Greek colony in Italy and Sicily.[8]

Hannibal tried to capture Puteoli in 214 B.C. so that his army could have a seaport to receive supplies from Carthage, but the Roman garrison there repulsed him. In 194 B.C. the Romans established a colony there, and the city became the first Roman seaport on the bay of Naples. With the growth in the importance of Rome Puteoli became its chief seaport even though it was 229 kilometres to the south. This was because of its safe harbour and the inhospitable coast near Rome. However Claudius (41–54 A.D.) built an artificial harbour called Portus Augusti (Port of Augustus) near the mouth of the Tiber river so that the grain ships could unload their cargoes nearer the capital. In Paul's time these ships put their passengers ashore at Puteoli and then sailed up the coast to Portus Augusti. At Puteoli Paul was allowed to stay with some Christians as at Sidon. These Christians were probably quite wealthy as Puteoli had flourished as a port and commercial centre, and the Jewish community there was apparently the oldest in Italy after that of Rome.[9] In any case it is not difficult to imagine these Christians giving coins to Paul, and these coins would have been those that circulated in Rome.

There is no evidence that Puteoli ever minted coins. Cumae had issued silver coins until 423 B.C. when it was captured by the Samnites, a group of Italian tribes. Neapolis, which had been founded by Greeks from Cumae about 650 B.C., continued to issue coins until 200 B.C. when Roman influence increased after the second Punic War. However, the Greek language and culture continued in Neapolis so that when Vesuvius erupted in 79 A.D. its citizens still spoke Greek.

At Pozzuoli many traces remain of the city which Paul saw although much lies under the sea due to earthquake activity in subsequent centuries. There is a market building which is partially submerged, and an amphitheatre. Several columns from the temple of Augustus (and Roma) are incorporated in the local cathedral. It must have been an impressive city, a foretaste of Rome itself.

33. Rome 60–62 A.D.

And so we came to Rome.
Acts 28:14b

Paul travelled to Rome on the Via Appia, the road named after Appius Claudius Caecus who began to build the road in 312 B.C. Parts of the road are still in use. Paul would have entered Rome through the Porta Capena, a gate in the south-east part of the wall which surrounded the city. Although it was traditionally attributed to Servius Tullius, a king of Rome in the sixth century B.C., this wall was constructed in the fourth century B.C. Servius may have built part of it. Sections of the Servian wall are still standing, although even in the time of Augustus it had become neglected and partially incorporated into the structure of private houses. In 271 A.D. Aurelian began to build a second outer wall, much of which is still standing.

On entering the city Paul would have found himself in a valley between the Palatine and Aventine Hills, two of the seven hills of Rome. This valley formed a natural site for the Circus Maximus which extended to the north-west for about 550 metres. It had been reconstructed by Julius Caesar and was used primarily for chariot races which were extremely popular with the Roman citizens. There was another stadium north of the Capitoline Hill and Caligula had begun to build a third one, which Nero completed, on the site where St Peter's Basilica now stands, on the other side of the Tiber River. Today the Circus

Maximus is an open, grassy space surrounded by multilaned highways 'where motorists play Ben Hur in Fiats and Lancias'.[1]

When Paul entered the city he would have seen the palaces of the emperors on top of the Palatine Hill on his right. There Nero would have been in residence enthusiastically anticipating the Neronian Games which were held later in the year 60 A.D. and were to be repeated every five years. These games involved contests in music, gymnastics and horsemanship. A semis, equal to half an as, was struck to celebrate the games. It has the laureate head of Nero on the obverse, and on the reverse a table bearing a wreath and a vase (prizes in the games), and the inscription CERTA QVINQ ROM CON (Certamen Quinqennale Romae Constitutum = The Five-yearly Contest Established at Rome).

Figure 104 – A semis of Nero. (Sear 691)

Nero was obsessed with singing and playing the lyre, and spent hours practising. According to Suetonius[2] he would lie on his back with a slab of lead on his chest, use enemas and emetics to keep his weight down, and refrain from eating apples and every other food considered deleterious to the vocal chords. He issued an as (Sear 689) with his head on the obverse, and on the reverse his own figure, as Apollo, in flowing robes advancing to the right, playing the lyre. The lyre was a symbol of Apollo, the patron of the arts, but here it is Nero who is depicted; for Suetonius[3] records that Nero 'set up several statues of himself playing the lyre. He also had a coin struck with the same device'.

Figure 105 – An as of Nero. (Sear 689)

The palace of Claudius had also been on the Palatine Hill. According to *RIC*[4] no copper or brass coins were struck at Rome in the reign of Nero until about 62 A.D., although gold and silver coins were produced from 54 to 64 A.D. So Paul probably did not see copper or brass coins of Nero during his two years in Rome. The coins most likely to have been handled by Paul would have been the common aes (copper or an alloy of copper) of Claudius. Apart from the goddess Minerva, these coins of Claudius tended to feature personified qualities such as Freedom (Libertas), Perseverance (Constantia), and Hope (Spes). A dupondius (Sear 636) has a beautiful portrait of Ceres, the corn-goddess, on its reverse. Sutherland[5] considers that these lower denominations 'presented a variety of simple types which would have been suggestive to the illiterate, and very positively so to the literate. There were few for whom a seated corn-goddess, a goddess holding a cap of liberty, an armed but patiently waiting amazon-goddess, or Athena in full panoply could have lacked a real significance.' Sutherland feels that whoever chose these types chose very well.

Figure 106 – A dupondius of Claudius. (Sear 636)

Ceres was the goddess of cereals, or more specifically the goddess of the growth of food plants. The yearly produce was represented by the goddess Annona. At Rome corn was very important because a vast amount was needed to feed the increasing population and a large proportion of the population was dependent on regular government hand-outs of corn. Corn was transported to Rome in grain ships like the one in which Paul was shipwrecked. Ceres was particularly important during Claudius' reign because there was a series of droughts which caused a scarcity of grain. This may be the famine referred to in Acts 11:28 when Paul brought famine relief to the Jerusalem Christians. Suetonius[6] records that a mob stopped Claudius in the Forum and pelted him so hard with curses and stale crusts that he had difficulty in regaining the palace by a side door. As a result he took all possible steps to import grain, even during the winter months, insuring merchants against the loss of their ships in stormy weather and offering a bounty for every new grain ship built. A festival, the Cerealia, was held every year in honour of Ceres. A cult of Ceres, Liber (the Roman earth god) and Libera (his female counterpart) was developed in imitation of the Greek trio of Demeter, Persephone and Iacchos worshipped at Eleusis. A temple built on the Aventine Hill, in the south-west part of the city was destroyed by fire in 31 B.C., but it was restored by Augustus.

Many of the sestertii of Claudius bear a countermark (**NCAPR**) and it has been assumed that they were so stamped in order to extend their life in circulation, in which case the letters stand for Nero Caesar Augustus Probavit (Nero Caesar Augustus Approved). But some of these countermarked coins are in very fine condition and Carson[7] has suggested that the countermark stands for Nero Caesar Augustus Populo Romano (Nero Caesar Augustus to the Roman People) and that the coins were distributed as gifts to the people in 57 A.D.

Figure 107 – A countermarked sestertius of Claudius.

The palace of Caligula was on the north-west edge of the Palatine Hill, overlooking the Forum, the political and spiritual centre of Rome. Caligula's coins tended to glorify himself or his family. A sestertius featured his three sisters on the reverse; another showed his mother, Agrippina, on the obverse, and an as which is fairly common today featured his father, Germanicus, on the obverse.

The large palace of Tiberius was also near the north-west part of the Palatine Hill. Tiberius was a very conservative man, and this attitude is reflected in his silver and gold coinage, which did not vary throughout his reign. Apart from an early denarius which showed him in a quadriga on the reverse, the reverse of all his silver and gold coins showed a seated woman, whose identity is still a matter of debate[8], and the inscription PONTIF MAXIM (Pontifex Maximus = High Priest). The aes coinage of Tiberius, however, shows a variety of types, e.g. a rudder and globe, or a winged caduceus.

Near the south-west edge of the Palatine Hill was the temple of Cybele and the temple of Apollo. Nearby was the modest house of Augustus who liked to maintain the fiction that he was merely the Princeps, the First Citizen. According to Suetonius[9] the temple of Apollo was erected in the part of the house to which, the soothsayers said, the god had drawn attention by having it struck with lightning. The coinage of Augustus featured a great variety of types and provided information on matters of importance to the whole empire. However, if the estimates of *RIC*[10] are correct, that silver had a life of 50 years and aes of 30 or 40 years, then Paul would not have seen the aes coins of Augustus in 60 A.D. although the later silver and gold issues of Augustus could still have been in circulation in 60 A.D. At that time Rome had a population close to a million inhabitants and coins, especially of the lower denominations, would have been subject to considerable wear.

Today the palaces on the Palatine Hill lie in ruins with grassy areas between broken walls. The citizens of modern Rome like to have picnics there. All that remains of the temple of Apollo is a mound of rubble, and there is virtually nothing to see of the temple of Cybele.

Many of the ancient monuments that we see in Rome today were built after Paul's time; for example, the Colosseum[11], the Pantheon[12], the Baths of Caracalla, and the arches of Titus, Severus, and Constantine. The Mausoleum of Augustus, where his ashes were interred, existed in Paul's day in the northern part of the city, and its ruined site can be seen today. Nearby is the Altar of Peace (Ara Pacis) that the Roman Senate in 13 B.C. vowed to build to celebrate the peace that Augustus had brought to the empire. Although broken into fragments over the centuries the altar has been carefully reconstructed from the fragments and is now housed in a glass building. This altar is probably the one which is shown on a copper as of Nero (*RIC* I, 458). The coin has the bare head of Nero with his titles on the obverse, and on the reverse a rectangular structure with the words **ARA PACIS** below and the letters **SC** on either side. What is shown on the coin is the enclosing wall, not the actual altar.

Figure 108 – An as of Nero. (*RIC* I, 458)

The city centre of Rome was the Forum, which was situated in the level area between the Palatine Hill to the south, the Capitoline Hill to the west, and the Esquiline Hill to the east. In the Middle Ages when Rome had fallen into decline, this valley had become filled with earth and debris so that the ground was about fifteen metres above the level of the Forum that Paul knew. The medieval Romans called it Campo Vaccino (Cow Field). In the late nineteenth century excavations began in the area, and the earth has been removed down to the level of the paving stones on which Paul walked. It is now possible to walk through the Forum and imagine it as it was in Paul's time.

The main Forum Romanorum was a roughly rectangular, open space about 200 metres long which extended in a west-north-westerly direction to end at the foot of the Capitoline Hill. If Paul entered this area at its east end he would have seen on his left the round temple of Vesta, the goddess of the hearth. This small temple, originally encircled by a double row of Corinthian columns, was partially reconstructed in the 1930s. Its circular shape imitated the round huts in which the earliest Romans lived. An inner chamber contained certain sacred objects such as the wooden statue of Athena Pallas[13] which, it was believed, Aeneas had brought from Troy. In the middle of the temple a sacred fire was kept burning by the Vestal Virgins, the six priest-esses chosen from the noble families of Rome. South of the temple of Vesta was the large House of the Vestal Virgins where there were statues[14] of Vesta. Just north of the temple of Vesta was the small building which housed the office of the Pontifex Maximus (High Priest), who supervised the Vestal Virgins as well as the other priestly colleges. Presumably in this building were kept the insignia of his office such as the simpulum and lituus which Paul had seen on the coins of Pontius Pilate in Jerusalem. After Augustus the Roman emperor was also the Pontifex Maximus. The cult of Vesta promoted family life and patriotism and Caligula, as Pontifex Maximus, conferred the honours of Vestal Virgins on his three sisters and his grandmother Antonia. He issued an as (Sear 616) which shows the goddess Vesta on the reverse with the inscription VESTA SC. The obverse has the laureate head of Caligula with his titles.

Figure 109 – An as of Caligula. (Sear 616)

The temple of Vesta was damaged in the great fire of Rome which occurred in 64 A.D. Nero issued a denarius (Sear 676) to advertise his rebuilding of it, although this was not actually completed until Vespasian (Sear 783). Nero's coin shows the goddess seated in a hexastyle temple.

Just north-west of the temple of Vesta was an archway built by Augustus, and Paul may have passed under it to enter the Forum. This archway no longer exists. The northern side of the archway abutted the temple of Divus Julius (Divine Julius) which was built near the site of the funeral pyre of Julius Caesar. This temple stood on a platform the front part of which was concave and faced the Forum. In the concave recess stood a commemorative altar. The rubbly remains of this temple stand at the eastern end of the Forum. Although portraits of Julius Caesar feature on some early coins of Augustus, the name Caesar became a title of the emperor and was generally a part of the inscription on all Roman coins, although from the time of Vespasian it became an office inferior to that of the Augustus.

When Paul walked into the Forum and stood in its south-east end, immediately on his left was the temple of Castor and Pollux. This was an impressive temple and three tall columns are still standing. The divinities worshipped in this temple came to be identified with the Greek Dioscuri but, according to Pierre Grimal[15], the divinity originally worshipped there was probably an equestrian spirit, the patron of the equites (horsemen), the richest members of the armed forces. This temple was the sanctuary of the knights of the equestrian order and their records were kept there. Pontius Pilate was a member of this order and he had probably visited this temple on many occasions.

Behind the temple of Castor and Pollux, i.e. to the south of it, stood the temple of Augustus, which Tiberius had begun to build but Caligula completed. Next to the temple of Castor and Pollux and filling most of the southern side of the Forum was the Basilica[16] of Julius. This was a large covered area, 95 metres long and 47.5 metres wide. It had been planned by Julius Caesar, but actually built by Augustus who dedicated the building in 12 A.D. It served a variety of purposes including court proceedings, and Paul's own case could well have been heard here. Today the Basilica of Julius is an open space, although much of the stone floor is still in place.

Next to the Basilica of Julius, at the western end of the Forum, stood the great temple of Saturn. Saturn was equivalent to the Greek Kronos, the father of Zeus (Jupiter). The temple was the centre of the week-long festival known as the Saturnalia. It was held from 17 to 23 December, and was the merriest festival of the year. There was feasting and exchange of gifts. Presents were given to children. Paul would have been present in Rome during this festival, but little did he realise that it would eventually evolve into the festivities of Christmas.

The treasury of the Roman state was kept in the temple of Saturn. The Roman term for this treasury was aerarium, from the Latin word 'aes' meaning copper or some alloy of copper.

Most of the northern side of the Forum was taken up by the Basilica Aemilia, named after one of the Roman officials who was responsible for its construction. At first this area was a market for shopkeepers, particularly butchers. In the second century B.C. the shopkeepers were moved elsewhere and the area was devoted to financial matters. The bankers and moneychangers did their business there. During Paul's time a gold aureus equalled 25 silver denarii. A denarius equalled four brass sestertii. A sestertius equalled two brass dupondii. A dupondius equalled two copper asses. An as equalled two semis and a semi equalled two quadrantes. Nero struck an as, semi and quadrans in brass as well as copper. Today the Basilica Aemilia is an open area littered with stones and broken columns. Ros Belford[17] remarks, 'The usurers were still at work in the fifth century when the Goths invaded, and clearly carried on business till the last moment. The pavement is spotted with tiny splashes of rust and verdigris: the remains of coins'.

Next to the Basilica Aemilia, on its western side, was the Curia, the building in which the Roman Senate met. Julius Caesar had begun to construct a new Curia, but was assassinated[18] in 44 B.C. The new Curia was completed by the Triumvirs (Antony, Octavian, and Lepidus) and dedicated by Octavian in 29 B.C. This Curia Julia was burnt down in the reign of Carinus (283–285 A.D.) and rebuilt by Diocletian (284–305 A.D.). The Curia of Diocletian has been reconstructed and stands complete, an ugly brick building which gives the Forum a gloomy, austere appearance. The letters SC for Senatus Consulto (by decree of the Senate) appear on many Roman coins. From the time of Augustus, SC was used only on aes coinage minted at Rome, although the SC coinage of Antioch was an exception. During the first part of Nero's reign, i.e. from 54 to 62 A.D., no aes coinage was minted at Rome and the gold and silver coins struck there showed the letters EX SC. Although SC was common on Roman coins its precise significance is still not understood. It probably means that the Senate authorised the release from the treasury of the metal for that coin. On some coins, however, it seems that it may refer to the titles and honours which are inscribed on the coin.

Next to the Curia, near the northern end of the Forum, was the temple of Janus. Actually it was not a temple in the usual sense of the word but a ceremonial gateway through which people could enter the Forum. The passageway through it was closed at both ends by double doors. An image of Janus stood beside the passageway in a sort of chapel. The god had two faces which looked in opposite directions, in keeping with his function as god of doorways, of coming and going, of beginnings and endings. He was an ancient, exclusively Roman god who was invoked first in every undertaking, even before Jupiter. January, the first month of the year, was named after him. The gates of his temple were kept open in times of war apparently because of a legend that when Rome was being invaded by Sabine soldiers Janus sent a gush of boiling water to stop them. As Rome was nearly always at war somewhere, there were very few occasions when the doors of Janus were shut. Such an occasion occurred during the reign of Nero. Suetonius states that this occurred when Tiridates, the king of Armenia, visited Rome in 66 A.D., but it must have occurred earlier because sestertii exist which show the doors shut and have the inscription TR POT XI, i.e. 64/65 A.D. In any case the doors of Janus were probably open during the period 60–62 A.D. when Paul was in Rome. Nero struck aurei, denarii, sestertii, dupondii, and asses with the type of the temple of Janus with closed doors on the reverse, indicating that he was proud of this achievement. These coins have the head of Nero on the obverse, and on the reverse the Janus temple with the inscription PACE P R TERRA MARIQ PARTA IANVM CLVSIT (Peace being provided on land and sea for the Roman People he closed the Janus). The peace that the Romans provided enabled the gospel that Paul was preaching to spread throughout the known world.

Figure 110 – An as of Nero. (*RIC* I, 307)

On the north-west side of the Forum, at the foot of the Capitoline Hill, stood the temple of Concordia (Harmony). It faced the temple of Divus Julius at the other end of the Forum. Tiberius embellished the temple and built an arch in the corner of the Forum just south of the temple. Neither this arch nor the temple of Concord exist today, but the goddess Concordia features on the reverse of aurei and denarii of Nero. She is a seated figure who holds a cornucopia with her left arm and a patera in her outstretched right hand. The inscription on the reverse is CONCORDIA AVGVSTA (Augustan Harmony).

Figure 111 – An aureus of Nero. (*RIC* I, 48)

There is a sestertius of Tiberius (*RIC* I, 67) which shows the front of the temple of Concord. It is a hexastyle temple with the goddess within. The temple has flanking wings with statues of Hercules and Mercury on either side of the entrance stairway. On top of the building, above the pediment, are statues of Jupiter, Juno, and Minerva, as well as Victories and other figures.

Figure 112 – A sestertius of Tiberius. (*RIC* I, 67)

Casson[19] mentions that there were paintings by the famous Greek artist Zeuxis[20] in the temple of Concord. He says that the building was fitted with large windows presumably to enable visitors to see the art inside. If Paul had looked through the windows he would have seen the paintings. It is known[21] that one of these paintings was of the bound figure of Marsyas. Marsyas, whose name may have derived from a word meaning 'battler', was a Phrygian man who happened to find the flute that Athena invented. Athena saw a reflection of herself in water when she was playing the flute and was disgusted at the way it distorted her cheeks, so she threw it away and put a curse on whoever might find it. Marsyas was delighted with it and charmed the whole of Phrygia with his music. He challenged Apollo with his lyre to a contest. Apollo agreed on condition that the winner could impose any punishment he wished on the loser. Apollo won and tied Marsyas to a tree and flayed him alive. All the woodland spirits and deities were so saddened by the cruel death of Marsyas that their tears became the river Meander, which flows to the sea between Ephesus and Miletus. The very flute which Marsyas played was venerated in a temple of Apollo at Sicyon, 20 kilometres north-west of Corinth. To the Greeks and Romans of Paul's time the story of Marsyas was a warning of what happens to those who challenge the gods. Arrogant presumption results in severe punishment.

It might seem strange that a painting of such a distressing scene should be on display in the temple of the goddess of harmony. Plato, in his *Republic*, explains that the flute is an instrument which evokes the darker, Dionysian, unruly passions, as opposed to Apollo's lyre, which represents harmony. The precise, crystal-clear notes of the lyre are like light and reason, compared to the sonorous, soulful sound of the flute. They are as different as heaven and earth and it is not surprising that Marsyas was thought to be a follower of Cybele[22] whose devotees loved to play the flute and the tambourine. The flaying of Marsyas was a frequent theme in Hellenistic art; and according to Mercatante[23], the figure of Marsyas bound to a tree influenced many portrayals of the crucifixion of Christ. So here through the window of a temple in the heart of Rome Paul could see the precursor of the crucifix which was to dominate Christian art in later centuries. Perhaps the sight of the unfortunate Marsyas acted as a premonition of his own execution.[24]

Immediately behind the temple of Concordia, on the slope of the Capitoline Hill, was the Public Records Office, the Tabularium. It had been erected by Sulla in the first century B.C. to hold the state archives as well as the laws promulgated by the Roman Senate. The summit of the Capitoline Hill was crowned by two great temples, the temple of Juno Moneta and the temple of Jupiter Optimus Maximus (Best and Greatest). Minerva was also worshipped with Juno and Jupiter in a Capitoline triad.

The Temple of Juno Moneta stood on the northern part of the

hill. Juno, known to the Greeks as Hera, was the wife of Jupiter. The month of June was named after her. The epithet 'Moneta' is thought to derive from the Latin word 'moneo' meaning 'I advise' or 'warn', and it may have referred to the legend of the sacred geese who lived in the temple grounds and woke the guards with their honking when the Gauls tried to capture the Capitol in 390 B.C. The mint of Rome was set up next to the temple, and by the late Roman Empire the word moneta had come to mean 'money'.

Jupiter was the equivalent of the Greek Zeus. He was the head of the Roman Pantheon, an all-powerful figure like the patriarchal head of a Roman family. When a Roman general was awarded a triumph, or celebratory procession, he rode in a chariot followed by his soldiers, and proceeded to the Temple of Jupiter on the Capitol. There he sacrificed white bulls to the god and took the crown of laurel leaves from his head and placed it before the idol. This temple was the largest in central Italy. The rock platform on which it stood was 62 by 53 metres, and can still be seen. Nero minted an aureus and a denarius (*RIC* I, 52, 53) which has the god on the reverse. He is seated on a throne and holds a thunderbolt in his right hand and leans on a long sceptre. The thunderbolt indicates that Jupiter was originally a sky god, as does his other symbol, the eagle. On the reverse of Nero's coin is the inscription IVPPITER CVSTOS (Jupiter Guardian). The figure on this coin is the idol which stood in the Capitoline temple, because it is similar to the figure on a denarius of Vitellius (RSC 39) which has the inscription I O MAX CAPITOLINVS (Jupiter Optimus Maximus Capitolinus). The god looked out over the Forum and the palaces of the emperors, and the citizens of Rome looked up to his temple as the centre of their religious world.

Figure 113 – An aureus of Nero. (*RIC* I, 52)

When Paul came to Rome it was a city of many temples. These temples were maintained in good condition since the Senate in 28 B.C. authorised Augustus to renovate 82 temples in need of repair. The deities worshipped in the temples in Rome all had their own mythologies and cults, and the Romans explained their world in terms of these myths. With his Hellenistic background Paul would have known about all these gods and the myths associated with them. He would have seen them on the many coins he handled during his missionary journeys.

If myth is defined as story that attempts to explain the world and the mysteries of life, then Paul brought a new myth to Rome. This myth eventually displaced all the others, destroying the Roman gods and goddesses and shattering their temples. The old myths were not strong enough to compete with it. In this context myth does not mean something false but something which reflects the human condition and is therefore profoundly true. The myth that Paul brought to Rome and in which he passionately believed was that Jesus was the divinely inspired Messiah, the Son of God, who was crucified and resurrected. As he insists in his letter to the Romans, 'If you confess with your lips that Jesus is Lord and believe in your heart that God raised him from the dead, you will be saved' (Romans 10:9). For Paul and for all Christians Jesus triggered off the ultimate myth of the God-Man who suffers and comes through that suffering (Acts 26:23). The implication of this myth is that human life has a spiritual dimension which is motivated by Love and gives value to man and the creation.

Human life is conditioned by myth, and everywhere symbols reflect this aspect of life. Even on coins, ancient and modern, the symbols speak of the worldview of those who produce and use them. It is interesting to note that in all of Paul's writings he scarcely mentions the historical Jesus: what is important to him is the story of the crucifixion and resurrection of Christ. For Paul it was this mythical element that had eternal significance, and it was this Christ myth that he gave to the world. When Paul was in Rome he taught about Jesus Christ and the kingdom of God (Acts 28:31), but the emphasis would have been on Christ crucified (I Cor. 1:23), the symbol of his faith.

At the end of the book of Acts Luke states that Paul stayed for two whole years in Rome in his own rented house and welcomed all who came to see him (Acts 28:30). Luke does not say what happened after this, but the implication of his statement is that when Paul's case was eventually heard, he was acquitted. He probably then left Rome and continued his missionary journeys.[25]

Today on the Capitoline Hill stands the church of Saint Maria d'Aracoeli[26] on the site of the temple of Juno Moneta. It is lined with columns from the ancient buildings and contains 'il Bambino', a small wooden statue which represents the Christ-child, the one who is forever being born anew into the world. The Christ myth that Paul preached speaks to every age, but it must be responded to in the way in which it was given, not only with the intellect but with the emotions and the soul. What the world needs as it enters the third millennium after the birth of Christ is a re-mythologised gospel, a religion of hope, based on the Christian faith transmitted from the past but presented in terms that answer the deep questions and meet the spiritual longings of modern men and women.

I pray that you may have the power to comprehend,
with all the saints, what is the breadth and length and height and depth,
and to know the love of Christ that surpasses knowledge,
so that you may be filled with all the fullness of God.
Paul's letter to the Ephesians 3:18,19

Notes

Introduction

1 Acts 18:3. Bible references are from the New Revised Standard Version, World Bible Publishers, 1989.
2 1 Thessalonians 2:9.
3 Matthew 22:19; Mark 12:16; Luke 20:24.
4 Socrates, *Hist. Eccl.*, 3:17.
5 MacMullen, R., *Paganism in the Roman Empire*, Yale University Press, New Haven, 1981, p 25.
6 Butcher, K., *Roman Provincial Coins*, Seaby, London, 1988, p 25.
7 Mattingly, H., et al., *Roman Imperial Coinage*, 10 volumes, Spink, 1923–1994.
8 Burnett, A., Amandry, M., Ripolles, P., *Roman Provincial Coinage*, British Museum Press and Bibliotheque Nationale, London and Paris, Volume I, 1992.
9 Some scholars question the historical accuracy of the account of the events in Acts because it does not seem to correlate with aspects of Paul's authentic letters. The arguments are complex, but for our purposes the account in Acts will be accepted at face value and supplemented by information from the letters. According to Ben Witherington III (*The Paul Quest*, InterVarsity Press, Downers Grove and Leicester, 1998, p 10), because the Pauline letters are not by and large autobiographical in *subject matter*, it is a mistake to consider them an overwhelmingly more primary source for reconstructing a picture of the historical Paul than Acts.
10 The chronology of Paul's life is considered in some detail in *Dictionary of Paul and his Letters*, Editors: G.F. Hawthorne and R.P. Martin, InterVarsity Press, Downers Grove and Leicester, 1993.

1. Tarsus 5–10 A.D.

1 Galatians 1:13–14.
2 *The International Standard Bible Encyclopedia*, Vol. I (1979), p 689.
3 Bruce, F.F., *Paul: Apostle of the Free Spirit*, Paternoster Press, Exeter, 1980, p 37.
4 Murphy-O'Connor, J., *Paul, A Critical Life*, Clarendon Press, Oxford, 1996, p 8. This is an important study of Paul's life.
5 Acts 21:39a.

6   The nearby mound of Gözlü Tepe has been excavated and its Hellenistic and Roman levels revealed only a poor suburb of ancient Tarsus (Goldman, H., *Excavations at Gözlü Tepe, Tarsus*, 6 volumes, 1950–1963). In 1947 the digging for the construction of a courthouse unearthed a large Roman building decorated with mosaics. Also a small Roman theatre has been excavated and the remains of a huge temple foundation have been found (Blaiklock, E.M., and Harrison, R.K., editors, *The New International Dictionary of Biblical Archaeology*, Zondervan, Grand Rapids, 1983, p 435). Before Alexander's conquest the coins of Tarsus bore the image of the Baal of Tarsus; and afterwards, virtually the same image was used on Alexander's coins to represent Zeus. So the principal deity of Tarsus was probably this Baal/Zeus and the huge temple was most likely dedicated to him. We do not know if it was standing in Paul's time.

7   Morton, H.V., *In the Steps of St Paul*, 5th edition, Methuen, London, 1949, p 55.

8   *RPC* 4151–4160, GIC 106. Also in 5 B.C. Antioch issued a silver tetradrachm with the head of Augustus on the obverse and a seated Zeus on the reverse (*RPC* 4150). *RPC* considers this coin to be a forerunner of the Tyche series and different from the Zeus tetradrachms of uncertain mint issued early in the first decade A.D. (*RPC* 4108).

9   *RPC*, p 29, states that there is no hoard or find evidence for any significant circulation of denarii in Syria before the late first century A.D.

10 *RPC* 4136–4149, Sear 7214. The last Seleucid king of Syria was Antiochus XIII (69–64 B.C.), but the last substantial issue of Seleucid tetradrachms was made by Philip Philadelphus (92–83 B.C.) who was regarded by the Romans as the last legitimate king, and they preferred to revive his coinage.

11 *RPC* could find only one specimen in the museums surveyed. Unless otherwise stated, the terms 'rare' or 'common' will refer to the present day, but a coin which is rare today may have been common in ancient times and vice versa.

12 Marshall, I.H., *New Bible Dictionary*, IVP, Leicester, 1982, p 589.

13 *RPC* 4097. Goldman H., op. cit., plate 92, no. 283.

14 Ferguson, J., *The Religions of the Roman Empire*, Thames and Hudson, London, 1970, p 79.

15 Ramsay, W.M., *The Cities of St Paul*, Armstrong and Son, New York, 1908, p 238.

16 Ferguson, J., op. cit., p 79.

17 Romans 8:28a.

18 Ferguson, J., op. cit., p 85.

2. Jerusalem 10–36 A.D.

1   Tiberius took the side of Herod Antipas in his war against Aretas. Herod had divorced his wife, the daughter of Aretas, to marry his niece, Herodias. Aretas was incensed enough to wage war against Herod. Tiberius ordered Vitellius, the Roman governor of Syria and father of a future emperor, to lead the Roman army against Aretas, but the campaign was called off at the news of Tiberius' death in 37 A.D. Although there is no record of it, Caligula probably reversed Tiberius' decision, granting Damascus, which had been part of the Roman province of Syria, to Aretas, in keeping with his general policy of favouring client kingdoms. It is unlikely that Aretas would have forcibly taken Damascus from the Romans who were at this time an expanding military power. Moreover when Vitellius marched against Aretas, he proceeded towards Petra, Aretas' capital south of Judaea, not towards Damascus, which suggests Damascus was still in Roman hands.

2   It is generally thought that the inclusive method was more usual in the ancient world for reckoning a time interval in years. According to our modern exclusive method, three years from 37 A.D. would be 34 A.D., but according to the inclusive method

it would be 35 A.D. See Carson, D.A., Moo, D.J., and Morris, L., *An Introduction to the New Testament*, Zondervan, Grand Rapids, 1992, p 225.

3 Hendin, D., *Guide to Biblical Coins*, 3rd edition, Amphora, New York, 1996, p 287.

4 Perkin, H.W., in ISBE, Volume III, 1986, p 406.

5 The anchor was used as a symbol of the Seleucid empire since the founder of the dynasty, Seleucus I (312–280 B.C.), employed it as his personal signet, perhaps because he had an anchor-shaped birthmark, or because it was a reminder of his service as Ptolemy's admiral (Head, B.V., *Historia Numorum*, p 756).

6 Perkin, H.W., op. cit., p 406.

7 Romanoff, P., *Jewish Symbols on Ancient Jewish Coins*, American Israel Numismatic Association, New York, 1944, p 3. Hendin D., op. cit., pp 71–76, also discusses these symbols.

8 Romanoff, P., op. cit., p 27.

9 Josephus, *Jewish Antiquities*, XVII, 151.

10 Livia was also called Julia, and Caesar was the adopted name of her husband, Octavian. So the legend is IOVΛIA KAICAPOC.

11 Suetonius, *The Twelve Caesars*, Tiberius, 51.

12 Ceres was the Roman corn goddess. Her Greek equivalent was Demeter, an earth goddess, whose cult was centred on Eleusis where the Eleusian Mysteries were celebrated. These mysteries probably involved revelations of future life, symbolised by the return of Demeter's daughter, Persephone, to the upper world, and by the corn seed which is first buried in the earth before shooting up into new life. In Rome Tiberius built the foundations of a temple to Ceres, Liber, and Libera. The Roman earth god Liber and his female counterpart Libera were associated with Ceres and presented as a similar trio to the Demeter, Persephone, and Iacchos at Eleusis. At Rome sacrifices were made to Ceres to purify a house where a death had occurred.

13 Ferguson, J., op. cit., p 93.

14 The term 'Roman Imperial Coinage' means coins issued from Rome, and similar issues from more than 20 other mints throughout the Empire, during the period of the Roman Empire founded by Augustus. They bore Latin legends, portraits of the emperor or his relatives, and designs which were culturally Roman. They could be made of any of the usual coinage metals and were legal tender throughout the Roman Empire except in closed currency areas like Egypt.

15 Ariel, D.T., *A Survey of Coin Finds in Jerusalem*, Liber Annuus 32, 1982, pp 273–326.

16 *RPC*, p 12.

17 The term 'Tribute Penny' is used by numismatists to refer to the coin mentioned in the Bible. The translators of the King James Version of the Bible chose to translate 'denarius' as 'penny' because at that time the English penny was a silver coin of similar diameter to a denarius. This course taken by the translators of the King James Version only supports the concept of the use of a term familiar to the listeners or readers. 'Tribute' is better translated in today's English as 'tax'.

18 Lewis, P.E., 'The Actual Tribute Penny', *JNAA*, Volume 10, 1999. See also Lewis, P.E., 'The Tribute Penny in the Gospel of Thomas', *JNAA*, Volume 10, 1999.

19 Shore, H., 'The Real Tribute Penny', *Australian Coin Review*, Issue Number 377, December 1995, p 34.

20 Exodus 30:13.

21 The account in Matthew begins with verse 24: 'When they reached Capernaum, the collectors of the temple tax [literally the collectors of the didrachma] came to Peter and said, "Does your teacher not pay the temple tax [literally: the didrachma]?"' The account ends with Jesus saying, 'Go to the sea and cast a hook; take the first fish that comes up; and when you open its mouth, you will find a coin [literally: a stater]; take that and give it to them for you and me'. As the stater was to pay the temple tax,

i.e. the didrachma for two men, it must have been a Tyrian tetradrachm. Some commentators consider that Jesus did not intend that his instructions to Peter be taken literally. As the text does not indicate that Peter actually carried out Jesus' instructions, they suggest that Jesus was making a playful comment on the disciples' lack of money. William Barclay (The Gospel of Matthew, Volume 2, p 190) is probably nearer the mark when he proposes that Jesus simply meant that the disciples should earn the money through fishing. According to Barclay, Jesus was saying, 'Back to your job, Peter; that's the way to pay your debts'.

22 *RPC*, p 586.
23 Meshorer, Y., in *Studies in Honour of Leo Mildenberg*, edited by Houghton, A., et al., Wetteren, 1984, pp 171–180.
24 Levy, B., 'Tyrian Shekels: the Myth of the Jerusalem Mint', *JSAN*, Volume XIX, No. 2, 1995, p 33.
25 Ferguson, J., op. cit., p 43.

3. Damascus 36–38 A.D.

1 A map of the caravan routes in Nabataean times occurs in *New Bible Dictionary*, op. cit., p 807.
2 Morton, H.V., op. cit., p 38.
3 *The New International Dictionary of Bible Archaeology*, op. cit., p 148.
4 *RPC* 4793–4796.
5 *RPC* 4797–4802.
6 This legend occurs on all the Damascus coins of Tiberius. Paul would have noticed that under Tiberius the old forms of the letters sigma and omega were no longer used.
7 Matsson, G.O., *The Gods, Goddesses and Heroes on the Ancient Coins of Bible Lands*, Numismatiska Bokforlaget, Stockholm, 1969, p 110.
8 Actually Petra was neither rose-red nor very old. Although there are Palaeolithic remains in the vicinity, the Nabataean city dates from the fourth century B.C. This famous line comes from Dean Burton's beautiful poem *Petra* written in the nineteenth century.
9 Meshorer, Y., 'Nabataean Coins', *QEDEM, Monographs of the Institute of Archaeology*, No.3, Hebrew University of Jerusalem, 1975.
10 There are good grounds for this accusation, e.g. 'Let a woman learn in silence with full submission. I permit no woman to teach or to have authority over a man; she is to keep silent' (1 Tim. 2:11,12). Also see 1 Cor. 11:2–16 and 14:33–36.
11 Browning, I., *Petra*, Chatto and Windus, London, 1973, p 44.
12 Bruce, F.F., op. cit., p 81.
13 Stark, F., *Rome on the Euphrates*, John Murray, London, 1966, p 108.

4. Tarsus 38–45 A.D.

1 Ramsay, op. cit. p 219, tells a story, originally related by Dio Cassius (163–235 A.D.) which reveals a lot about Athenodorus: He chanced one day to enter the house of a noble Roman friend, and found the family in distress. An order had come from Augustus that the wife of this noble must go instantly to meet Augustus in the palace, and a closely covered litter was waiting to convey her. It was not doubtful that the purpose was a dishonourable one; but no one in this high-born family dared to think of disobeying the autocrat. It was the village-born philosopher who was bold enough to do so. Athenodorus immediately offered his services. He took her place in the litter, with a drawn sword in his hand. When he had been carried thus into Augustus's chamber and the litter was set down, he leapt out suddenly, sword in

hand, exclaiming, 'Are you not afraid lest someone may enter like this and assassinate you?' Augustus was impressed and Athendorus's influence increased.
2 Ramsay, op. cit. p 222.
3 Sydenham, E.A., *The Coinage of Caesarea in Cappadocia*, London, 1933, p 3.
4 Ramsay, op. cit., p 185.
5 *Larousse Encyclopedia of Mythology*, Hamlyn, London, 1959, p 114.
6 Ferguson, op. cit., p 16.
7 Ferguson, op. cit., p 19.
8 Chapter 1, footnote 6.
9 *New Dictionary of Theology*, IVP, Leicester, 1988, p 290.
10 Peters, F.E., *The Harvest of Hellenism*, Allen and Unwin, 1972, p 496.
11 Ramsay, op. cit., p 235.

5. Antioch 46 A.D.

1 Downey, G., *A History of Antioch in Syria from Seleucus to the Arab Conquest*, Princeton University Press, Princeton, 1961, p 287. This book is authoritative and comprehensive and has been used as the source for the historical information in this chapter.
2 Downey, op. cit., p 187.
3 *RPC*, p 620.
4 *RPC*, p 369.
5 Butcher, op. cit., p 100.

6. Seleucia 47 A.D.

1 Head. B., *Historia Numorum*, Clarendon Press, Oxford, 1910, p 783.
2 Bromiley, G.W., Editor, *The International Standard Bible Encyclopedia*, Volume 4, Eerdmans, Grand Rapids, 1988, p 384.
3 Morton, H.V., *In the Steps of St Paul*, Methuen, London, 1936, p 99.
4 Brosnahan, T., *Turkey, a travel survival kit*, Lonely Planet, Hawthorn, 1993, p 504.
5 Morton, H.V., op. cit., p 101.
6 Walker, D.R., *The Metrology of the Roman Silver Coinage*, Part 1, BAR Sup. 5, 1976, p 65.
7 *RPC*, p 631.
8 From Appian's book *Syria*, section 24. The Greek text of this passage is in Head, op. cit., p 783.
9 The name 'Daphne' means laurel tree, and there was a Greek myth about a beautiful nymph who was pursued by Apollo but changed into a laurel tree when he overtook her. Hence the favourite tree of Apollo is the laurel, and he wears the leaves on his head.
10 Matsson, G.O., *The Gods, Goddesses and Heroes on the Ancient Coins of Bible Lands*, Stockholm, 1969, p 11.
11 At Delphi in Greece the priestess of Apollo prophesied when sitting near or on a tripod.

7. Cyprus 47 A.D.

1 It is not clear from the text whether the fourteen years should be counted from Paul's conversion or from his brief visit to Judaea after his escape from Damascus. The former is considered more likely by the *International Standard Bible Encyclopedia*, Chronology of the New Testament, Volume 1, p 689, and this is the chronology followed here. Actually the chronology of the early part of Paul's career depends very much on whether the visit to Jerusalem of Galatians 2:1–10 refers to the famine-relief visit of Acts 11:27–30 or to the visit for the Apostolic Council related in Acts 15. The latter is more likely as the famine relief probably consisted of food, like the corn

and figs sent by Queen Helena of Adiabene to the Jews, and these provisions would have been accompanied by Paul, a Roman citizen, as far as the Judaean border where he would have been met by Christian elders. It is significant that Acts 11:27–30 does not state that Paul actually went to Jerusalem. Paul probably wrote his letter to the Galatians soon after the Apostolic Council and before he revisited the area on his second missionary journey. So he writes a passionate letter reflecting the heated debate of the Council, unlike Luke's white-washed account written many years later. Paul's letter was meant for the Christians in the cities of South Galatia (Pisidian Antioch, Iconium, and Lystra). North Galatia was a remote area.

2   See *Some Archaeological Observations on Paul's First Missionary Journey* by B. Van Elderen, in *Apostolic History and the Gospel*, eds. W.W. Gasque and R.P. Martin, Paternoster Press, Exeter, 1970.

3   There is a description and map of the ruins of Salamis in *Cyprus: from the Stone Age to the Romans*, by V. Karageorghis, Thames and Hudson, London, 1982.

4   'What a disappointing site it is! There are a few stones, mostly the bases of statues standing on a slight hill some distance from the sea. It is impossible to make anything of them or to gain an idea of the temple that once stood there.' H.V. Morton, op. cit., p 139.

5   Tacitus, *The Annals of Imperial Rome*, translated by Michael Grant, Penguin, 1975, p 158.

6   Suetonius, *The Twelve Caesars*, Tiberius, 52.

7   Tacitus, op. cit., p 158.

8   Paper presented by Dr Mehmet Taslianlan at Macquarie University on 12 May 2000. Dr Taslianlan is Supervisor of Excavations at the site of Pisidian Antioch and Director of the Museum at nearby Yalvaç.

8. Perga 48 A.D.

1   See *The Cities of the Eastern Roman Provinces*, by A.H.M. Jones, Clarendon Press, Oxford, 1971. According to *RPC*, p 535, the Romans annexed Lycia in 43 A.D. and Pamphylia was detached from the Roman province of Galatia and joined with Lycia to make the new province of Lycia-and-Pamphylia. Pamphylia was returned to Galatia in the 50s when Cappadocia was also added, thus making a huge province covering most of central and eastern Anatolia. This lasted for about ten years when Cappadocia was detached and Pamphylia returned to its previous province with Lycia. So, in 48 A.D., Pamphylia was part of the Roman province of Lycia-and-Pamphylia.

2   The ruins of Perga are described in *Classical Turkey*, by John Freely, Penguin, London, p 126; and there is a map of the ancient city in *Turkey, a Travel Survival Kit*, by Tom Brosnahan, Lonely Planet, Hawthorn, 1993.

3   Originally the Greek goddess Artemis was an agricultural deity concerned with forests and hunting. From the beginning she was associated with her twin brother, Apollo, and participated in his nature. So, just as Apollo was a divinity of light, especially sunlight, Artemis was the goddess of moonlight, and in this capacity she is shown holding a flaming torch. This light-giving function was gradually taken over by a separate moon goddess, Selene.

4   Matsson, op. cit., p 20.

9. Pisidian Antioch 48 A.D.

1   Ramsay, op. cit., p 247.

2   This temple with its image of Mên is shown on a coin of Gordian III (238–244 A.D.). The coin is figure 265 in *Coins and their Cities* by M.G. Price and B.L. Trell, Vecchi & Sons, London, 1977.

3 Ramsay, op. cit., p 287.
4 Morton, op. cit., p 183.
5 *RPC*, op. cit., p 541.
6 *RPC*, op. cit., p 29.
7 Sydenham, op. cit., p 2.
8 Sydenham, op. cit., p 8.
9 Sydenham, op. cit., p 13.
10 Sydenham, op. cit., p 20.
11 *Corpus Nummorum Romanorum*, 18 volumes, edited by Banti, A., and Simonetti, L., Firenze, 1972–1979, Vol. XI, p 63.
12 Tacitus, op. cit., p 162.
13 Caligula's mother, Agrippina, was the daughter of Agrippa and Julia, who was the daughter of Octavian.
14 Suetonius, op. cit., p 205.
15 The analysis of this Latin phrase is that the preposition 'de' means 'concerning' and is followed by the ablative case. 'Britannis' is the ablative case, plural, of the adjective, 'Britannus, -a, -um', which means 'British', according to the *Latin Dictionary* by Lewis and Short, Clarendon Press, Oxford, 1879.
16 Ramsay, op. cit., p 426.
17 Suetonius, op. cit., p 206.
18 See Romans 13:1–7.

10. Iconium 48 A.D.
1 Ramsay, op. cit., p 326.
2 Ramsay, op.cit., p 369.
3 Ramsay, op. cit., p 357.
4 Ramsay, op. cit., p 327.
5 Tacitus, op. cit., p 253
6 Scullard, H.H., *From the Gracchi to Nero: A History of Rome from 133 B.C. to A.D. 68*, Methuen, New York, 5th edition, 1982, p 303.
7 Kinross, Lord, *Within the Taurus: A Journey in Asiatic Turkey*, Murray, London, 1954, p 175.
8 Ramsay, op. cit., p 330.
9 Jones, J.M., *A Dictionary of Ancient Greek Coins*, Seaby, London, p 164.
10 Stapleton, M., *The Hamlyn Concise Dictionary of Greek and Roman Mythology*, Hamlyn, London, 1982, p 116.
11 Ferguson, op. cit., p 135.

11. Lystra 48 A.D.
1 Ramsay, op. cit., p 408.
2 LaSor, W.S., in *The International Standard Bible Encyclopedia*, Volume 3, p 188.
3 From the translation in Morton, op. cit., p 199.
4 Ramsay, op. cit., p 142.
5 Ramsay, op. cit., p 141.
6 Morton, op. cit., p 201.
7 Ramsay, op. cit., p 411.
8 There is a photograph of the stone in Morton, op. cit., between pages 200 and 201. The stone now stands in the Museum for Classical Antiquities at Konya.
9 A statue of Concord (Harmony) sent by Lystra in the second century A.D. to its sister colony of Pisidian Antioch has been recovered. *The International Standard Bible Encyclopedia*, Volume 3, p 193.
10 Ferguson, op. cit., p 25.

12. Derbe 48 A.D.

1 For example the map on p 628 of *Greek Imperial Coins* by D.R. Sear, Seaby, London, 1982. The map in Jones, A.H.M., op.cit., is correct.
2 Ballance, M., *Anatolian Studies* 7, 1957, pp 147–51.
3 Van Elderen, op. cit., p 158.
4 Ballance, M., *Anatolian Studies* 14, 1964, pp 139–40.
5 Jones, A.H.M., op. cit., p 133
6 Jones, A.H.M., op. cit., p 133
7 Magie, D., *Roman Rule in Asia Minor*, Princeton University Press, 1950, p 1368. Magie says that in the lists (Volume 6, 16) of Ptolemy, the Egyptian geographer of the second century A.D., there is a military district (strategia) of Cappadocia called Antiochiane, situated in the part of Lycaonia just north of Cilicia and containing the cities of Laranda and Derbe. Presumably this district had been subject to Antiochus IV whose name had subsequently been given to it.
8 Head, op. cit., p 775. The signs of the Zodiac were important to the kings of Commagene. Antiochus I (c. 69–31 B.C.) who ruled Commagene at the zenith of its power was born under the sign of the Lion, and on the reliefs at his mausoleum on the top of Nimrud Dagh (Nemrut Dagi), a mountain in south-east Turkey, he wears an Armenian-type tiara ornamented with a lion.
9 Lindgren, H.C., and Kovacs, F.L., *Ancient Bronze Coins of Asia and the Levant*, 1985.
10 The star sign of Capricorn (Latin: goat-horned) governs the period 22 December to 19 January. It is a peculiar animal with the foreparts of a goat and the hindpart of a fish. Its strange form is explained by a Greek myth which relates how the god Pan was in the process of changing into an animal when he was frightened by a monster and jumped into the water, whereupon the part of him above water changed into a goat while the part below changed into a fish.
11 Augustus was born on 23 September and his victory at Actium occurred on 2 September but Capricorn does not govern these dates. J.M. Jones (*A Dictionary of Ancient Roman Coins*, Seaby, London, 1990) explains that, according to an astronomical work written about the time of Tiberius' reign, the moon, not the sun, determined the signs of the Zodiac at that time, and the moon was in Capricorn at that time.
12 According to Sear (*GIC*, p 544) the Armenian tiara may refer to Antiochus' acquisition of part of Armenia in 60 A.D. in reward for services rendered to the Roman general Corbulo against the Parthians, but this type of pointed headdress may simply have been favoured by rulers in this part of the world and may not have referred directly to Armenia.
13 Cornucopias were commonly used in antiquity to symbolise fertility and abundance, but are rarely seen today. Similarly, the swaddling of infants is no longer practised today, but the human-headed cornucopias may have appealed to the ancient mind as a sort of fusion of fertility and swaddled infants.
14 Paul's two questions in this statement may allude to Hosea 13:14. Nevertheless the scorpion of Commagene could well have prompted Paul to ask the questions.

13. Attalia 48 A.D.

1 Jones, A.H.M., op. cit., p 129.
2 Jones, A.H.M., op. cit., p 130.
3 Matsson, op. cit., p 33.
4 Ferguson, op. cit., p 23.
5 Ferguson, op. cit., p 13.
6 Smith, W., *A Smaller Classical Dictionary*, Murray, London, 1880. Reprinted 1996 by Wordsworth Editions, Ware.

14. Antioch and Jerusalem 49 A.D.

1 Chapter 7, end note 1.
2 *The Penguin Dictionary of Ancient History*, ed. Speake, G., Penguin, London, 1994, p 487.
3 Hendin, D., op. cit., p 159, Errata.
4 Four of the five coins are in Sear, D.R., *Greek Imperial Coins*, Seaby, 1982; numbers 5567, 5568, 5569, 5570.
5 Bruce, F.F., in *New Bible Commentary*, Guthrie, D. and Motyer, J.A., (eds) IVP, 1970, p 1163.

15. Troas 49 A.D.

1 Magie, D., op.cit., p 472.
2 Freely, J., *Classical Turkey*, Penguin, London, p 19.
3 Brosnahan, T., *Turkey, a Travel Survival Kit*, Lonely Planet, Hawthorn, 1993, p 286.
4 Borchert, G.L., in *ISBE*, Volume 4, p 923.
5 Jones, J.M., *A Dictionary of Ancient Greek Coins*, Seaby, London, 1986, p 21.
6 *Larousse Encyclopedia of Mythology*, Hamlyn, London, 1959, p 120.
7 Matsson, op. cit., p 10.
8 *RPC* p 365. Five possible arrangements are listed: traditional tribal region (Troas, Ionia, etc.); Roman conventus or administrative district; style; patterns of circulation; cultural groupings. According to *RPC* there is too little information about patterns of circulation and coin finds have not shown that the conventus explains the pattern of circulation.
9 'Cistophoros' means basket-bearer, and the term was applied to silver coins which bore on the obverse the cista mystica or basket used in the mystical rites of Dionysus. The basket was shown with its lid open and a snake sliding out of it. The coins were issued by the kings of Pergamum in the second century B.C., but under the early Roman empire coins of the same weight were still called cistophori even though they had different types on the obverse.
10 Apollonos Smintheus. The first letter of Smintheus is the archaic form of the Greek letter zeta, which is equivalent to the English letter Z. It looks like 'I' with a bar at each end. Also note that there is no 'N' before the Greek letter theta, so the zeta before 'M' may indicate an 'N' sound before the following consonant.
11 Smith, W., op. cit., p 43.
12 Matsson, op. cit., p 11.

16. Philippi 50 A.D.

1 Bruce, F.F., *The Book of the Acts*, Eerdmans, Grand Rapids, 1988, p 351.
2 Blaicklock, E.M., and Harrison, R.K., op. cit., p 331.
3 C. Cavedoni, writing in the *Naples Archaeological Bulletin* (August, 1855) and quoted by *CNR* (Volume VII, p 186), says that the lateral altars had been erected by Mark Antony in the encampments situated along the road from Philippi to Amphipolis prior to the battle of Actium and that these altars still existed during the reign of Tiberius.
4 The praetorian guard was the Roman Emperor's bodyguard. In 27 B.C. it was organised by Augustus into nine cohorts, each consisting of 500 veteran soldiers. Under Caligula the number of praetorian cohorts was increased to twelve. Sejanus, the prefect (or commander) of the praetorian guard under Tiberius, concentrated the cohorts in a single camp just outside Rome and this enabled them to become politically very powerful, and both Caligula and Claudius were installed by the praetorian guard.
5 Blaiklock, E.M. and Harrison, R.K. op. cit., p 362.

17. Amphipolis and Apollonia 50 A.D.

1 Bruce, F.F., *The Book of the Acts*, op. cit., p 322.
2 Head, op. cit., p 215, says that the magnificent series of full-face heads of Apollo on the coins of Amphipolis, as works of art, perhaps excel the types of any other city of Northern Greece. So Amphipolis would have had a tradition of producing quality coins, and there could well have been a family of master engravers who called this city home.
3 Ferguson, J., op. cit., p 113.
4 *Liddell and Scott's Abridged Greek-English Lexicon*, Clarendon Press, Oxford, 1871, p 693.
5 Jones, J.M., *A Dictionary of Ancient Greek Coins*, op. cit., p 28.
6 It is an interesting fact that the reverse showing Artemis Tauropolis is similar to that on contemporary coins of Sidon showing Europa riding a bull (compare figures 49 and 100). According to Greek legend Europa was abducted from Phoenicia by Zeus in the form of a bull. King Minos of Crete was the son of Europa and Zeus, and his daughter, Ariadne, had several sons by Dionysos, the god of wine. These sons became the ancestors of tribes living on certain Aegean islands and on the north Aegean coast. One of these ancestors was Tauropolis (Graves, op. cit., 27.8). Ariadne, Europa and Artemis should all be regarded as manifestations of the moon goddess, who in turn is a manifestation of the Great Mother. The Great Mother was very important in Phoenician and Cretan religion. In Crete her cult involved young men and women leaping over a bull, which was later sacrificed. The type of a woman riding a bull and holding up a veil which encircles her head represents the moon goddess surrounded by the firmament of stars. The bull represents the sun.
7 *RPC*, p 43.
8 Head, op. cit., p 204, says Imhoof's attribution of certain coins inscribed ΑΠΟΛΛΩΝΟΣ to the Apollonia south of Lake Volvi is very doubtful. Despite the inscription the head on the obverse is that of Dionysus as it is crowned with ivy. The situation is complicated because there were several cities in the ancient world called Apollonia and three of them were in Macedonia.
9 Coins minted in Rome will be dealt with in the chapter entitled 'Rome'.
10 Stapleton, op. cit., p 37.

18. Thessalonica and Beroea 50 A.D.

1 *RPC* p 288.
2 Sear, D.R., *Greek Coins and their Values*, Volume I, Seaby, 1978, p xxiii.
3 Stevenson, S.W., *A Dictionary of Roman Coins*, Bell, 1889, reprinted by Seaby, 1982, p 55.
4 Suetonius, op. cit., p 165.
5 According to the Roman poet Virgil (Eclogues 4: 1–62), a golden age had been ushered in by Augustus. Not only did Augustus bring peace to the Roman world but an era of prosperity and promise had been inaugurated. According to J.R. Harrison (*Paul, Eschatology and the Augustan Age of Grace*, Tyndale Bulletin 50/1, 1999, pp 79–91) an overpowering sense of eschatological destiny had gripped the minds of the contemporaries of Augustus when they honoured him, and he suggests that, by the time of Paul, Romans were confronted by two competing eschatological hopes: the imperial version of Augustan beneficence, and Christ's reign of grace (Romans 521). The fact that Augustus built a temple to Julius Caesar in Thessalonica testifies to the importance of the imperial cult there, and several scholars consider that the popular slogan, 'Peace and Security' (I Thessalonians 5:3), referred to the imperial cult. Pax and Securitas are common types on imperial coins. In view of the strength of the Augustan ideology it is not surprising that Paul had to flee the city.

6   The politarchs (Acts 17:6) were the city magistrates. The title is attested on inscriptions from Thessalonica and other Macedonian cities.

7   *RPC* p 303.

19. Athens 50 A.D.

1   Morton, op. cit., p 268.

2   According to *ISBE*, Volume I, p 287, there were two traditions as to how the hill got its name. Areopagus may mean 'hill of Ares', the god of war, or it may mean 'hill of the Arai'. The Arai, more popularly known as the Furies, were goddesses whose task was avenging murder.

3   *ISBE*, Volume I, p 288.

4   Thompson, H.A., and Wycherley, R.E., *The Agora of Athens*, 1972.

5   Head, op. cit., p 389.

6   Pausanias, Book I, 24:5.

7   Kroll, J.H., *The Athenian Agora*, Volume XXVI (the Greek Coins), Princeton, 1993.

8   Suetonius (Augustus: 50) states, 'The first seal Augustus used for safe-conducts, dispatches, and private letters was a sphinx; next came a head of Alexander the Great; lastly, his own head, cut by Dioscurides, the seal which his successors continued to employ'. The sphinx was a mythical creature which the Greeks had taken over from the Egyptians, and it was said that Augustus stopped using the sphinx signet because of its unpleasant associations with Egypt and Cleopatra, and because the sphinx was associated with dark, riddling prophecies (Jones, *A Dictionary of Ancient Roman Coins*, p 295.)

9   Jones, op. cit., (Greek Coins), p 172.

20. Corinth October 50 A.D. to April 52 A.D.

1   This fragmentary inscription has the number XXVI in the title of Claudius, referring to the 26th acclamation of him as imperator, i.e. 52 A.D., before August. After August his inscriptions have XXVII. In the inscription Claudius refers to 'my friend Gallio, proconsul of Achaia' in terms which suggest that Gallio has recently held the office but no longer holds it. As Gallio would have held the office for only a year (or perhaps less as Seneca says he left Achaia because of a fever) a reasonable estimate for the beginning of his period of duty is June 51 A.D. This date is favoured by Bruce (op. cit. Acts) and *ISBE*.

2   Bruce, *The Book of the Acts*, op. cit., p 351.

3   Murphy-O'Connor, J., op. cit., p 14.

4   The coin is figure 152 in Price, M.J., and Trell, B.L., *Coins and their Cities*, Vecchi and Sons, London, 1977.

5   Peirene was a nymph whose tears at the death of her son were so abundant that she was changed into a fountain.

6   Price and Trell, op. cit., p 81.

7   Tritons were mythical beings who were men in the upper part of their bodies and fish in the lower part. They were the sons of Poseidon and at the command of Poseidon they blow their shell trumpets to soothe the restless waves of the sea.

8   Vos, H.V., *Archaeology in Bible Lands*, Moody Press, Chicago, 1977, p 356.

9   According to Mattson, op. cit., 'His offspring were, generally, either rough and brutal men or monsters ... On the whole the impression of this god that one receives, while it reflects strength, leaves one with the feeling that he was not one of the more admirable deities.'

10   Poseidon was the father of Pegasos, the winged horse. In the form of a stallion he seduced the beautiful maiden Medusa in the precincts of a temple of Athena. The goddess was furious and changed the hair of Medusa into snakes. When Perseus

decapitated Medusa Pegasos sprang from her blood. The 'asos' ending of Pegasos is not Greek and the idea of a winged horse may have come from the east. Hippocamps feature on coins of Phoenicia and horses are very prominent on the coins of Carthage, a Phoenician foundation.

11 Cadmus was the son of Agenor, king of Phoenicia. His sister was Europa who was carried off to Crete by Zeus in the form of a bull. Agenor sent Cadmus in search of her, but unable to find her he settled in Greece founding the city of Thebes.

12 Price and Trell, op. cit., p 86.

13 Pentheus in Greek means 'grief'.

14 Graves, Robert, *The Greek Myths*, Penguin Books, Revised Edition, 1960. See 71.4 (p 233) and 156.2 (p 256).

15 There is little doubt about this. At Carthage thousands of urns containing the burned bones of children have been found in the Sanctuary of Tanit, and similar findings have been made in other Phoenician cities in North Africa. The children were sacrificed to the god Baal, but the goddess Tanit was described as the 'face of Baal' (Larousse, p 85).

16 This bronze coinage has been studied by Amandry, M., *Le Connayage des duovirs corinthiens*, BCH Supp. XV (1988).

17 Acts 18:3. They were probably more than tent-makers. Bruce suggests leather-workers, but their work probably involved the repair of sails, a skill no doubt in demand in Corinth.

18 *RPC*, p 246.

19 *RPC*, p 246.

20 (i) Agrippa Postumus. He was the youngest son of Augustus' daughter, Julia, and his friend Agrippa. He was born in 12 B.C. His two elder brothers Caius and Lucius died in 4 A.D. and 2 A.D. respectively. In 4 A.D he and Tiberius were adopted by Augustus, and Corinth issued coins in honour of Agrippa Postumus, Tiberius, Drusus Minor (Tiberius' son), and Germanicus (Tiberius' nephew whom he adopted in 4 A.D.). Therefore all of these coins have the surname Caesar in the inscription. When Augustus died in 14 A.D. Tiberius had Agrippa Postumus murdered. Stevenson (op. cit.) says that this is the only coin of Agrippa Postumus but *CNR* lists also a coin of Pella in Macedonia and a coin of Apameia in Bithynia. (ii) Tiberius. (iii) Drusus Minor. (iv) Germanicus.

21 Stevenson, op. cit., p 282.

22 (i) Julius Caesar, who had adopted Augustus in 44 B.C. (ii) Caius and Lucius, grandsons of Augustus.

23 M ANTONIO HIPPARC (M. Antonius Hipparchus) and M NOVIO BASSO (M. Novius Bassus). In Roman colonies the governing authority was often a pair of magistrates and this system was probably modelled on the two consuls at Rome.

24 (i) Livia, as Pietas or Salus. (ii) Augustus, radiate. (iii) ?Drusus Minor.

25 A staff surmounted by a pine cone or a bunch of ivy leaves. It was carried by Bacchus (Dionysus), the god of wine, or his associates. Stevenson (op. cit.) says that it was the custom of his votaries at their sacrificial feasts to have the thyrsus borne in triumphant procession by the Bacchantes, who employed it in the frenzied ceremonies of their wild and licentious worship. According to Larousse (op. cit.) the cult of Bacchus involved human sacrifice at Boeotia, Chios and Lesbos, but it was later replaced by flagellation. Bacchus was the son of Semele who was one of the sisters of Ino, the mother of Melicertes.

26 (i) Livia. (ii) Caligula and Tiberius Gemellus, who was the son of Drusus Minor and grandson of Tiberius. Gemellus was born in 19 A.D. When Drusus died in 23 A.D. he was designated to succeed Tiberius but Caligula had him murdered in 37 A.D.

27 LABE PEREG IIVIR for L. Furius Labeo and L. Arrius Peregrinus, duovirs.

28 L ARRIO PEREGRIN IIV (to or by L. Arrius Peregrinus, duovir).

29 L FVRIO LABEONE IIV (to or by L. Furius Labeo, duovir).
30 These were the sons of Germanicus and Agrippina Senior, and the brothers of
    Caligula. They died in 31 A.D. and 33 A.D. respectively and are honoured here
    posthumously by their brother.
31 (i) Agrippina Senior, Caligula's mother. (ii) Germanicus, Caligula's father. (iii)
    Antonia Junior, Caligula's grandmother
32 P VIPSANIO AGRIPPA IIV (P. Vispanius Agrippa, duovir) or M BELLIO
    PROCVLO IIV (M. Bellius Proculus, duovir).
33 FLAM RE IIVIR for L. Paconius Flam and Cn. Publicius Regulus, duovirs.
34 LICINO ITER OCTAVIO IIVIR for Licinius again (or for a second time) and
    Octavius, duovirs.

21. Cenchreae, Ephesus, Jerusalem, Antioch 52 A.D.

1   A lituus was a curved staff used by an augur in his divinations. On this coin it may
    indicate that the office of augur was given to Nero.
2   A simpulum was a ladle used by a priest in sacrificial ceremonies. On this coin it may
    indicate that the office of priest was given to Nero.
3   Tradition asserts that Paul was killed during the persecution under Nero that
    occurred in 64 A.D. As a Roman citizen Paul would have been executed by
    beheading with a sword.

22. Ephesus 53–54 A.D.

1   Vos, H.V., op. cit., p 318.
2   Robert Graves (*The Greek Myths*, 2 Volumes, Penguin, 1948) suggests that the
    Amazons were originally the priestesses of the local moon goddess who resisted the
    coming of new gods with the arrival of the Greeks in Ionia. They probably even bore
    arms, giving rise to the myth of a race of warrior women. According to the Larousse
    Encyclopedia of Mythology (p 132) the early Greeks thought the name Amazon
    meant 'no breast', and explained that they removed the right breast to draw a bow
    more easily; but probably the prefix 'a' is augmentative referring to the multiple
    breasts of the goddess.
3   Yamauchi, E.M., *The Archaeology of New Testament Cities in Western Asia Minor*,
    Pickering and Inglis, Glasgow, 1980, p 79.
4   Ibid, p 103.
5   One of these column bases can be seen in the British Museum. Although badly
    damaged it still evinces the skill of the sculptor and the greatness of the temple of
    Artemis at Ephesus.
6   See for example G.K. Jenkins, *Ancient Greek Coins*, Seaby, London, 1990, p 13.
7   Yamauchi, E.M. op. cit., p 104.
8   Price and Trell, op. cit., p 130.
9   The pediment in a Greek temple was the triangular area crowning the front of the
    building below the roof.
10 Two fine marble examples can be seen in the Ephesus Museum at Seljuk near
    Ephesus.
11 According to Head, op. cit., p 571, Artemis was considered to be the queen bee and
    her priestesses (melissae) the honey bees. From about 600 B.C. to 85 B.C. the bee
    appears regularly on Ephesian coinage.
12 Temple keeper in Greek is ΝΕΩΚΟΡΟΣ which literally means temple sweeper.
    This word sometimes appears on later coins of Ephesus, e.g. Sear 1409, a coin of
    Antoninus Pius.
13 Sutherland, C.H.V., *The Emperor and the Coinage*, Spink and Son, London, 1976, p 81.
14 Ibid, p 85.

15 Ibid, p 81.

16 *RPC*, p 368.

17 Sutherland, C.H.V., *The Cistophori of Augustus*, RNS Special Publication No. 5, London, 1970.

18 Jones, J.M., *A Dictionary of Ancient Roman Coins*, p 294. Suetonius, op. cit., p 83, says that the first seal Augustus used for safe-conducts, dispatches and private letters was a sphinx; next came a head of Alexander the Great; lastly, his own head, cut by Dioscurides, the seal which his successors continued to employ.

19 According to Suetonius, op. cit., p 107, Theogenes the astrologer predicted such a great future for Augustus that he struck a silver coin stamped with Capricorn, the sign under which he had been born. This coin is probably the denarius Sear 477.

20 Foss, C., *Roman Historical Coins*, Seaby, London, 1990, p 49.

21 *Corpus Nummorum Romanorum*, Volume V, p 100.

22 Jones, J.M., *A Dictionary of Ancient Roman Coins*, p 65.

23 Ibid., p 175.

24 Sutherland, C.H.V., *The Emperor and the Coinage*, p 84.

25 Mattingly, H., quoted in *RPC*, p 380.

26 The CA coinage was an extensive series of brass and bronze coins which circulated in Asia, northern Syria and Cyprus. These coins are distinguished by a large CA within a laurel wreath on the reverse, and a head of Augustus on the obverse. The meaning of CA is disputed but it is probably an abbreviation for Commune Asiae.

27 Bruce, F.F., *The Book of the Acts*, Eerdmans, Grand Rapids, 1988, p 377.

28 Walls, A.F., *New Bible Dictionary*, IVP, Leicester, 1982, p 24.

29 Bruce, F.F., *The Book of the Acts*, p 376.

30 Bruce, F.F., *New Bible Dictionary*, p 12.

31 There is a detailed discussion of the term ΕΠΙΣΚΟΠΟΣ in *Theological Dictionary of the New Testament* by Gerhard Kittel, translated by G.W. Bromley, Eerdmans, Grand Rapids, 1964, Volume 2, p 608. Kittel mentions that the second century A.D. historian Appian tells us in his history of Rome (Mithridateios, 48) that Mithridates VI (120–63 B.C.) appointed a certain Philopoimen to be ΕΠΙΣΚΟΠΟΣ ΕΦΕΣΙΩΝ (Supervisor of the Ephesians). Kittel also discusses this coin (*RPC* 2623), listing three German references.

32 For example Philippians 1:1.

23. Macedonia, Greece, Troas 55–57 A.D.

1 Carson, D.A., et al., *An Introduction to the New Testament*, Zondervan, Grand Rapids, 1992, p 242.

2 Bruce, F.F., *The Book of the Acts*, Eerdmans, Grand Rapids, 1992, p 381.

3 For example *The International Standard Bible Encyclopedia*, Volume 1, p 691.

4 Ramsay, W.M., *Pauline and Other Studies in Early Christian History*, London 1907, pp 348ff.

5 Carson, D.A., et al., op. cit., p 230.

6 Bruce, F.F., op. cit., p 449.

7 *RPC*, p 303.

8 Tacitus, op. cit., p 343.

9 Stevenson, S.W., op. cit., p 409.

10 In *Roman Coins and their values*, by David Sear, the figure on the reverse of the coin with Octavia on the obverse (Sear 712) is said to be female. However, the Latin word 'genius' is masculine, and the figure on the photographed coin in *RPC* seems to be male.

11 Jones, J.M., *A Dictionary of Ancient Roman Coins*, p 236.

12 Bruce, F.F., op. cit., p 384.

Notes

24. Assos 57 A.D.

1 Murphy-O'Connor (op. cit., p 345) mentions the gold daric as one of the few internationally accepted currencies, and cites Casson (op. cit., p 75) as the reference; but Casson was discussing the coinage of an earlier era and darics would not have been circulating in Paul's time.

2 Burnett, A., *Coinage in the Roman World*, Seaby, London, 1987, p 50.

3 Casson, L., *Travel in the Ancient World*, Allen and Unwin, London, 1974, p 176. When Jesus sends his twelve disciples to preach in various towns in Palestine he says, 'Take no gold, or silver, or copper in your belts' (Matthew 10:9). This suggests that Paul wore a money-belt.

4 Murphy-O'Connor, J., op. cit., p 346.

5 The Stoic school of philosophy was founded about 300 B.C. by Zeno who was succeeded by Cleanthes as head of the school in Athens. According to the *Encyclopedia Britannica*, Cleanthes produced little that was original but he brought a religious fervour to the teachings of Zeno, stressing the belief that the universe is a living entity and that God is the vivifying ether of the universe.

6 Vos, H.F., op. cit., p 317.

7 See Yamauchi, E.M., op. cit., pp 21–29. See also Akurgal, E., *Ancient Civilizations and Ruins of Turkey*, Mobil Oil, Istanbul, 1970.

8 There is a report on excavation coins found at Assos in *Excavations at Assos*, 1921, by H.W. Bell.

9 Pausanias, book 1, 24:5.

10 Stapleton, M., op. cit., p 57.

11 Herodotus, book 3, section 116 and book 4, section 13.

12 *Encyclopedia Britannica*: griffin.

13 Mercatante, A.S., *The Facts on File Encyclopedia of World Mythology and Legend*, Facts on File, New York, 1988: griffin.

25. Miletus 57 A.D.

1 Yamauchi, E.M., op. cit., p 118.

2 The daughter of King Minos was Deione, also called Acacallis. By Apollo she bore a son called Miletus whom she carried into a forest because she was afraid of Minos. Protected by Apollo he was reared by wolves until discovered by shepherds. He later fled to Asia Minor where he founded the city of his name.

3 Head, B.V., op. cit., p 585.

4 Freely, J., op.cit., p 72. There are excellent plans of the ancient city in Freely's book.

5 Yamauchi, E.M., op. cit., p 126.

6 The epithet 'Didymeus' was used as a surname for Apollo. It was equivalent to the adjective 'Didymaean' meaning 'of Didyma'.

7 There is a myth about the nymph, Daphne, who was the daughter of the river Peneius. She was as chaste as she was beautiful, and Apollo fell deeply in love with her. However, when he tried to seduce her, she fled. Just as he was overtaking her and she felt his arms around her, she cried out to Mother Earth who changed her into a laurel tree. A wonderful marble statue by Bernini in the Villa Borghese in Rome captures the moment of her changing.

8 There is only one known specimen of this coin and only the end of the name]INA is discernible. So the woman can be either Messalina or Agrippina II.

9 L. Robert in *Houtes Etudes Numismatique. Monnaies Grecques*, 1967, pp 47–52, has pointed out that the name Tiberius Claudius Damas is known from two Milesian inscriptions, one of which gives the name of his magistracy, archiprytanis (chief president). According to Robert he was interested in restoring old customs.

10 On the coin Miletus appears as a young man with his foot on the prow of a ship. He is holding a spear and an aphlaston (an ornament on the stern part of a ship). A river god swims in the background.

26. Patara, Tyre, Ptolemais, Caesarea 57 A.D.

1 There is an account of the ruins of Patara in Blaiklock, op. cit., p 356.
2 *Larousse Encyclopedia of Mythology*, op. cit., p 119.
3 The coinage of the Lycian League has been studied by Troxell, H.A., *The Coinage of the Lycian League*, New York, 1982.
4 Josephus, F., *Contra Apionem*, book I, 18:116–120.
5 Herodotus, *History*, book 2, section 44.
6 The silver coinage of Tyre continued until the outbreak of the First Jewish War in 66 A.D. *RPC* (p 656) maintains that the Jewish War was not the cause of the cessation of Tyrian silver: it was because the Roman authorities decided to increase the output of silver from Antioch in 60 A.D.
7 Meshorer, Y., *Ancient Jewish Coinage*, Volume 2, Amphora, New York, 1982, pp 6–9.
8 Hendin, D., *Guide to Biblical Coins*, 3rd Edition, Amphora, New York, 1996, p 290.
9 Talmud, *Tosephta Kethuboth*, 13, 20.
10 Levy, B., 'Tyrian Shekels: the Myth of the Jerusalem Mint', in the *Journal of the Society for Ancient Numismatics*, Vol. XIX, No. 2, 1995. pp 33–35.
11 According to *RPC* (p 656) the dates for the 21 millimetre size are 37/36 B.C., 9/8, 6/5, 3/2, 1 B.C./1 A.D., 4/5 A.D., 25/6, 30/31, 52/53, 53/54, 56/57, 62/63, 66/67 A.D. The dates for the 19 millimetre size range from 37/36 B.C. to 66/67 A.D. The dates for the 15 millimetre size range from 18/17 B.C. to 64/65 A.D.
12 Chebab, M., *Tyre*, Editions Librairies Antoine, Beirut, 1969.
13 Vos, op. cit., p 256.
14 The translation of ΓΕΡΜΑΝΙΕΩΝ is difficult. It really needs K between I and E to make sense. Head (p 793) and Sear (GIC 497) do in fact state that the inscription on the coins is ΓΕΡΜΑΝΙΚΕΩΝ, but the inscriptions on these worn coins are not easy to read, and the information in *RPC* is probably correct. Perhaps the engraver omitted the K because of limited space. If K is to be understood, the suggestion of *RPC* that the name is Germanicia is more probable than Head's suggestion of Germanica because Germanica is simply the feminine form of Germanicus and it would be less appropriate for the name of a city than Germanicia (ΓΕΡΜΑΝΙΚΕΙΑ).
15 On the reverse of the two coins minted at Ptolemais under Nero there are four standards each of which carries the number of a Roman legion. The numbers are often worn and not easy to read, but *RPC* states that III, VI, X, and XI seem sure. Head (p 793) and Sear (GIC 626) have XII instead of XI. Hendin (p 236) has III, V, X and XII. An account of the various legions of the early Roman empire can be found in *The Making of the Roman Army from Republic to Empire* by Lawrence Keppie, 1998 edition. Soon after Julius Caesar's arrival in Gaul as proconsul in 58 B.C. two legions (XI and XII) were raised to fight the Helvetii. Legion XII Fulminata (Bearing Thunder) was later sent to Egypt and then to Syria. It was called Fulminata because the shields of the soldiers bore the device of Jupiter brandishing a thunderbolt. Legions V and VI were raised in 52 B.C. and Legion VI Ferrata (Iron-Clad) was later sent to Syria. Legion III Gallica (Gallic, of Gaul) was formed about 48 B.C. and served in Spain, Italy and Parthia. In 30 B.C. it was assigned to duty in Syria. Legion X Fretensis (Marine) was formed by Octavian about 41 B.C. It operated in Macedonia during the early part of Augustus' reign and was transferred to Syria in the early part of the first century A.D. It was involved in the First Jewish War (66–70 A.D.) and participated in the destruction of Jerusalem and Masada.

16 The harpa was the sickle-shaped sword which Hermes gave Perseus to slay the Gorgon.

17 Pliny the Elder, *Natural History*, 5, 14, 69.

18 This coin (*RPC* 4749) also has IMP XIV in the inscription, which must be a mistake because Nero did not receive an IMP XIV acclamation. His reign ended at IMP XII. Perhaps XIV became confused with VIIII in the engraver's mind. Nero was IMP VIIII when he was COS IIII.

27. Jerusalem May 57 A.D.

1 Before 41 A.D. the official title of the Roman governor of Judaea was prefect. This has been confirmed by the finding of an inscription at Caesarea which refers to Pontius Pilate as prefect. After 41 A.D. the official title is procurator. So Felix was procurator of Judaea. Later writers tended to refer anachronistically to the earlier governors as procurators; for example Tacitus (Ann. 15, 44) calls Pontius Pilate procurator. Josephus sometimes uses the correct term 'eparchos'. These governors were usually drawn from the equestrian order, but Felix, a freedman, was an exception.

2 Romanoff, P., op.cit., p 16.

3 Grant, Michael, *The Jews in the Roman World*, Weidenfeld and Nicolson, London, 1973, p 159.

4 Mattill, A.J., 'The Purpose of Acts: Schneckenburger Reconsidered', in *Apostolic History and the Gospel*, W.W. Gasque and R.P. Martin (eds), Exeter, Grand Rapids, 1970, p 116.

5 Klausner, J., *From Jesus to Paul*, English Translation, London, 1944, p 400, suggests that the Gentile Christians may in fact have crossed the barrier.

28. Caesarea 57–59 A.D.

1 The town was apparently built in the fourth century B.C. by a king of Sidon, called Straton.

2 In the temple there was also an impressive statue of the goddess Roma because Augustus did not allow worship of himself alone. 'Thus while deprecating worship of himself alone, Augustus welcomed the cult of Roma et Augustus when it emerged spontaneously in the East, and he encouraged its spread to the West' (Scullard, H.H., *From the Gracchi to Nero*; Methuen, London, 1982, p 236). In this, Augustus was very astute as he linked his destiny with that of the goddess Roma herself, and the myth of the greatness of Rome was the most powerful myth of the age.

3 Grant M., *The Visible Past*; Scribner, New York, 1990, p 103.

4 There is a map of the ruins in *Israel and the Palestinian Territories: A Lonely Planet Travel Survival Kit* by Andrew Humphreys and Neil Tilbury; Lonely Planet; Hawthorn, 1993, p 238. There is also an excellent account in *The Holy Land: An Archaeological Guide from Earliest Times to 1700* by Jerome Murphy-O'Connor, Oxford University Press, 1986 (2nd Edition). A comprehensive account of the coins excavated at Caesarea Maritima can be found on the internet at <http://www.asor.org/BA/Evans.html>. The account was written by Jane DeRose Evans and is entitled, 'Ancient Coins from The Drew Institute of Archaeological Research Excavations of Caesarea Maritima, 1971–1984'. It includes an extensive bibliography.

5 Smallwood. E.M., *The Jews under Roman Rule from Pompey to Diocletian: A Study in Political Relations* (SJLA 20) Brill, Leiden, 1981, p 269, note 40.

6 Josephus, *Antiquities of the Jews*, book XX, chapter VIII, section 9.

7 Josephus, *Antiquities of the Jews*, book XX, chapter VII, section 2.

8 There is no scholarly consensus on the date when the book of Acts was written. It must have been written between 62 A.D., the date at which the last event in the

book takes place, and the middle of the second century when the first clear reference to it occurs in Christian literature (Justin's *Apology*, 1.50.12.). According to Carson et al. (*Introduction*, op. cit., p 192) most scholars now date the book of Acts in the 80s, or a bit later. These authors themselves favour a date in the early or mid 60s, just after the book ends. Bruce (*Commentary*, op cit., p 12) says that it is difficult to fix the date of composition of Acts more precisely than at some point within the Flavian period (A.D. 69–96), possibly about the middle of the period. King Agrippa II died about 100 A.D. (ISBE, vol. 2, p 698).

9 According to Hendin (op. cit., p 125) archaeological evidence bears out the fact that this coin (Hendin 553) was struck for use in those of his territories largely populated by Jews. The other coins of Agrippa I are rarely found in the territory of Ancient Judaea, but instead are found in the far north of Israel and in Jordan.

10 Stevenson, op. cit., p 582.

11 See the argument for this by Bo Reicke, *Caesarea, Rome, and the Captivity Epistles* in Gasque et al., op. cit., p 277.

29. Sidon 59 A.D.

1 Diodorus, *History*, Book XVI.41. Diodorus was a Greek historian in the first century B.C.

2 There is a map of modern Sidon in *Lebanon* by Anne Jousiffe, Lonely Planet, Hawthorn, 1998. Much of the historical information in this chapter comes from Jousiffe's book.

3 Graves, Robert, op. cit., p 391.

4 Ibid., p 80 (21.3).

5 Jousiffe, op. cit., p 205.

6 Some scholars maintain that the name 'Ashtoreth' is simply Astarte with the vowels from bosheth, a Hebrew word meaning 'shame'. The Hebrew scribes did this to indicate the abhorrence they felt for the Canaanite goddess of fertility.

7 This Egyptian influence suggests that Astarte was being identified with Isis at that time. Matsson (op. cit., p 30) comments that it was natural for the great Palestinian goddess Astarte, who like Isis was also a nature-goddess and sky-goddess, to be associated with Isis. Astarte was sometimes portrayed with the Egyptian headdress of Isis, a disc set between cow's horns.

8 A baetyl was a stone, probably of meteoric origin, which represented a divinity. Although it is assumed that the baetyl in this case represents Astarte, it is not explicitly stated on the coins.

9 Butcher, Kevin, *Roman Provincial Coins*, Seaby, London, 1988, p 101.

10 *RPC*, op.cit., p 651.

11 Graves, Robert, op. cit., p 196 (58.2).

12 Matsson, op. cit., p 30.

13 Graves, Robert, op. cit., p 197 (58.3).

14 Herodotus, *History*, Book 1, section 2. Herodotus was a fifth-century B.C. Greek historian. The translation used in this book is by George Rawlinson.

30. Myra 59 A.D.

1 *Inscriptiones Graecae, ad res Romanas pertinentes*, 3.719, 721. (Quoted in Blaiklock et al., op. cit., p 324)

2 *RPC*, op. cit., p 527.

3 Jones, J.M., *A Dictionary of Ancient Greek Coins*, op. cit., p 26.

4 See Liddell and Scott's Greek-English Lexicon, op, cit., p 215.

5 St Nicholas is the patron saint of children, virgins, sailors, merchants and pawnbrokers. He is also the patron saint of Russia and Greece. Sailors in peril off the coast

of Lycia prayed to him. The three bags of gold that he gave to three destitute girls are supposed to have given rise to the pawn-brokers' sign of three balls. In the eleventh century A.D. Italian merchants stole the reputed relics of St Nicholas from Myra and took them to Bari in Italy where they are still enshrined in the Basilica of San Nicola. At Demre there is still a church of Saint Nicholas which dates from the third century A.D. It was restored by Tsar Nicholas I in the nineteenth century.

6   Attwater, D., *The Penguin Dictionary of Saints*, Penguin, 1965, p 251.

31. Malta 59 A.D.

1   W. Burridge has inspected the area and in *Seeking the Site of St Paul's Shipwreck* (Valetta, 1952) argues that the site of Paul's landing was not the traditional site, St Paul's Bay, but the next bay to the north, Mellieha Bay.

2   W.P. Workman, *A New Date-Indication in Acts*, Expository Times 11 (1899–1900), pp 316–319.

3   Head, op. cit., p 883.

4   *RPC*, p 180. *RPC* mentions that the coins of Melita have most recently been studied by Coleiro (*Numismatic Chronicle*, 1971, pp 67–91), but comments that he dated them by false analogy with weight standards in use elsewhere.

5   *RPC* 674 is identical except that the veiled female head faces to the left.

6   MELITAS is a transliteration into Latin letters of the Greek word, ΜΕΛΙΤΗΣ, which is the genitive form of ΜΕΛΙΤΗ. One would have expected MELITES but the pronunciation of the Greek letter η (H) varied from time to time and from place to place, and the transliterator here considered it sounded more like the Latin A. This suggests that the common language of the Maltese at this time was koine (common) Greek.

7   This is probably the Phoenician god, Melqart (Hercules) who was also the god of the sea. A coin of Malta with a Punic inscription (Sear 6585) features a bearded Heracles on the obverse. The reference to Paul being a murderer suggests that on Malta convicted murderers had been sacrificed to Melqart and Astarte.

8   There are no venomous snakes on Malta. Various explanations have been put forward, but it is difficult to imagine the natives being mistaken in this regard. Their ancestors had lived on the island for centuries. Perhaps there were venomous snakes which have since become extinct.

9   Or conversely Paul's experience with the snake might have influenced the writer of this passage, which scholars generally consider was added to the end of Mark's Gospel.

32. Syracuse, Rhegium, Puteoli 60 A.D.

1   Arethusa was a beautiful nymph who was pursued by the river-god Alpheus. Alpheus was the chief river in the Peloponnesus and in some parts of its course it flowed underground. This gave rise to the story of the river-god flowing under the sea to reach Arethusa whom Artemis changed into a fountain on Ortygia. Thus Alpheus merged with Arethusa in the waters of the fountain.

2   Guido, Margaret, *Syracuse, A Handbook to its History and Principal Monuments*, Max Parrish: London, 1958.

3   Foss, Clive, *Roman Historical Coins*, Seaby, London, 1990, p 67.

4   There was a large temple to Zeus on the mainland just south of the city.

5   Butcher, Kevin, *Roman Provincial Coins*, Seaby, London, 1988, p 17.

6   Jones, J.M., *A Dictionary of Ancient Roman Coins*, Seaby, London, 1990, p 186.

7   The Dioscuri (Castor and Pollux) were sons of Zeus. When the Romans defeated the Etruscans in 484 B.C. it was said that the brothers appeared and fought in the battle. A temple was built to them in Rome. In mythology they took part in various

adventures, for example they sailed in the Argo in search of the Golden Fleece. They were popular gods with sailors and the vessel that Paul sailed in from Malta had the Dioscuri as its figurehead (Acts 28:11).

8 See 'When the Greeks Went West', by Rick Gore, in *National Geographic Magazine*, November 1994, (Volume 186, No. 5).

9 Bruce, F.F., *The Book of the Acts*, Eerdmans: Grand Rapids, 1988, p 502.

33. Rome 60–62 A.D.

1 Belford, Ros, *Rome*, Virago Press, London, 1993, p 228.

2 Suetonius, *The Twelve Caesars*, Nero:20. Translated by Robert Graves, revised by Michael Grant, Penguin Books, 1979.

3 Suetonius, op. cit., Nero:25.

4 Sutherland, C.H.V., and Carson, R.A.G., *The Roman Imperial Coinage*, Volume I, Spink, London, 1984, p 7.

5 Sutherland, C.H.V., *The Emperor and the Coinage, Julio-Claudian Studies*, Spink, London, 1976, p 116.

6 Suetonius, op. cit., Claudius:18.

7 Carson, R.A.G., *Coins of the Roman Empire*, Routledge, London, 1990, p 285.

8 According to *RIC*, op. cit., p 87, 'Modern scholars are not agreed upon its interpretation, some regarding the seated female figure as Livia in the guise of Pax, some as Pax-Justitia, some simply as the priestess Livia, revered as the wife of the first imperial pontifex maximus and the stepmother of the second'.

9 Suetonius, op. cit., Augustus: 29.

10 *RIC*, op. cit., p 10.

11 The building of the Colosseum was begun by Vespasian and officially opened in 80 A.D. It was named after a colossal statue of Nero which stood nearby. This statue was erected in the extensive grounds of the new palace which Nero built after the great fire of 64 A.D.

12 The Pantheon as it now stands was built by Hadrian (117–138 A.D.). Agrippa, the Roman general, originally built a temple on the site dedicated to all the gods; hence the name from pan (all) and theos (god). This was a small rectangular temple with columns, and was damaged by fire in 80 A.D. Hadrian built an almost completely new structure roofed by an enormous concrete dome.

13 The meaning of Pallas is unknown. According to Jones (op. cit., *A Dictionary of Ancient Roman Coins*, p 233) it may mean 'brandisher' or 'maiden'. Some scholars consider that it was originally the name of another goddess who became identified with Athena. The myth of Athena killing a giant called Pallas simply attempted to explain the name. A small wooden statue of Athena was called a Palladium. Aeneas was supposed to have brought such a statue from Troy. Jones (op. cit., p 319) says that when Vesta is shown holding a Palladium, it is the Vesta enshrined in a second temple which Augustus built near his home on the Palatine Hill.

14 According to Pierre Grimal (*The Civilization of Rome*, Allen and Unwin, London, 1963, p 264), there was no image of Vesta in the temple, but statues of her stood in the House of the Vestal Virgins.

15 Grimal, op. cit., p 265.

16 The word 'basilica' was a Greek adjective meaning 'royal'. It was the term used for a royal portico (Greek: stoa). Such porticos were provided by Hellenistic monarchs for the convenience of their subjects, and the word came to be applied to colonnaded halls where people could collect if the sun was too hot or the rain too heavy for outdoor activities. Later such buildings were used as Christian churches. In Rome the word was applied to the seven churches built by Constantine in the fourth century A.D.

17 Belford, op. cit., p 182.

18 The assassination did not occur in the Senate building but at a meeting of the Senate held in the theatre of Pompey which was three kilometres north-west of the Capitoline Hill. Caesar received multiple stabwounds and died at the foot of Pompey's statue. Pompey's theatre was standing in Paul's time.

19 Casson, L., *Travel in the Ancient World*, Allen and Unwin, London, 1974, p 249.

20 Zeuxis was a Greek painter active in the last 25 years of the fifth century B.C. He was considered to be one of the greatest painters of antiquity. Although none of his paintings survive, the descriptions indicate that he painted mythological scenes and figures such as the punishment of Marsyas. There is an ancient sculpture of Marsyas, naked and tied to a tree, in the Conservatori Museum in Rome, which gives an idea of what Zeuxis' portrait might have been like. There was a statue of Marsyas among the various monuments which stood in the Forum. Although Zeuxis' portrait of Marsyas must have been tragic in the extreme, there is an anecdotal report that he was so amused by a painting he had just finished of a funny-looking old woman that he laughed himself to death.

21 *Encyclopedia of World Art*, McGraw-Hill Book Coy, New York, 1967, Volume XIV, p 934.

22 Robert Graves (op. cit., 25:5) considers that Apollo's victory over Marsyas commemorates the Hellenic conquest of Phrygia, and that Marsyas' punishment may refer to the ritual flaying of a sacred king or to the removal of the entire bark from an alder-shoot (the alder was a tree related to birch) to make a shepherd's pipe, the tree being personified as a god or demi-god.

23 Mercatante, A.S., *The Facts on File Encyclopedia of Mythology and Legend*, Facts on File, New York, 1988, p 436.

24 It is not known what eventually happened to Paul. Tradition associates his execution with the persecution of the Roman Christians after the great fire of 64 A.D. He was probably beheaded in about 65 A.D. His headless body is supposed to lie under the High Altar of the Basilica of St Paul Outside the Walls. 'This church has the peace of great dignity, the majesty of perfect proportions . . . I approached the high altar, where, beneath a canopy, upheld by four columns of the purest alabaster, is the vault of Roman times in which St Paul lies buried. Through the kindness of those who guard his tomb, I was allowed to kneel at the fenestella and to gaze for a moment into that dim space below, where the words PAULO APOSTOLO MART, are written on a stone' (H.V. Morton, op. cit., p 414).

25 Many scholars consider that Paul journeyed to Spain in order to carry the gospel to every part of the known world before the Second Coming of Christ (1 Thessalonians 4:15–18). A.N. Wilson (*Paul: The Mind of the Apostle*, Pimlico, London, 1998, p 249) likes to think that Paul was somehow saved from the gruesome fate of the Roman Christians: 'While the human torches screeched in agony in the Vatican Gardens of a sadistic emperor, some will have imagined Paul already dead; others have perhaps supposed he died with them. But I prefer to think of him, far away in the west wholly oblivious to what he had started, eagerly gazing towards the heaving sea on which he had so often been tossed and awaiting the coming of Christ'.

26 Ara coeli means 'altar of heaven'. The name of this church apparently came from an unlikely story, recorded in a twelfth-century guidebook, which related how Augustus, when standing on the Capitoline Hill, saw the heavens open to reveal a vision of the Virgin Mary holding a baby whom heavenly voices declared the Saviour of the World. Augustus then built an altar on the site.

Glossary

Aes	The term used for copper or alloys of copper. Some coins of pure copper were minted in the first century A.D. but usually they were of bronze.
Agora	The Greek term for the place of assembly in a city. It was an open area usually in the centre of the city where people gathered for activities such as debating, court cases, and business. It was especially used as a market place, and was the equivalent of the Latin forum.
Aureus	A gold Roman coin at the top of the hierarchy of Roman coinage. An aureus equalled twenty-five silver denarii. A denarius equalled four bronze sestertii. A sestertius equalled two bronze dupondii. A dupondius equalled two bronze asses. An as was the standard unit of bronze coinage and one as equalled four bronze quadrantes. A quadrans was the smallest denomination which circulated in Italy.
Baetyl	A stone used to represent a god or goddess. Many such divine stones were probably originally meteorites.
Basilica	A large colonnaded building used for such purposes as court cases and business of various kinds including moneychanging. The name derives from the Greek word 'basileus', which means 'king'. Hellenistic monarchs provided these buildings for public use. They were later used as churches. The seven churches built in Rome by Constantine the Great were also called basilicas.
Brass	An alloy of copper and zinc. It was called orichalcum in ancient times.
Bronze	An alloy of copper. The other metal was usually tin, but lead and zinc were also used.
Bust	Portrait of a person which includes the shoulders.
Consul	The highest official in the Roman Republic. From the foundation of the Republic in 509 B.C. two consuls were appointed annually to take over the powers of the king. During the Empire the position remained important, the emperor himself being one of the consuls. On coins the word is usually abbreviated to COS.
Denarius	See Aureus.
Dupondius	See Aureus.

Exergue	The small segment on a coin usually on the reverse and below the design. It is often separated by a line and usually contains the name of the city in abbreviated form (mintmark) or the date.
Field	The smooth area surrounding the main design on either side of a coin.
Flan	The blank piece of metal before it is struck with a die to form a coin.
Forum	The public square in a Roman city. It was equivalent to the Greek agora.
Head	Portrait of a person which does not include the shoulders.
Imperator	Commander. A victorious general was acclaimed imperator by his troops. Emperors assumed the title, and the abbreviation IMP is common on coins. The Roman numerals following IMP indicate the number of times the emperor was so acclaimed.
Laureate	Crowned with a wreath made of leaves from the laurel tree. The wreath was a symbol of victory.
Legend	The inscription on a coin.
Lepton	Plural: lepta. A small bronze coin which circulated in Palestine till the First Jewish Revolt (66–70 A.D.). The word 'lepton' is a Greek word which means 'small'. In Mark 12:42 it is explained that two lepta equal one quadrans, which was the smallest bronze coin which circulated in Italy. In Palestine two lepta equalled one prutah, which from 6 A.D. was equal to a quadrans. See Prutah.
Mint	The place where coins were made.
Obverse	The 'head' side of a coin usually bearing the ruler's portrait or the more significant deity or city symbol. For ancient coins the obverse die was generally fixed on an anvil and the reverse die, engraved on a punch, was struck with a hammer.
Patera	A bowl with a boss in the centre for pouring libations (liquid sacrifices) to the gods.
Prutah	Plural: prutot. A bronze coin which circulated in Palestine till the fall of Jerusalem in 70 A.D. 'Prutah' was a Hebrew word which meant a grape pip. One prutah equalled two lepta, the lepton being the lowest denomination. After 6 A.D. the prutah was equivalent to the Roman quadrans. David Hendin has explained the relationship between the various denominations in his article, 'Prutahs, Leptons and Mites', in *The Celator*, Vol. 14, No. 4, April 2000, pp 46, 47, 50.
Quadrans	Plural: quadrantes. A small bronze coin which circulated in Italy. Quadrans was a Latin word meaning a quarter. In Palestine from 6 A.D. a quadrans was equivalent to a Prutah. See Aureus.
Quadriga	Chariot pulled by four horses.
Radiate	Wearing a crown with spikes representing the sun's rays. It denoted an association with the sun god Sol (Greek, Helios), and deified emperors were usually shown in this way.
Reverse	The 'tail' side of a coin. It is the side opposite the Obverse.
Semis	A bronze coin which circulated mostly in Italy. The word is a Latin one which means 'half'. It was equal to half an as. See Aureus.
Sestertius	Plural: sestertii. See Aureus.
Stoa	A long, covered walkway open and colonnaded on one side. The Latin equivalent was a portico. They were commonly built near public squares to provide shelter from the sun and rain. They served a variety of functions, e.g. classroom, lawcourt, market. In Athens the Stoa of Attalus, originally built in the second century B.C., has been completely restored and serves as a museum for the Agora.

Tetradrachm	A Greek word meaning four drachms. It was a large silver coin common in areas which had come under Greek influence. The drachm (Greek: drachmon, plural drachma) was a silver coin equivalent to the Roman denarius.
Tribunicia Potestate	This is the Latin phrase meaning 'with tribunician power'. A tribune was originally the leader of a tribe, but the term came to be used in a military sense (tribunus militum) and for a leader of the common people (tribunus plebis). From the time of Augustus emperors assumed the power of the latter. On coins it is usually abbreviated to TR. P or TR. POT.
Type	The main design on either side of a coin.

Bibliography

Akurgal, E., *Ancient Civilizations and Ruins of Turkey*, Mobil Oil, Istanbul, 1970.
Amandry, M., *Le Connayage des duovirs corinthiens*, BCH Supp. XV, 1988.
Appian (second century A.D.), *History of Rome's Wars*.
Ariel, D.T., *A Survey of Coin Finds in Jerusalem*, Liber Annuus 32, 1982.
Attwater, D., *The Penguin Dictionary of Saints*, Penguin, 1965.
Ballance, M., *Anatolian Studies 14*, 1964.
Ballance, M., *Anatolian Studies 7*, 1957.
Banti, A., & Simonetti, L., *Corpus Nummorum Romanorum*, 18 volumes, Firenze, 1972–1979.
Belford, R., *Rome*, Virago Press, London, 1993.
Bell, H.W., *Excavations at Assos*, 1921.
Blaiklock, E.M. & Harrison, R.K. (eds), *The New International Dictionary of Biblical Archaeology*, Zondervan, Grand Rapids, 1983.
Bromiley, G.W. (ed.), *The International Standard Bible Encyclopedia*, 4 Vols, Eerdmans, Grand Rapids, 1979–1988.
Brosnahan, T., *Turkey – a travel survival kit*, Lonely Planet, Hawthorn, 1993.
Browning, I., *Petra*, Chatto and Windus, London, 1973.
Bruce, F.F., *Paul: Apostle of the Free Spirit*, Paternoster Press, Exeter, 1980.
Bruce, F.F., *The Book of the Acts*, Eerdmans, Grand Rapids, 1988.
Burnett, A., Amandry, M., Ripolles, P., *Roman Provincial Coinage*, British Museum Press and Bibliotheque Nationale, London and Paris, Volume 1, 1992.
Burnet, A., *Coinage in the Roman World*, Seaby, London, 1987.
Burridge, W., *Seeking the Site of St Paul's Shipwreck*, Valetta, 1952.
Butcher, K., *Roman Provincial Coins*, Seaby, London, 1988.
Carson, D.A., Moo, D.J., and Morris L., *An Introduction to the New Testament*, Zondervan, Grand Rapids, 1992.
Carson, R.A.G., *Coins of the Roman Empire*, Routledge, London, 1990.
Casson, L., *Travel in the Ancient World*, Allen and Unwin, London, 1974.
Cavedoni, C., *Naples Archaeological Bulletin*, August 1855.
Chebab, M., *Tyre*, Editions Librairies Antoine, Beirut, 1969.
Coleiro, *Numismatic Chronicle*, 1971.
Dio Cassius (third century A.D.), *Romaika*.

Dio Chrysotom (second century A.D.), *Orations*.

Diodorus Siculus (first century B.C.), *History*.

Douglas, J.D. (ed.), *New Bible Dictionary*, Inter-Varsity Press, Leicester, 1982.

Downey, G., *A History of Antioch in Syria from Seleucus to the Arab Conquest*, Princeton University Press, Princeton, 1961.

Eusebius (260–340 A.D.), *Ecclesiastical History*.

Ferguson, J., *The Religions of the Roman Empire*, Thames and Hudson, London, 1970.

Ferguson, S.B., & Wright, D.F., *New Dictionary of Theology*, IVP, Leicester, 1988.

Foss, C., *Roman Historical Coins*, Seaby, London, 1990.

Freely, J., *Classical Turkey*, Penguin, London.

Gasque, W.W., & Martin, R.P. (eds), *Apostolic History and the Gospel*, Paternoster Press, Exeter, Exeter, 1970.

Goldman, H., *Excavations at Gözlü Tepe, Tarsus*, 6 Vols, 1950–1963.

Gore, R., 'When the Greeks Went West', in *National Geographic Magazine*, November 1994.

Grant, M., *The Jews in the Roman World*, Weidenfeld and Nicholson, London, 1973.

Graves, R., *The Greek Myths*, 2 Vols, Penguin, 1960.

Grimal, P., *The Civilization of Rome*, Allen and Unwin, London, 1963.

Guido, M., *Syracuse, A Handbook to its History and Principal Monuments*, Max Parrish, London, 1958.

Guirand, F. (ed.), *Larousse Encyclopedia of Mythology*, Hamlyn, London, 1959.

Guthrie, D., and Motyer, J.A. (eds), *New Bible Commentary*, IVP, Leicester, 1970.

Hawthorne, G.F., and Martin, R.P. (eds), *Dictionary of Paul and his Letters*, IVP, Downers Grove and Leicester, 1993.

Head, B.V., *Historia Numorum*, Clarendon Press, Oxford, 1910, (Reprinted 1977).

Hendin, D., *Guide to Biblical Coins*, 3rd Edition, Amphora, New York, 1996.

Herodotus (fifth century B.C.), *History*, translated by George Rawlinson, *Encyclopedia Britannica*, 1952.

Humphreys, A., & Tilbury, N., *Israel and the Palestinian Territories: A Lonely Planet Travel Survival Kit*, Lonely Planet, Hawthorn, 1993.

Jenkins, G.K., *Ancient Greek Coins*, Seaby, London, 1990.

Jones, A.H.M., *The Cities of the Eastern Roman Provinces*, Clarendon Press, Oxford, 1971.

Jones, J.M., *A Dictionary of Ancient Greek Coins*, Seaby, London, 1986.

Jones, J.M. *A Dictionary of Ancient Roman Coins*, Seaby, London, 1990.

Josephus, F., (first century A.D.), *The Antiquities of the Jews*. Translation by William Whiston, published by Hendrickson, Peabody, Massachusetts, 1987.

Josephus, F., (first century A.D.), *The Wars of the Jews*. Translation as above.

Josephus, F., (first century A.D.), *Flavius Josephus Against Apion*. Translation as above.

Jousiffe, A., *Lebanon*, Lonely Planet, Hawthorn, London, 1998.

Justin Martyr, (second century A.D.), *Apology*.

Karageorghis, V., *Cyprus: from Stone Age to the Romans*, Thames and Hudson, London, 1982.

Keppie, L., *The Making of the Roman Army from Republic to Empire*, 1998.

Kinross, Lord, *Within the Taurus: A Journey in Asiatic Turkey*, Murray, London, 1954.

Kittel, G., *Theological Dictionary of the New Testament*, translated by G.W. Bromiley, Eerdmans, Grand Rapids, 1964.

Klausner, J., *From Jesus to Paul*, English Translation, London, 1944.

Kroll, J.H., *The Athenian Agora*, Volume XXVI (the Greek Coins), Princeton, 1993.

Lewis, C.T. & Short, C.A., *Latin Dictionary*, Clarendon Press, Oxford, 1879.

Lewis, P.E., 'The Actual Tribute Penny', *Journal of the Numismatic Association of Australia*, Vol 10, July 1999, p 3.

Lewis, P.E., 'The Tribute Penny in the Gospel of Thomas', *Journal of the Numismatic Association of Australia*, Vol 10, July 1999, p 14.

Levy, B., 'Tyrian Shekels: the Myth of the Jerusalem Mint', *Journal of the Society for Ancient Numismatics*, Vol XIX, No 2, 1995, p 33.

Liddell, H.G. & Scott, R., *Greek–English Lexicon (Abridged)*, Clarendon Press, Oxford, 1944.

Lindgren, H.C., and Kovacs, F.L., *Ancient Bronze Coins of Asia Minor and the Levant*, Chrysopylon, San Mateo, 1985.

MacMullen, R., *Paganism in the Roman World*, Yale University Press, New Haven, 1981.

Magie, D., *Roman Rule in Asia Minor*, Princeton University Press, 1950.

Marshall, I.H., in *New Bible Dictionary*, IVP, Leicester, 1982, p 589.

Matsson, G.O., *The Gods, Goddesses and Heroes on the Ancient Coins of Bible Lands*, Numismatiska Bokforlaget, Stockholm, 1969.

Mattill, A.J., *The Purpose of Acts: Schneckenburger Reconsidered*, in *Apostolic History and the Gospel*, W.W. Gasque & R.P. Martin (eds), Paternoster Press, Exeter, 1970.

Mattingly, H., et al., *Roman Imperial Coinage*, 10 Vols, Spink, 1923–1994.

Mercatante, A.S., *The Facts on File Encyclopedia of World Mythology and Legend*, Facts on File, New York, 1988.

Meshorer, Y., *Ancient Jewish Coinage*, 2 Vols, Amphora, New York, 1982.

Meshorer, Y., *Studies in Honour of Leo Mildenberg*, edited by A. Houghton et al., Wetteren, 1984.

Meshorer, Y., 'Nabataean Coins', *QEDEM, Monographs of the Institute of Archaeology*, No 3, Hebrew University of Jerusalem, 1975.

Morton, H.V., *In the Steps of St Paul*, 5th Edition, Methuen, London, 1949.

Murphy-O'Connor, J., *Paul, a Critical Life*, Clarendon Press, Oxford, 1996.

Murphy-O'Connor, J., *The Holy Land: An Archaeological Guide from Earliest Times to 1700*, Oxford University Press, 1986.

Ovid (43 B.C.–17 A.D.), *Metamorphoses*.

Pausanias (second century A.D.), *Description of Greece*, 10 books.

Perkin, H.W., in *The International Standard Bible Encyclopedia*, G.W. Bromiley (ed.), Volume III, 1986, p 406.

Peters, F.E., *The Harvest of Hellenism*, Allen and Unwin, 1972.

Pliny the Elder, (23–79 A.D.), *Natural History*.

Price, M.G. & Trell, B.L., *Coins and their Cities*, Vecchi and Sons, London, 1977.

Ramsay, W.M., *Pauline and other Studies in Early Christian History*, London, 1907.

Ramsay, W.M., *The Cities of St Paul*, Armstrong and Son, New York, 1908.

Reicke, B., *Caesarea, Rome, and the Captivity Epistles*, in *Apostolic History and the Gospel*, W.W. Gasque & R.P. Martin (eds), Exeter, Grand Rapids, 1970.

Robert, L., *Houtes Etudes Numismatique. Monnaies Greques*, 1967.

Romanoff, P., *Jewish Symbols on Ancient Jewish Coins*, American Israel Numismatic Association, New York, 1944.

Sallustius (fourth century A.D.) *De Dis et Mundo 9*.

Scullard, H.H., *From the Gracchi to Nero: A History of Rome from 133 B.C. to A.D. 68*, Methuen, New York, 1982.

Sear, D.R., *Greek Imperial Coins and their Values*, Seaby, London, 1982.

Sear, D.R., *Greek Coins and their Values*, 2 Vols, Seaby, London, 1978 and 1979.

Sear, D.R., *Roman Coins and their Values*, Seaby, London, !988.

Shore, H., *The Real Tribute Penny*, in *Australian Coin Review*, No 377, December 1995, p 34.

Smallwood, E.M., *The Jews under Roman Rule from Pompey to Diocletian: A Study in Political Relations*, SJLA 20, Brill, Leiden, 1981.

Smith, W., *A Smaller Classical Dictionary*, Murray, London, 1880.

Socrates (fifth century A.D.), *Historia Ecclesiastica* (Church History).

Speake, G., *The Penguin Dictionary of Ancient History*, Penguin, London, 1994.

The Pocket Guide to St Paul

Stapleton, M., *The Hamlyn Concise Dictionary of Greek and Roman Mythology*, Hamlyn, London, 1982.
Stark, F., *Rome on the Euphrates*, John Murray, London, 1966.
Stevenson, S.W., *A Dictionary of Roman Coins*, Bell, 1889, reprinted by Seaby, 1982.
Strabo (64 B.C.–24 A.D.), *Geography*, 17 books.
Suetonius (second century A.D.), *The Twelve Caesars*. Translation by Robert Graves, revised by Michael Grant, published by Penguin, London, 1979.
Sutherland, C.H.V., *The Cistophori of Augustus*, RNS Special Publication No 5, London, 1970.
Sutherland, C.H.V., *The Emperor and the Coinage*, Spink, London, 1976.
Sydenham, E.A., *The Coinage of Caesarea in Cappadocia*, London, 1933.
Tacitus (c 56–c 120 A.D.), *The Annals of Imperial Rome*. Translation by Michael Grant, Penguin, London, 1975.
Thompson, H.A. & Wycherley, R.E., *The Agora of Athens*, 1972.
Thucydides (c 455–c 400 B.C.) *History of the Peloponnesian War*. Translated by Richard Crawley, *Encyclopedia Britannica*, 1952.
Troxell, H.A., *The Coinage of the Lycian League*, New York, 1982.
Van Elderen, B., *Some Archaeological Observations on Paul's First Missionary Journey* in *Apostolic History and the Gospel*, W.W. Gasque & R.P. Martin (eds), Paternoster Press, Exeter, 1970.
Vos, H.V., *Archaeology in Bible Lands*, Moody Press, Chicago, 1977.
Walker, D.R., *The Metrology of the Roman Silver Coinage*, Part 1, BAR Sup. 5, 1976.
Wilson, A.N., *Paul: The Mind of the Apostle*, Pimlico, London, 1998.
Witherington, B., *The Paul Quest*, IVP, Downers Grove and Leicester, 1998.
Workman, W.P., *A New Date-Indication in Acts*, Expository Times 11, 1899–1900.
Yamauchi, E.M., *The Archaeology of New Testament Cities in Western Asia Minor*, Pickering and Inglis, Glasgow, 1980.

Eastern Mediterranean

Western Asia Minor

Greece

Italy and Sicily

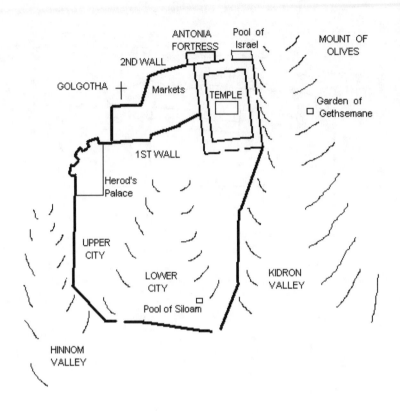

ANTONIA
FORTRESS

Pool of
Israel

MOUNT OF
OLIVES

2ND WALL

GOLGOTHA

Markets

TEMPLE

Garden of
Gethsemane

1ST WALL

Herod's
Palace

UPPER
CITY

LOWER
CITY

KIDRON
VALLEY

Pool of Siloam

HINNOM
VALLEY

Jerusalem 10 A.D.

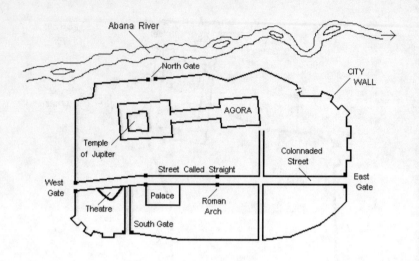

Damascus 36 A.D.

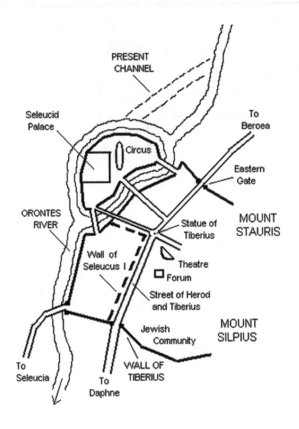

Antioch 46 A.D.

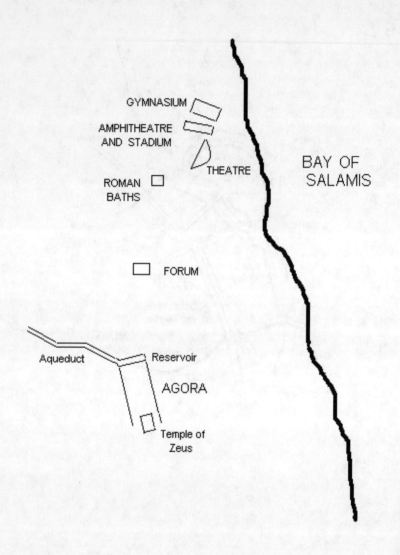

GYMNASIUM

AMPHITHEATRE
AND STADIUM

THEATRE

ROMAN
BATHS

BAY OF
SALAMIS

FORUM

Aqueduct

Reservoir

AGORA

Temple of
Zeus

Salamis 47 A.D.

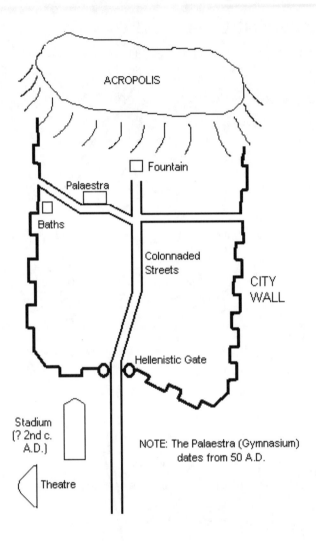

ACROPOLIS

Fountain

Palaestra

Baths

Colonnaded
Streets

CITY
WALL

Hellenistic Gate

Stadium
(? 2nd c.
A.D.)

NOTE: The Palaestra (Gymnasium)
dates from 50 A.D.

Theatre

Perga 48 A.D.

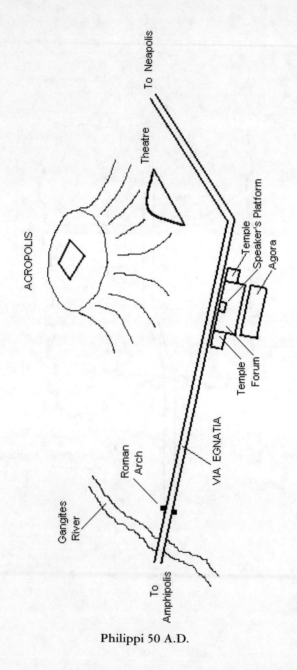

Philippi 50 A.D.

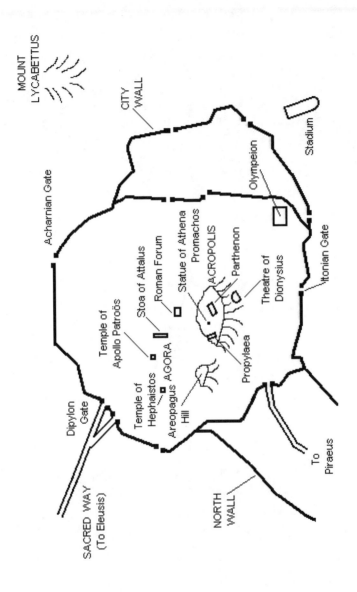

Athens 50 A.D.

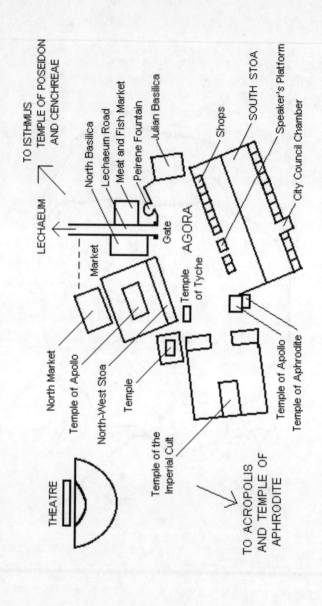

Corinth 50 A.D.

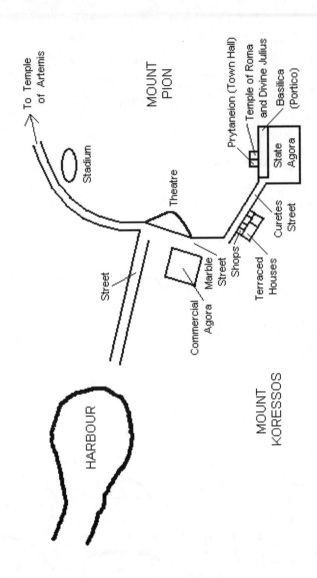

Ephesus 53 A.D.

273

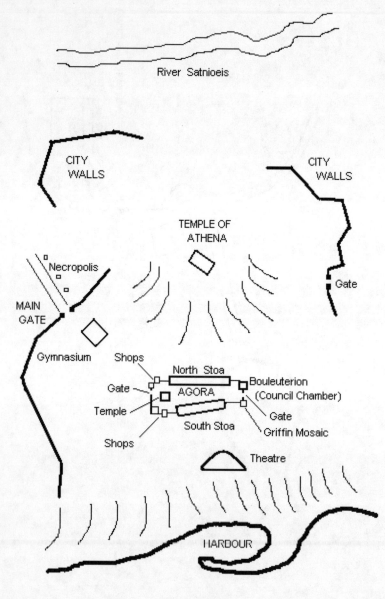

River Satnioeis

CITY WALLS

CITY WALLS

TEMPLE OF ATHENA

Necropolis

Gate

MAIN GATE

Gymnasium

Shops

North Stoa

Bouleuterion
(Council Chamber)

Gate

AGORA

Temple

Gate

Shops

South Stoa

Griffin Mosaic

Theatre

HARBOUR

Assos 57 A.D.

Miletus 57 A.D.

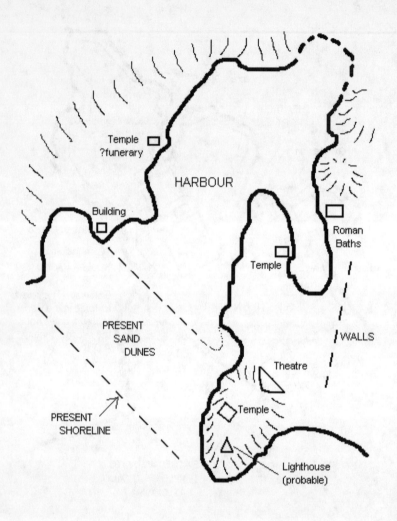

Patara 57 A.D.

NORTH
HARBOUR

ISLAND
CITY

ROCKS

ORIGINAL
COASTLINE

MAINLAND
CITY

Temple of
Melqart

SOUTH
HARBOUR

Tyre 57 A.D.

277

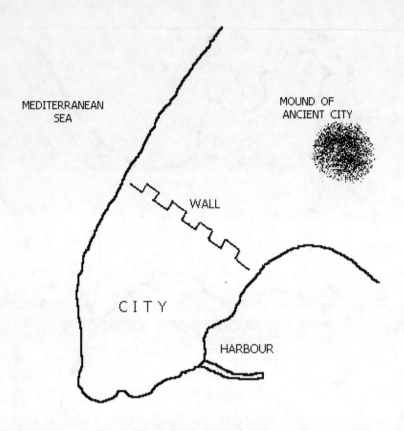

MEDITERRANEAN
SEA

MOUND OF
ANCIENT CITY

WALL

C I T Y

HARBOUR

BAY OF HAIFA

Ptolemais 57 A.D.

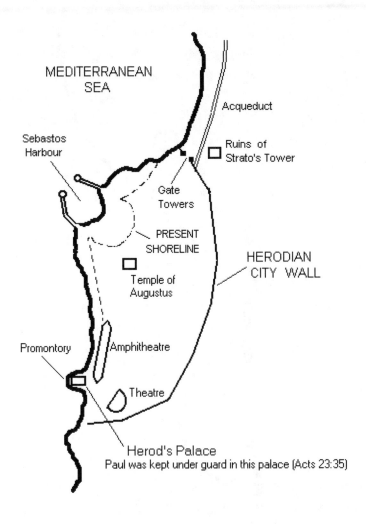

MEDITERRANEAN
SEA

Acqueduct

Sebastos
Harbour

Ruins of
Strato's Tower

Gate
Towers

PRESENT
SHORELINE

HERODIAN
CITY WALL

Temple of
Augustus

Promontory

Amphitheatre

Theatre

Herod's Palace
Paul was kept under guard in this palace (Acts 23:35)

Caesarea Maritima 57 A.D.

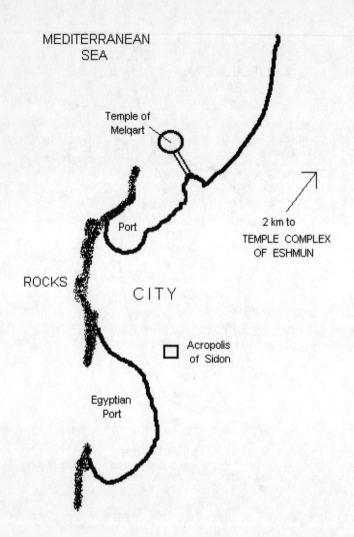

MEDITERRANEAN
SEA

Temple of
Melqart

2 km to
TEMPLE COMPLEX
OF ESHMUN

Port

ROCKS

CITY

Acropolis
of Sidon

Egyptian
Port

Sidon 59 A.D.

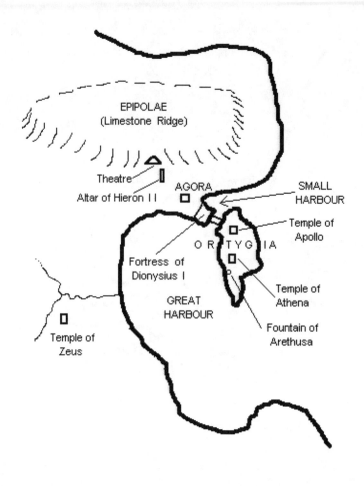

EPIPOLAE
(Limestone Ridge)

Theatre

Altar of Hieron II

AGORA

SMALL
HARBOUR

Temple of
Apollo

O R T Y G I A

Fortress of
Dionysius I

GREAT
HARBOUR

Temple of
Athena

Temple of
Zeus

Fountain of
Arethusa

Syracuse 60 A.D.

281

To ROME

Capua

CAMPANIA

Cumae

Baiae

Neapolis

Herculaneum

Mount
Vesuvius

Puteoli

Misenum

AENARIA
(ISCHIA)

Pompeii

Stabiae

Aequana

Suarentum

CAPREAE

MEDITERRANEAN
SEA

Bay of Naples 60 A.D.

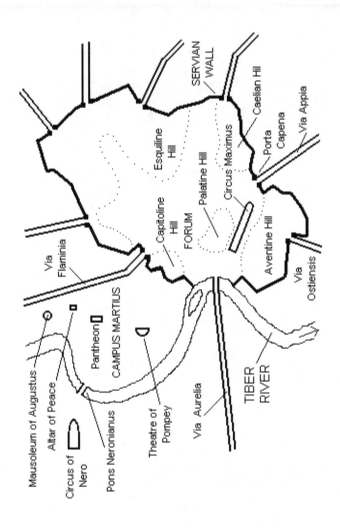

Rome 60 A.D.

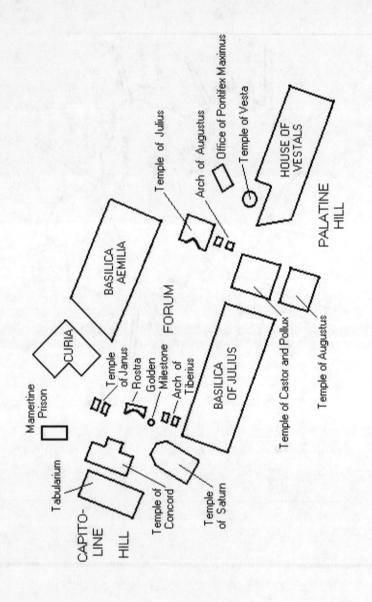

Roman Forum 60 A.D.

Index

Map pages are in *italics*.

A

Absalom 31
Acacallis 247
Achaia 116, 126, 130, 156, *263*
Acre 182
Acrocorinth 131, 137
Acropolis (Athens) 125, 167
Actaeon 152
Actium, Battle of 70, 109, 110, 117, 119, 146, 212, 241
Acts, Book of 2, 190, 191, 233, 250
Adonis 200
Aelia Capitolina 10
Aeneas 105, 223, 252
aerarium (treasury) 225
Agave 133
Agenor 203, 244
Agonothesia 121
agora 254
Agrippa (Roman general) 239, 244, 252
Agrippa I 98–101, 151, 153, 154, 187
Agrippa II 187, 195, 196, 250
Agrippa Postumus 244
Agrippina I 43, 44, 69, 78, 239, 245

Agrippina II 44, 69, 77–79, 140, 150, 153, 154, 158–60, 162, 187, 197, 198, 221
Ahenobarbus, Cn Domitius 78
Akko 182; see also Ptolemais
Alcmena 23
Alexander Jannaeus 10, 11
Alexander of Ephesus 152, 153
Alexander Tiberius (procurator) 3, 41, 98
Alexander the Great 4, 22, 23, 41, 118, 143, 160, 170, 178, 183, 199, 243
Alexandria (Egypt) 205, *261*
Alexandria Troas; see Troas
Al-Jazzar, Ahmed Pasha 183
Allaeddin Hill 75
alphabet 132, 203, 204
Alpheus 251
Altar of Peace (Ara Pacis) 222
Al Uzza 31
Amarna letters 181, 199
Amazons 142, 144, 245
Amphipolis 113, 158, *236*
Amphora 128
Amyntas 65, 88

Ananias 27
Anaximander 169
Anaximenes 169
anchor 10, 90, 235
Andriake 205, 207
Androclus 142
Andromeda 184
angel 28
Annius Afrinus 77, 78
Annona 220
Antakya 41, 48
Antalya 93
Anthius river 64
Antigonus I 103
Antioch
  in South Galatia; see Pisidian Antioch
  in Syria 40, 96, 112, 139, *261, 267*
Antiochiane 240
Antiochus (father of Seleucus I) 41
Antiochus I 32, 64
Antiochus I (king of Commagene) 240
Antiochus II 143
Antiochus III 47, 181
Antiochus III (king of Commagene) 88
Antiochus IV 37, 42, 171, 181
Antiochus IV (king of Commagene) 88–90, 240

Index